Britain's Railways

British Railway Atlas 1955

Ian Allan
PUBLISHING

INTRODUCTION

This is the second in Ian Allan Publishing's new series of railway atlases and is designed to show the state of the nation's railway network as at 1 January 1955. The mid-1950s represented a watershed in the history of British Railways. The first effects of Nationalisation had been felt, with the elimination of some duplicate lines and stations, but the network still stretched into much of the countryside. The massive closures that were to occur as a result of the Beeching report, *The Reshaping of Britain's Railways*, were still some years away and many wayside stations, which had lost their passenger services many years previously, still retained quite extensive freight facilities.

The compilation of this atlas had, perforce, been based around a number of source documents, of which the most important was undoubtedly the official BR register of stations. Information on closures has been gathered from as many different sources as possible in order, where necessary, to try and double-check the often contradictory data available. Whilst every effort has been made to ensure that the information contained within these maps is as accurate as possible, there will — no doubt — be some errors and the publishers will welcome corrections for updates in future editions.

The lines of the various regions are coloured as followed:

Eastern — blue
London Midland — purple
North Eastern — orange
Scottish — blue
Southern — green
Western — brown

Passenger lines are indicated by solid lines and freight only lines by broken (or pecked) lines of the appropriate colours. A number of routes over which excursion services only operated have been treated as freight only for the purposes of this volume as all local passenger traffic had ceased and the excursion services only operated largely during the summer months. Station names are distinguished as follows:

Black — passenger stations
Red — stations from which regular passenger services had been withdrawn or freight locations

Wherever possible the full station name (based upon the official BR nomenclature for the location) is given. However, in a number of cases, this is not possible due to the complexity of the local railway network; the index, however, does list the full title as officially recorded. There are a number of stations where the BR spelling of the location appears to be at variance with the recognised spelling of a particular location; where this does occur the book records the official BR spelling.

There are a number of stations included that were unadvertised in public timetables and in the official register. These stations, which were used by railway staff or for workmen's services, have been included, as far as possible, to reflect the complete railway scene at the time.

As with all atlases, every effort has been made to ensure accuracy. There are, no doubt, errors and the Publishers would welcome any corrections or comments so that these can be incorporated into future editions of the work.

First published 2000

ISBN 0 7110 2726 9

© Ian Allan Publishing Ltd 2000

Published by Ian Allan Publishing

an imprint of Ian Allan Publishing Ltd, Terminal House, Shepperton, Surrey TW17 8AS; and printed by Ian Allan Printing Ltd, Hersham, Surrey KT12 4RG.

Code: 0011/C2

Back cover photograph by courtesy of Colour-Rail

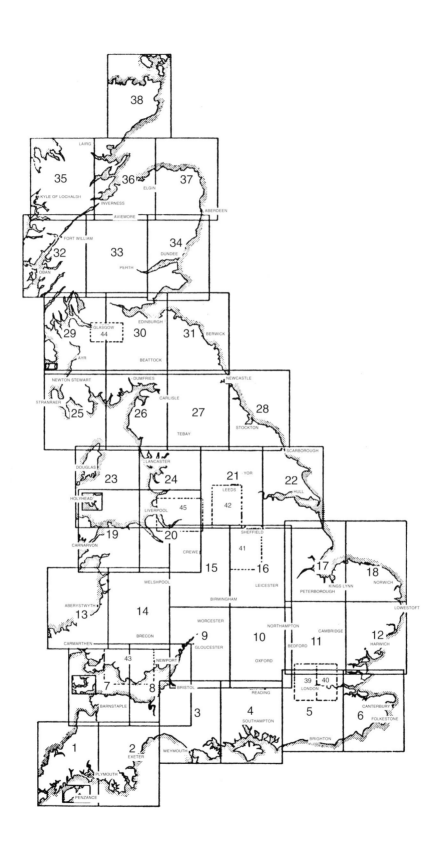

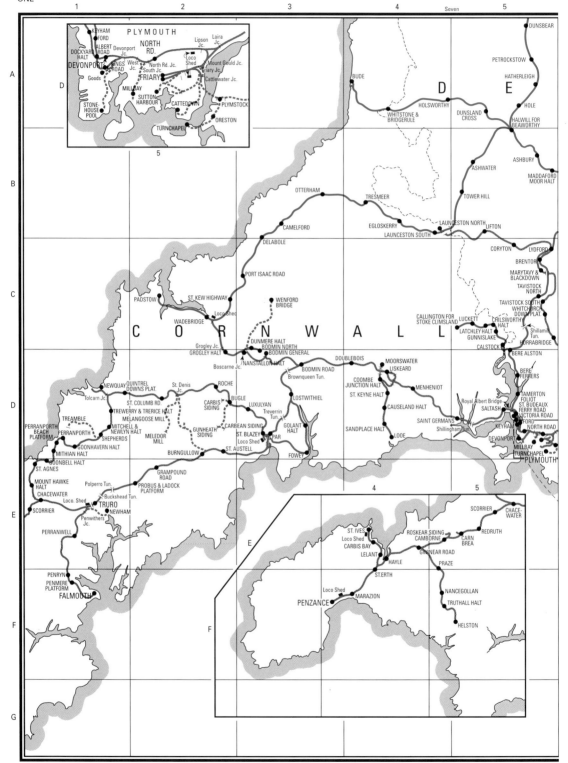

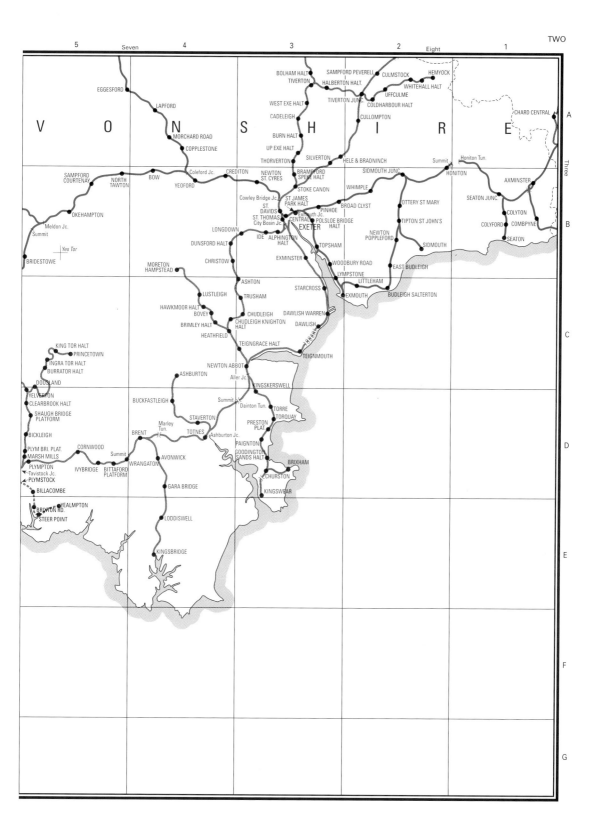

1   2   3   Eight   4   Nine   5

W I L T S

S O M E R S E T

D O R S E T S H I R E

CHRISTIAN MALFORD HALT
PORTISHEAD
AVONMOUTH
SHIREHAMPTON
SEA MILLS
FILTON JUNC.
HORFIELD
ASHLEY HILL
STAPLE HILL
Westerleigh Junc.
PORTBURY
PILL
CLIFTON DOWN
FISH PONDS
MANGOTSFIELD
CHIPPENHAM
STANLEY BRIDGE HALT
HAM GREEN HALT
St Annes Park Jun.
WARMLEY
OLDLAND COMMON
BLACK DOG SIDING
BRISTOL
St Annes Park
CLIFTON BR.
TEMPLE MEADS
ST. ANNES PARK
BITTON
BOX MILL LANE PLATFORM
Box Tun.
Thingley Jc.
LACOCK HALT
CALNE
FLAX BOURTON
St. Annes Wood Tun.
SEE INSET
Middle Hill Tun.
CORSHAM
CLEVEDON
BRISLINGTON
KEYNSHAM & SOMERDALE
Brislington Gdns.
Twerton Tun.
BATHFORD HALT
I Loco Shed
WESTON
BATHAMPTON
BEANACRE HALT
NAILSEA & BACKWELL
WHITCHURCH HALT
SALTFORD
BATH SPA
GREEN PARK
MELKSHAM
YATTON
CONGRESBURY
PENSFORD
OLDFIELD PARK
Devonshire Tun.
Combe Down Tun.
HOLT JUNC.
BROUGHTON GIFFORD HALT
DEVIZES
WESTON MILTON HALT
Worle Jun.
WRINGTON
CLUTTON
MIDFORD
LIMPLEY STOKE
BRADFORD ON AVON
Bradford Jcs.
SEMINGTON HALT
SEEND
BROMHAM & ROWDE
WOODBOROUGH
WESTON - SUPER - MARE GENERAL
Uphill Junc.
SANDFORD & BANWELL
HALLATROW
WELLOW
FRESHFORD
AVONCLIFF HALT
STAVERTON HALT
PANS LANE HALT
PATNEY & CHIRTON
BLEADON & UPHILL
WINSCOMBE
FARRINGTON GURNEY HALT
RADSTOCK NORTH
SHOSCOMBE & SINGLE HILL HALT
TROWBRIDGE
BRENT KNOLL
AXBRIDGE
CHEDDAR
MIDSOMER NORTON & WELTON
RADSTOCK WEST
LAVINGTON
DRAYCOTT
Chilcompton Tun.
MIDSOMER SOUTH
MELLS ROAD
WESTBURY
BURNHAM ON SEA
Level Crossing
HIGHBRIDGE EAST
LODGE HILL
CHILCOMPTON
Loco. Shed
DILTON MARSH HALT
Loco Shed
BASON BRIDGE
WOOKEY
BINEGAR
Masbury Summit
VOBSTER
HIGHBRIDGE & BURNHAM ON SEA
EDINGTON BURTLE
MASBURY HALT
WELLS PRIORY RD
FROME
WARMINSTER
DUNBALL
SHAPWICK
WELLS, TUCKER ST halt
Winsor Hill Tun.
CRANMORE
WANSTROW
HEYTESBURY
ASHCOTT
SHEPTON MALLET HIGH STREET
SHEPTON MALLET CHARLTON ROAD
WITHAM
CODFORD
BRIDGWATER NORTH
GLASTONBURY & STREET
WEST PENNARD
PYLLE
EVERCREECH (NEW)
WYLYE
BRIDGWATER
EVERCREECH JUNC.
WISHFORD
WILTON NORTH
CASTLE CARY
BRUTON
LYNG HALT
Athelney Junc.
KEINTON MANDEVILLE
ALFORD HALT
COLE
Castle Cary Junc.
DINTON
WILTON SOUTH
DURSTON
ATHELNEY
LANGPORT EAST
SOMERTON
CHARLTON MACKRELL
WINCANTON
TISBURY
Curry Rivell Junc.
LANGPORT WEST
LONG SUTTON & PITNEY
SPARKFORD
Loco Shed
Goods
GILLINGHAM
SEMLEY
THORNEY AND KINGSBURY HALT
MARTOCK
MARSTON MAGNA
TEMPLECOMBE
Buckhorn Weston Tun.
HATCH
MONTACUTE
Summit
MILBORNE PORT
HENSTRIDGE
ILTON HALT
PEN MILL
STALBRIDGE
ILMINSTER
HENDFORD HALT
Loco Shed
Clifton Maybank Junc.
SHERBORNE
DONYATT HALT
TOWN STA. Joint
STURMINSTER NEWTON
DAGGONS ROAD
YEOVIL JUNC.
YEOVIL
CHARD CENTRAL
SUTTON BINGHAM
Loco Shed
THORNFORD BRIDGE HALT
SHILLINGSTONE
VERWOOD
L & S.W/ Goods
CREWKERNE
YETMINSTER
STOURPAIN & DURWESTON HALT
CHARD TOWN
CHETNOLE HALT
BLANDFORD FORUM
ASHLEY HEATH HALT
CHARD JUNC.
EVERSHOT
CHARLTON MARSHALL HALT
WEST MOORS FOR FERNDOWN
CATTISTOCK HALT
SPETISBURY
BAILEY GATE
CARTERS SIDING
WIMBORNE
MAIDEN NEWTON
Corfe Mullen Junc.
CORFE MULLEN HALT
BOSCOMBE
TOLLER
BROADSTONE
BRIDPORT
POWERSTOCK
GRIMSTONE & FRAMPTON
CREEKMOOR HALT
Hales Bay Jc.
Gasworks Jc.
LYME REGIS
BRADFORD PEVERELL & STRATTON HALT
HAMWORTHY JUNC.
POOLE
WEST
HAMWORTHY
BOURNE-MOUTH
WEST BAY
DORCHESTER WEST
DORCHESTER SOUTH
Goods
MORETON
HOLTON HEATH
PARKSTONE
Loco Shed
Dorchester Jc.
MONKTON & CAME HALT
WAREHAM
WOOL
Worgret Junc.
Bincombe Tuns.
UPWEY GOODS
UPWEY WISHING WELL HALT
UPWEY & BROADWEY
CORFE CASTLE
RADIPOLE HALT
Weymouth Jc.
Loco Shed (G.W.)
MELCOMBE REGIS
TOWN STA.
QUAY
WEYMOUTH
RODWELL
SWANAGE
PORTLAND
EASTON

BRISTOL

REDLAND
CLIFTON DOWN
MONTPELIER
Ashley Hill Jc.
STAPLETON RD.
CANNON'S MARSH GDS
ST. PHILIP'S
AVONSIDE Gds.
WHARF
Kingswood Jc.
CLIFTON BRIDGE
Lawrence Hill Jc.
LAWRENCE HILL
Dr Days Bridge Jc.
ASHTON GATE PLATFORM
Ashton
TEMPLE MEADS
Goods
Feeder Br. Jc.
PYLLE HILL (Gds)
Loco Sheds
St. Anne's Park Jc.
PARSON STREET
ST. PHILIPS MARSH (Gds)
BEDMINSTER
Bedminster Jc.

Eight

Two

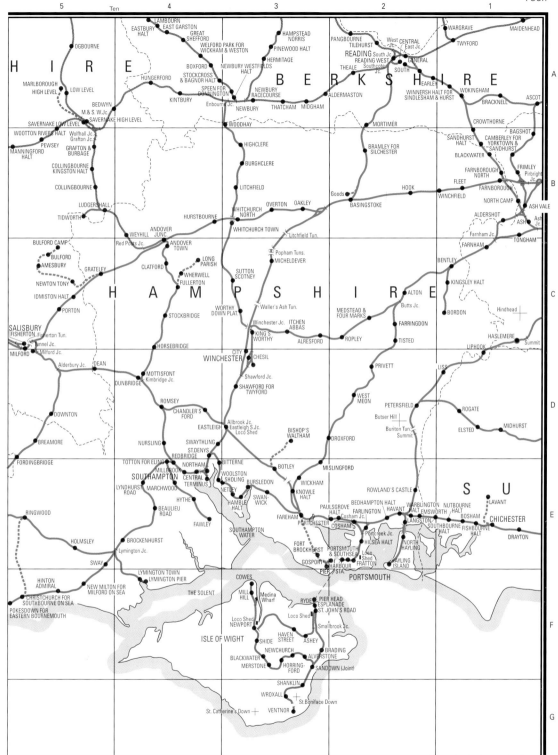

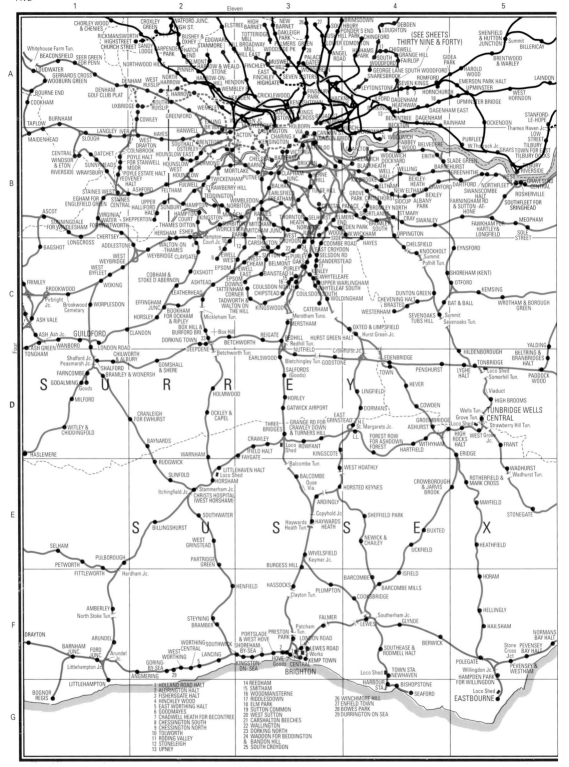

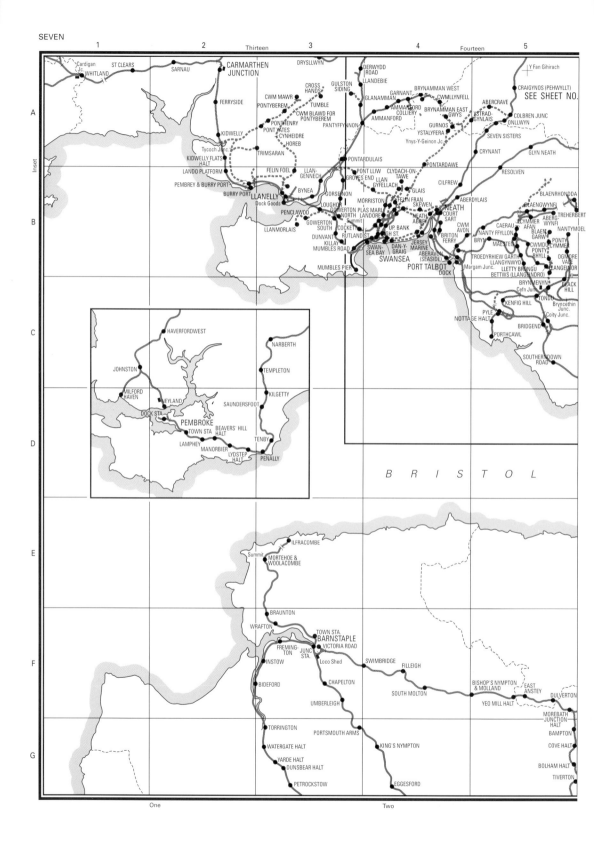

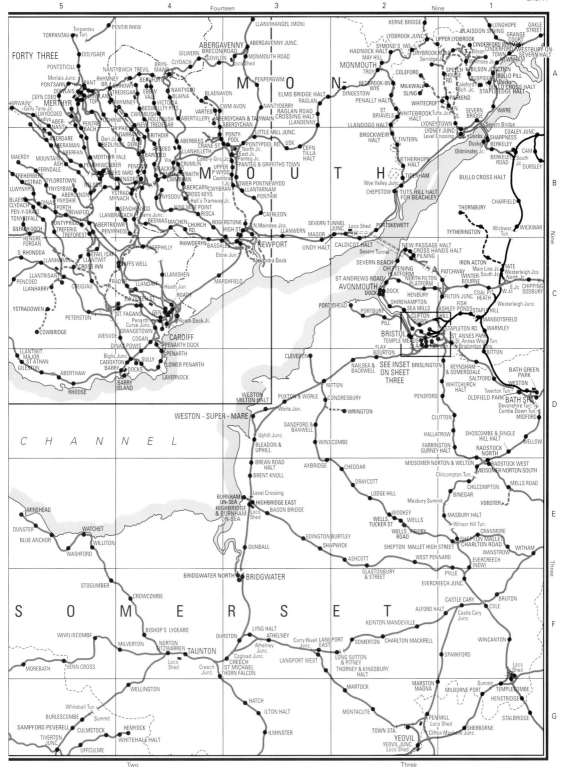

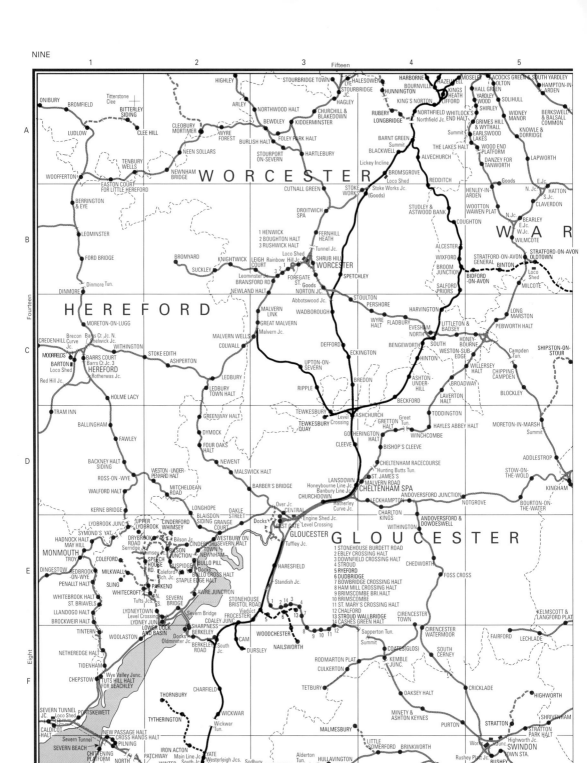

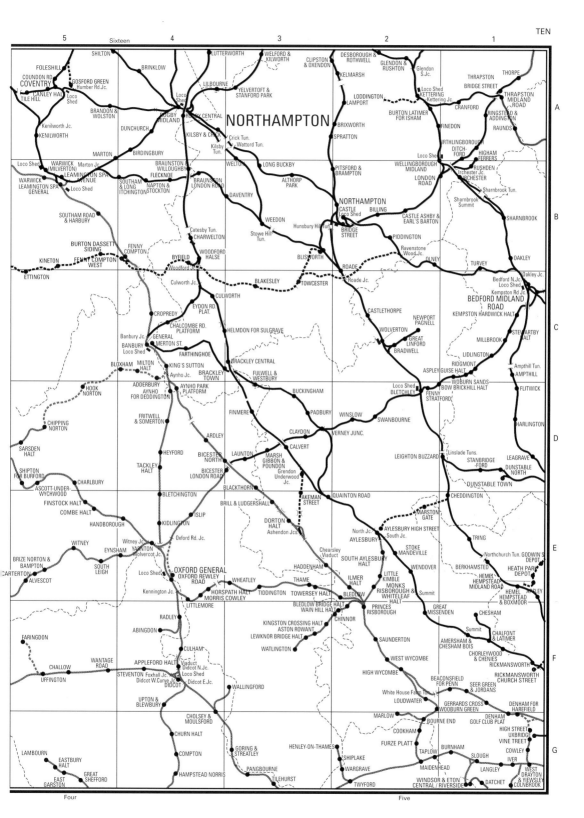

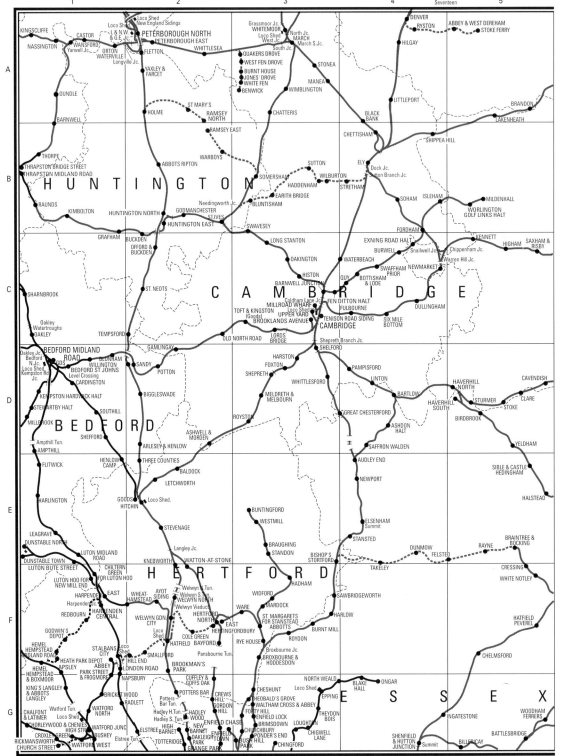

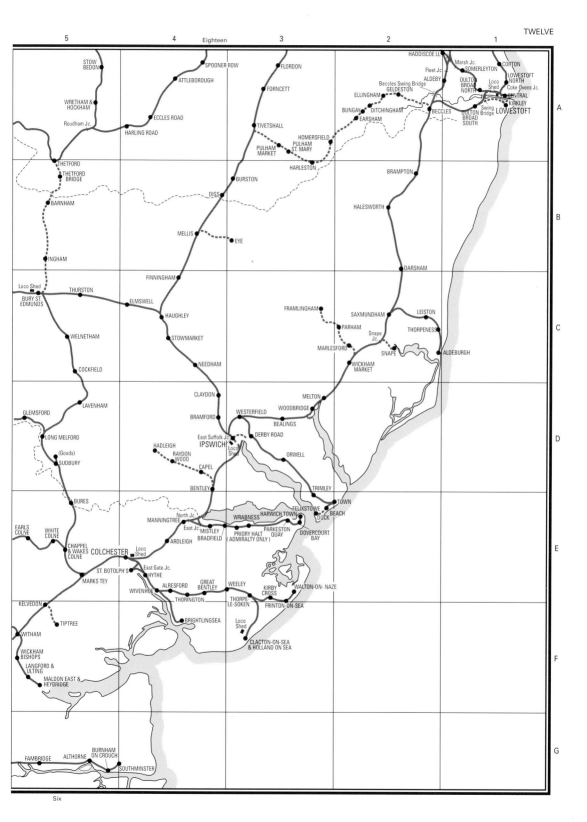

1 2 3 4 5

A B C D E F G

BIRMINGHAM DISTRICT
(INSET ON SHEET No. FIFTEEN)

PRIESTFIELD
Goods DARLASTON
WALSALL/ LONGSTREET
MIDLAND ROAD
WALSALL
BILSTON WEST
BILSTON CENTRAL
PLECK
East Jc.
West Jc.
DAISY BANK & BRADLEY
Goods
South Jc.
BESCOT JUNCTION
DEEPFIELDS & COSELEY
Goods Branch Jc.
WEDNESBURY TOWN
WEDNESBURY CENTRAL
PRINCE'S END & COSELEY
TIPTON (OWEN STREET)
GREAT BRIDGE NORTH
GREAT BARR
Horsleyfield Jc.
GREAT BRIDGE SOUTH
North Jc.
TIPTON FIVE WAYS
DUDLEY PORT (LOW LEVEL)
SWAN VILLAGE
Sedgley Jc.
DUDLEY PORT (HIGH LEVEL)
PERRY BARR
DUDLEY CASTLE
DUDLEY TOWN
ALBION
Goods
WEST BROMWICH & SPON LANE
Handsworth Jc.
WITTON FOR VILLA PARK
BLOWERS GREEN
DUDLEY
OLDBURY & BROMFORD LANE
Goods
THE HAWTHORNS (WEST BROMWICH) PLATFORM
Soho Pool Jc.
ASTON
Loco Shed
ASTON GOODS
NETHERTON
OLDBURY
SPON LANE FOR WEST BROMWICH
Handsworth Jc.
HANDSWORTH & SMETHWICK
WINDSOR STR. WHARF
BAPTIST END HALT
SMETHWICK JUNC.
SMETHWICK
SOHO POOL
SALTLEY Loco Shed
WINDMILL END HALT
Galton Jc.
SOHO
SOHO & WINSON GREEN
VAUXHALL & DUDDESTON
WITHYMOOR BASIN
OLDBURY & LANGLEY GREEN
Soho Soap Works Jc.
Soho East Jc.
HOCKLEY
Saltley Jc.
DARBY END HALT
LANGLEY GREEN & ROOD END
SOHO
Aston Curve Jc.
LLANDRE
HIGH STREET HALT
WINSON GREEN
MONUMENT LANE
SNOW HILL
CURZON STR.
LAWLEY STR.
ADDERLEY PARK
BOW STREET
OLD HILL
Harborne Jc.
Loco Shed
Prodhouse Jc.
Cun. Str.Jc.
St. Andrew's Jc.
ROWLEY REGIS & BLACKHEATH
HAGLEY RD.
CENTRAL STA.
NEW ST. MOOR ST.
St.Jc.
BORDESLEY
Bordesley Jc.
CAMP HILL
Camp Hill Jc.
HARBORNE

DYFFRYN ARDUOWY
LLANABER HALT
Barmouth Bridge
BARMOUTH
BARMOUTH JUNC. FAIRBOURNE
ARTHOG
Cader Idris
LLWYNGWRIL
LLANGELYNIN HALT
ABERGYNOLWYN
TONFANAU
DOLGOCH
BRYNGLAS
RHYDYRONEN
CYNFAL HALT
TOWYN
PENORE WHARF STA.
GOGARTH HALT
ABERTAFOL HALT
ABERDOVEY
PENHELIG HALT
YNYSLAS
BORTH
LLANDRE
BOW STREET
ABERYSTWYTH
Loco Shed
GLANRAFON
LLANBADARN
CAPEL BANGOR
LLANRHYSTYD RD.
LLANILAR
FELINDYFFRYN HALT
TRAWSCOED

ABERAYRON
CILIAU- AERON
PONT LLANIO
FELIN FACH
OLMARCH HALT
LLANGYBI
DERRY ORMOND
Aberayron Jc.
LAMPETER
PENCARREG HALT
LLANYBYTHER

C A R D I G A N

CARDIGAN
KILGERRAN
HENLLAN
MAES-Y-CRUGIAU
NEWCASTLE EMLYN
LLANDYSSUL
BRYN TEIFY
BONCATH
FISHGUARD HARBOUR
FISHGUARD & GOODWICK
GLOGUE
PENCADER
P E M B R O K E
CRYMMYCH ARMS
JORDANSTON HALT
Letterston Jc.
PUNCHESTON
LLANFYRNACH
C A R M A R T H E N
LETTERSTON
LLANPUMPSAINT
MATHRY ROAD
RHYDOWEN
WELSH HOOK HALT
WOLF'S CASTLE HALT
LLANGLYDWEN
CONWIL
BRONWYDD ARMS
TALLEY ROAD
LOGIN
LLANDILO BRI.
LLANDILO
Spittal Tun.
CLARBESTON ROAD
ABERGWILI
LLANARTHNEY HALT
Clarbeston Jc.
CLYNDERWEN
LLANFALTEG
TOWN STA.
NANTGAREDIG
GOLDEN GROVE
FFAIRFACH
Cardigan Jc.
ST.CLEARS
SARNAU
CARMARTHEN
DRYSLLWYN
WHITLAND
JUNC.
Myrtle Hill Jc.
Loco Shed
DERWYDD ROAD

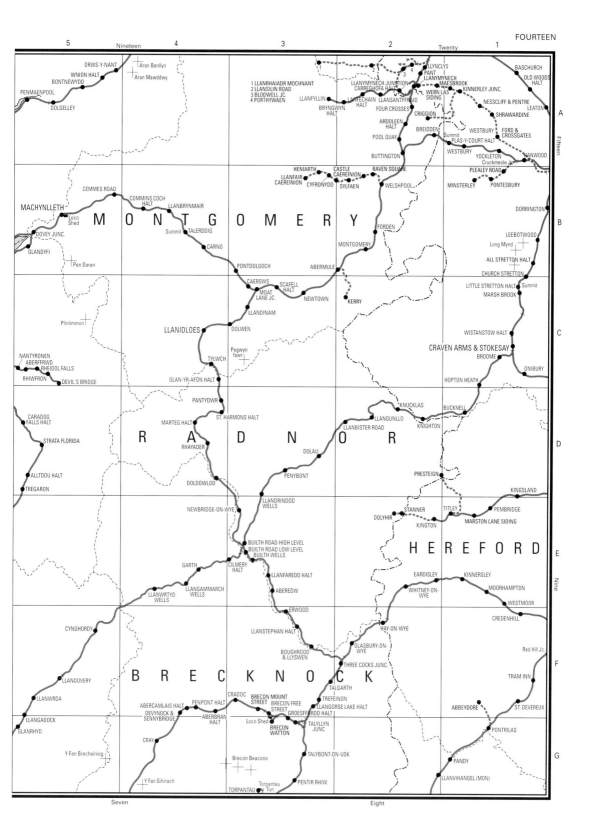

DRWS-Y-NANT
WNION HALT
BONTNEWYDD
Aran Benllyn
Aran Mawddwy
PENMAENPOOL
DOLGELLEY

1 LLANRHAIADR MOCHNANT
2 LLANSILIN ROAD
3 BLODWELL JC.
4 PORTHYWAEN

LLYNCLYS
PANT
LLANYMYNECH
BASCHURCH
OLD WOODS HALT
LLANYMYNECH JUNCTION
CARREGHOFA HALT
MAESBROOK
KINNERLEY JUNC.
WERN LAS SIDING
NESSCLIFF & PENTRE
LEATON
LLANFYLLIN
LLANFECHAIN HALT
LLANSANTFFRAID
LLANFAIN
BRYNGWYN HALT
FOUR CROSSES
CRIGGION
SHRAWARDINE
ARDDLEEN HALT
CRIGGION
BREIDDEN
WESTBURY
FORD & CROSSGATES
POOL QUAY
Summit
PLAS-Y-COURT HALT
BUTTINGTON
WESTBURY
YOCKLETON
Cruckmeole Jc.
HANWOOD
Fifteen

A

HENIARTH
CASTLE CAEREINION
RAVEN SQUARE
PLEALEY ROAD
LLANFAIR CAEREINION
CYFRONYDD
SYLFAEN
WELSHPOOL
MINSTERLEY
PONTESBURY

MACHYNLLETH
CEMMES ROAD
COMMINS COCH HALT
LLANBRYNMAIR
DORRINGTON
Loco Shed

MONTGOMERY

Summit TALERDDIG
LEEBOTWOOD
Long Mynd
ALL STRETTON HALT
DOVEY JUNC.
CARNO
CHURCH STRETTON
GLANDYFI
Pen Daren
PONTDOLGOCH
FORDEN
MONTGOMERY
LITTLE STRETTON HALT Summit
MARSH BROOK
CAERSWS
SCAFELL HALT
ABERMULE
MOAT LANE JC.
NEWTOWN
KERRY
LLANDINAM
WISTANSTOW HALT
Plinlimmon
LLANIDLOES
DOLWEN
CRAVEN ARMS & STOKESAY
BROOME
NANTYRONEN
ABERFFRWD
RHEIDOL FALLS
Pegwyn fawr
TYLWCH
ONIBURY
RHIWFRON
DEVIL'S BRIDGE
GLAN-YR-AFON HALT
HOPTON HEATH

C

CARADOG FALLS HALT
PANTYDWR
KNUCKLAS
BUCKNELL
MARTEG HALT
ST. HARMONS HALT
LLANGUNLLO
KNIGHTON
STRATA FLORIDA
RHAYADER
LLANBISTER ROAD

RADNOR

DOLAU
ALLTDDU HALT
DOLDOWLOD
PENYBONT
PRESTEIGN
KINGSLAND
TREGARON
NEWBRIDGE-ON-WYE
LLANDRINDOD WELLS
STANNER
TITLEY
PEMBRIDGE
DOLYHIR
MARSTON LANE SIDING
KINGTON

BUILTH ROAD HIGH LEVEL
BUILTH ROAD LOW LEVEL
BUILTH WELLS

HEREFORD

GARTH
CILMERY HALT
EARDISLEY
KINNERSLEY
LLANFAREDD HALT
MOORHAMPTON
LLANGAMMARCH WELLS
ABEREDW
WHITNEY-ON-WYE
LLANWRTYD WELLS
WESTMOOR
ERWOOD
CREDENHILL

Nine

E

CYNGHORDY
LLANSTEPHAN HALT
HAY-ON-WYE
GLASBURY-ON-WYE
Red Hill Jc.
BOUGHROOD & LLYSWEN
THREE COCKS JUNC.

BRECKNOCK

TALGARTH
TRAM INN
LLANDOVERY
TREFEINON
BRECON MOUNT STREET
CRADOC
LLANGORSE LAKE HALT
LLANWRDA
ABERCAMLAIS HALT
PENPONT HALT
BRECON FREE STREET
GROESFFORDD HALT
ABBEYDORE
ST. DEVEREUX
DEVYNOCK & SENNYBRIDGE
ABERBRAN HALT
Loco Shed
LLANGADOCK
BRECON WATTON
TALYLLYN JUNC.
PONTRILAS
GLANRHYD
CRAY
Y Fan Brecheiniog
TALYBONT-ON-USK
PANDY
Brecon Beacons
LLANVIHANGEL (MON)
Y Fan Gihirach
Torpantau Tun
PENTIR RHIW
TORPANTAU

G

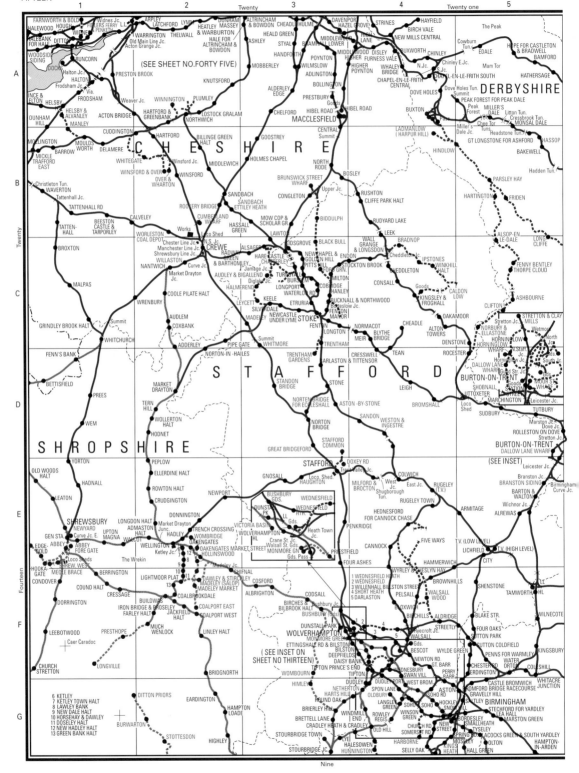

5   Twenty one   4   3   Twenty two   2   1

Row A

SHEFFIELD VICTORIA, WHARF STREET, QUEENS RD., DARNALL, Treeton Jc., TREETON, THURCROFT, DINNINGTON & LAUGHTON, RANSKILL, South Jc., North Jc., GAINSBOROUGH CENTRAL, GAINSBOROUGH LEA ROAD, MIDLAND, HEELEY, WOODHOUSE, BEIGHTON, WALESWOOD, Southern Jc., Dimington Jc., STURTON, LEA, Pyewipe Jc., W.Holmes Jc., W.HOLMES, CENTRAL, HOLMES, Durham Ox Jc.

MILL HOUSES, BEAUCHIEF, KILLAMARSH, KIVETON BRIDGE, KIVETON PARK, G.C.& Mid. SHIREOAKS, Clarborough Jc., LEVERTON, Boultham Jc., WEST, ST.MARKS, EAST, Sincil Jc., Level Crossing

DORE & TOTLEY, Dore S.Jc., Broadway Tun., DRONFIELD, SPINKHILL, Brancliffe, WORKSOP, Goods NorthJc., Loco Shed, RETFORD, SouthJc., Clarborough Tun., STOW PARK FOR MARTON, LANGWORTH

Totley Tun., UNSTONE, BARROW HILL, WHITWELL, CHECKER HOUSE, Loco Shed, COTTAM, TORKSEY, SAXILBY, West Holmes Jc., Wipe Jc., LINCOLN, REEPHAM, Level Crossing, Durham Ox Jc.

GRINDLEFORD, Broomhouse Tun., CLOWNE, Whiskerhill Jc., Level Crossing, Askham Tun., Sykes Jc., SKELLINGTHORPE, Sincil Jc., Boultham Jc., Durham Ox Jc.

Row B

SHEEPBRIDGE, STAVELEY WORKS, BRIMINGTON, CRESWELL & WELBECK, ELMTON & CRESWELL, TUXFORD NORTH, FLED BOROUGH, CLIFTON-ON-TRENT, DODDINGTON & HARBY, BRANSTON & HEIGHINGTON, POTTER-HANWORTH

CHESTERFIELD, MARKET PLACE, DEN, Tapton Jc., MIDLAND, ARKWRIGHT TOWN, BOLSOVER, LANGWITH Jc., LANGWITH, WARSOP, CLIPSTONE SIDING, TUXFORD CENTRAL, BOUGHTON, CROW PARK FOR SUTTON-ON-TRENT, SWINDERBY, THORPE-ON-THE-HILL, HYKEHAM, WADDINGTON

BRAMPTON, GRASSMOOR, HASLAND, HEATH, GLAPWELL, SHIREBROOK, EDWINSTOWE, OLLERTON, CARLTON-ON-TRENT, HARMSTON, NOCTON & DUNSTON, BLANKNEY & METHERINGHAM

ROWSLEY, CLAY CROSS TOWN, Pass., PLEASLEY, MANSFIELD WOODHOUSE, COLLINGHAM, NAVENBY

DARLEY DALE, STRETTON, TIBSHELF TOWN, TEVERSAL, SKEGBY, MANSFIELD, BLIDWORTH & RAINWORTH

Row C

MATLOCK, High Tor Tunnels, DOE HILL, SUTTON Jc., FARNSFIELD, KIRKLINGTON

MATLOCK BATH, CROMFORD, Willersley Tun., WESTHOUSES, SUTTON-IN-ASHFIELD, KIRKBY-IN-ASHFIELD, SOUTHWELL, Level Crossing, NEWARK CASTLE, NEWARK NORTH GATE, LEADENHAM

STEEPLE HOUSE, Lea Wood Tun., High Peak Jc., WINGFIELD, Wingfield Tun., ALFRETON, (SEE SHEET NO. FORTY ONE), FISKERTON, ROLLESTON JUNC.

WIRKS-WORTH, WHATSTANDWELL, West Jc., AMBERGATE, South Jc., East Jc., BUTTERLEY, PINXTON, PYE BRIDGE, PYE HILL, JACKSDALE, NEWSTEAD, LINBY, BLEASBY, THURGARTON, CLAYPOLE, CAYTHORPE, SLEAFORD

BELPER, SHOTTLE, Milford Tun., RIPLEY, CODNOR PK & IRONVILLE, DENBY, EASTWOOD, HUCKNALL, BUTLER'S HILL, LOWDHAM, HOUGHAM, HONINGTON, ANCASTER, RAUCEBY

DUFFIELD, COXBENCH, HEANOR, ILKESTON, KIMBERLEY, AWSWORTH, BESTWOOD COLLY., Moorbridge, BULWELL FOREST, BULWELL COMMON, DAYBROOK, COTHAM, BARKSTON

Row D

LITTLE EATON, Little Eaton Jc., WEST HALLAM, ILKESTON JUNC., BASFORD, BULWELL, CARLTON & NETHERFIELD, GERLING, BURTON JOYCE, ELTON & ORSTON, N.Jc., BOTTESFORD, Belvoir Jc., Peascliffe Tun.

DERBY (FRIARGATE), MICKLEOVER, Derby N.Jc., TROWELL, Wedn'day, VICTORIA Gds., RADCLIFFE-ON-TRENT, Saxondale Jc., BINGHAM, W.Jc., E.Jc., Barr Road Jc., GREAT PONTON

DERBY, ST ANDREWS, MIDLANDS, BREADSALL, NOTTINGHAM ROAD, STANTON GATE, STANTON GATE, ARKWRIGHT STREET, Rectory Jc., BINGHAM ROAD, ASLOCKTON, REDMILE, BONERBY SIDING, Loco shed, GRANTHAM

PEARTREE & NORMANTON, Spondon Jc., SPONDON, STAPLEFORD & SANDIACRE, BEESTON, NOTTINGHAM, EDWALTON, BARNSTONE, SELSEDGEBROOK

ETWALL, London Road Jc., BORROWASH, LONG EATON, ATTENBOROUGH, RUDDINGTON, PLUMTREE, DENTON SIDING, SPROXTON, Stoke Tun.

CHELLASTON & SWARKESTONE, DRAYCOTT, SAWLEY, SAWLEY JUNC. FOR LONG EATON, Attenborough Jc., Long Eaton Jc., Stanton Tun., WIDMERPOOL, HARBY & STATHERN, Summit, GREAT PONTON

EGGINTON, East Jc., Stenson Jc., Willington Jc., WESTON ON TRENT, Trent Jc., Sheet Stores Jc., GOTHAM, Gotham Jc., WALTHAM-ON-THE-WOLD, Wycombe Jc., STAINBY, CORBY GLEN

REPTON & WILLINGTON, CASTLE DONINGTON & SHARDLOW, RUSHCLIFFE PLATFORM

Row E

MELBOURNE, TONGE & BREEDON, KEGWORTH, HATHERN, EAST LEAKE, OLD DALBY, SCALFORD

BRETBY COLLIERY, WORTHINGTON, LOUGHBOROUGH DERBY ROAD, LOUGHBOROUGH MIDLAND, Grimston Tun., GRIMSTON, Saxe Iby Tun., SAXBY, SOUTH WITHAM, Little Bytham

SWADLINCOTE, SHEPSHED, LOUGHBOROUGH CENTRAL, HOLWELL JUNCTION, NORTH, WYMONDHAM Jc., CASTLE BYTHAM

GRESLEY, WOODVILLE, LOUNT COLLIERY, BARROW ON SOAR & QUORN, FRISBY, ASFORDBY, MELTON MOWBRAY TOWN, EDMONDTHORPE & WYMONDHAM, LITTLE BYTHAM

MOIRA, WHITWICK, BROOKSBY, Asfordby Tun., Melton Jc., WHISSENDINE

DONISTHORPE, MEASHAM, SWANNINGTON, COALVILLE TOWN, COALVILLE EAST, QUORN & WOODHOUSE, SILEBY, REARSBY, ASHWELL, COTTESMORE

HEATHER & IBSTOCK, HUGGLESCOTE, BARDON HILL, BAGWORTH & ELLISTOWN, ROTHLEY

SNARESTONE, BELGRAVE & BIRSTALL, SYSTON N.Jc., Syston E. Jc., JOHN O'GAUNT, RUTLAND, OAKHAM, ESSENDINE, RYHALL

Row F

SHACKERSTONE, GLENFIELD, Glenfield Tun., SYSTON S. Jc., SYSTON, LEICESTER, THURNBY & SCRAPTOFT, HUMBERSTONE, N.Jc., Morefield Jcs., STAMFORD EAST

POLESWORTH, MARKET BOSWORTH, RATBY, WEST BRI., BELGRAVE ROAD, CENTRAL, HUMBERSTONE RD, W., KETTON & COLLYWESTON, STAMFORD TOWN

SHENTON, DESFORD, KIRBY MUXLOE, Leicester Goods Jc., LONDON ROAD, TILTON, Manton Tun., MANTON, LUFFENHAM

ATHERSTONE, STOKE GOLDING, Knighton S.Jc., Knighton Jc., Knighton Central Jc., Knighton N.Jc., Wing Tun., UPPINGHAM, Glaston Tun., MORCOTT

ELMESTHORPE FOR BARWELL & EARL SHILTON, ENDERBY, NARBOROUGH, BLABY, Wigston N.Jc., Wigston S.Jc., EAST NORTON, Seaton Tun., WAKERLEY & BARROWDEN

NUNEATON ABBEY STREET, Weddington Jc., HINCKLEY, WHETSTONE, GLEN PARVA, WIGSTON MAGNA, SEATON, KINGSCLIFFE

S.Leicester Jc., Summit, CROFT, WIGSTON SOUTH, GREAT GLEN, Welland Viaduct, NASSINGTON

STOCKINGFORD, Summit, Stockingford Tun., COUNTESTHORPE, HALLATON, Hallaton Jc., GRETTON

Row G

SHILSTOKE, NUNEATON TRENT VALLEY, BROUGHTON ASTLEY, KIBWORTH, Summit, WELHAM Jc., Drayton Jc., ROCKINGHAM, Corby Tun., OUNDLE

ARLEY & FILLONGLEY, CHILVERS COTON, LEIRE HALT, ASHBY MAGNA, EAST LANGTON, ASHLEY & WESTON, CORBY & WELDON, Summit

BEDWORTH, ULLESTHORPE, LUBENHAM, MARKET HARBOROUGH, NORTHAMPTON, BARNWELL

HAWKESBURY LANE, SHILTON, THEDDINGWORTH, Summit, DESBOROUGH & ROTHWELL

LUTTERWORTH, WELFORD & KILWORTH, CLIPSTON & OXENDON, GLENDON & RUSHTON, Glendon S.Jc.

NOTT-ING-HAM, LINCOLN, RUTLAND, LEICESTER

1   2   3   4   Twenty two   5

A

MARKET RASEN
FOTHERBY HALT
SALTFLEETBY
LOUTH
Loco Shed
GRIMOLDBY
THEDDLETHORPE
HALLINGTON
WITHCALL
WICKENBY
SOUTH WILLINGHAM & HAINTON
LEGBOURNE ROAD
MABLETHORPE
SNELLAND
DONINGTON-ON-BAIN
AUTHORPE
SUTTON-ON-SEA
WRAGBY
EAST BARKWITH
ABY FOR CLAYTHORPE
LANGWORTH
ALFORD TOWN
KINGTHORPE
MUMBY ROAD

B

REEPHAM
Level Crossing
Durham Ox. Jc.
FIVE MILE HOUSE
WILLOUGHBY
Greet-well Jcs.
BRANSTON & HEIGHINGTON
Sincil Jc.
BARDNEY
SOUTHREY
HORNCASTLE
BURGH-LE-MARSH
POTTERHANWORTH
SPILSBY
FIRSBY
SKEGNESS
WADDINGTON
STIXWOULD
WOODHALL SPA.
HALTON HOLGATE
Firsby S. Jc.
SEACROFT
NOCTON & DUNSTON
WOODHALL JUNC.
LITTLE STEEPING
THORPE CULVERT
RAVENHOUSE
BLANKNEY & METHERINGHAM

C

NAVENBY
SCOPWICK & TIMBERLAND
TATTERSHALL
CONINGSBY
STICKNEY
MIDVILLE
Bellwater Jc.
WAINFLEET
DIGBY
DOGDYKE
TUMBY WOODSIDE
NEW BOLINGBROKE
EAST VILLE
RUSKINGTON
OLD LEAKE
ANCASTER
North Jc.
SLEAFORD
LANGRICK
SIBSEY
RAUCEBY
East Jc.
South Jc.
HECKINGTON
SWINESHEAD
HUBBERT'S BRIDGE
Loco Shed
BOSTON
Sleaford Jc.

D

ASWARBY & SCREDINGTON
HELPRINGHAM
KIRTON
HUNSTANTON
DOCKING
HEACHAM
SEDGEFORD
BILLINGBOROUGH & HORBLING
DONINGTON ROAD
ALGARKIRK & SUTTERTON
SNETTISHAM
GOSBERTON
SURFLEET
DERSINGHAM
RIPPINGALE
WOLFERTON

E

PINCHBECK
CORBY GLEN
MORTON ROAD
South Jc.
North Jc.
WHAPLODE
HOLBEACH
FLEET
NORTH WOOTTON
HILLINGTON FOR SANDRINGHAM
NORTH DROVE
SPALDING TOWN
Goods
LONG SUTTON
GEDNEY
GRIMSTON ROAD
COUNTER DRAIN
East Jc.
Cuckoo Jc.
WESTON
MOULTON
Sutton Bridge Jc.
SUTTON BRIDGE
Loco Shed
KING'S LYNN
GAYTON ROAD
CASTLE BYTHAM
Little Bytham Jc.
BOURNE
West Jc.
TWENTY
Welland Bank Jc.
TERRINGTON
CLENCHWARTON SOUTH LYNN
MIDDLETON TOWERS
LITTLE BYTHAM
COWBIT
TYDD
WALPOLE
HARDWICK ROAD SIDING
EAST WINCH

F

LITTLEWORTH
FERRY
NARBOROUGH & PENTNEY
POSTLAND FOR CROWLAND
ESSENDINE
FRENCH DROVE & GEDNEY HILL
WISBECH ST. MARY
WISBECH NORTH
EMNETH
MAGDALEN ROAD
RYHALL & BELMISTHORPE
ST. JAMES DEEPING
WISBECH EAST
SMEETH ROAD
MIDDLE DROVE
TALLINGTON
PEAKIRK
ELMBRIDGE
STOW BARDOLPH
STAMFORD EAST
UFFINGTON & BARNACK
Level Crossing
MURROW EAST
BOYCES BRI.
OUTWELL BASIN
STAMFORD TOWN
HELPSTON
THORNEY
OUTWELL VILLAGE
KETTON & COLLYWESTON
WRYDE
COLDHAM
DOWNHAM
WALTON
Werrington Jc.
EYE GREEN, FOR CROWLAND
GUYHIRNE
UPWELL
Loco Shed
New England Sidings
ABBEY & WEST DEREHAM
KINGSCLIFFE
Loco Shed G.N.
PETERBOROUGH NORTH
L & N.W. & G.E. Jc.
WHITEMOOR
North Jc.
DENVER
STOKE FERRY
CASTOR
PETERBOROUGH EAST
MARCH
RYSTON
NASSINGTON
WANSFORD
Yarwell Jc.
ORTON WATERVILLE
FLETTON
WHITTLESEA
March S.Jc.
South Jc.
HILGAY

G

ELTON
YAXLEY & FARCET
QUAKERS DROVE
WEST FEN DROVE
STONEA
BLACKHORSE DROVE SIDING
BURNT HOUSE
JONES' DROVE
OUNDLE
WHITE FEN
BENWICK
MANEA
WIMBLINGTON
LITTLEPORT
BRANDON
BARNWELL
HOLME
ST. MARY'S RAMSEY NORTH
CHATTERIS DOCK
BLACK BANK
LAKENHEATH
CHATTERIS

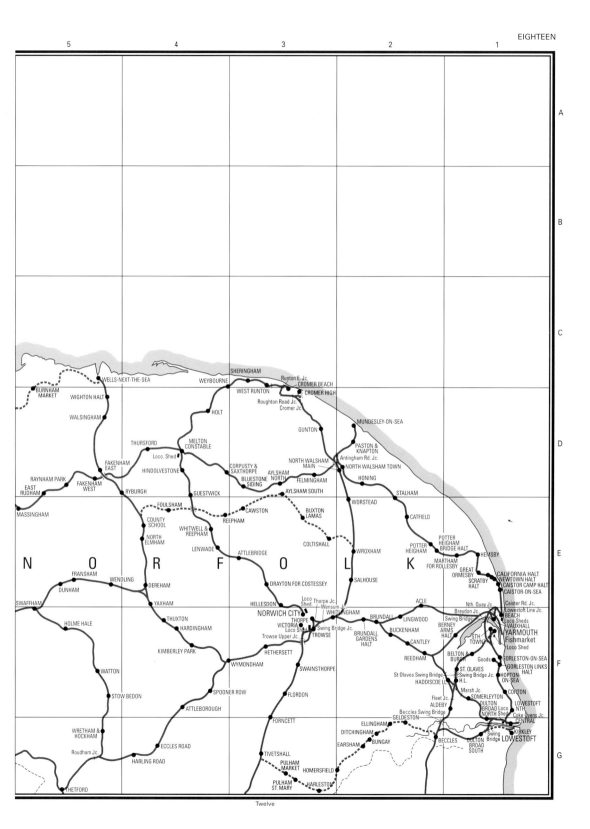

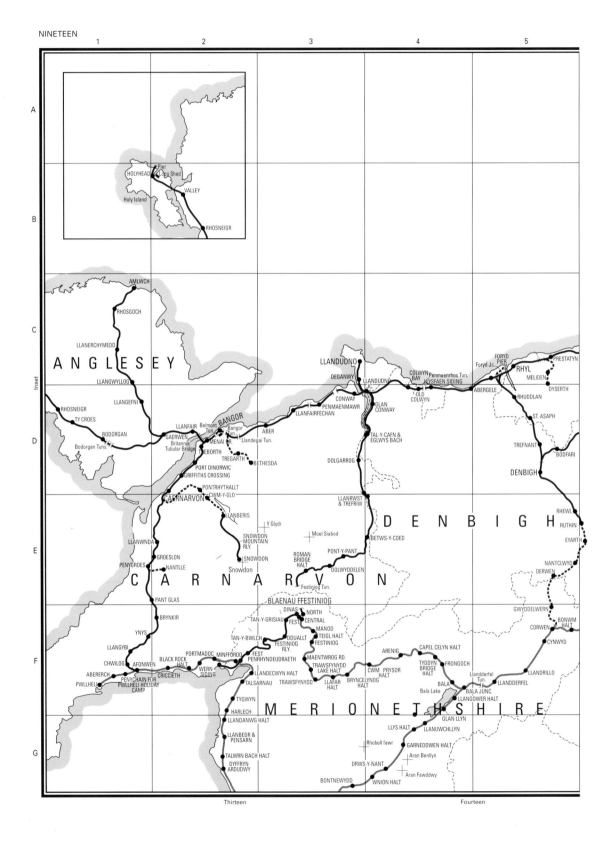

ANGLESEY

AMLWCH
RHOSGOCH
LLANERCHYMEDD
LLANGWYLLOG
LLANGEFNI
RHOSNEIGR
TY CROES
BODORGAN
Bodorgan Tuns.
LLANFAIR
Belmont Tun.
GAERWEN
Britannia
Tubular Bridge
MENAI BR.
TREBORTH
Llandegai Tun.
BANGOR
Bangor
Tun.
ABER

HOLYHEAD Pier
Loco Shed
VALLEY
Holy Island
RHOSNEIGR

CARNARVON

PORT DINORWIC
GRIFFITHS CROSSING
PONTRHYTHALLT
CWM-Y-GLO
CAERNARVON
LLANBERIS
Y Glydr
SNOWDON
MOUNTAIN
RLY.
SNOWDON
Snowdon
LLANWNDA
GROESLON
PENYGROES
NANTLLE
PANT GLAS
BRYNKIR
YNYS
LLANGYBI
CHWILOG
AFONWEN
ABERERCH
PWLLHELI
PENYCHAIN FOR
PWLLHELI HOLIDAY
CAMP
CRICCIETH
BLACK ROCK
HALT
PORTMADOC
MINFFORDD
FEST
PENRHYNDEUDRAETH
WERN
SIDING
LLANDECWYN HALT
TALSARNAU
TYGWYN
HARLECH
LLANDANWG HALT
LLANBEDR &
PENSARN
TALWRN BACH HALT
DYFFRYN
ARDUDWY

TREGARTH
BETHESDA
DOLGARROG

CONWAY
PENMAENMAWR
LLANFAIRFECHAN
GLAN
CONWAY
TAL-Y-CAFN &
EGLWYS BACH
LLANRWST
& TREFRIW
BETWS-Y-COED
PONT-Y-PANT
ROMAN
BRIDGE
HALT
DOLWYDDELEN
Festiniog Tun.
ROMAN
Moel Siabod

LLANDUDNO
DEGANWY
LLANDUDNO
JC.
COLWYN
BAY
Penmaenrhos Tun.
LYSFAEN SIDING
OLD
COLWYN
ABERGELE
FORYD
PIER
Foryd Jc.
RHYL
MELIDEN
DYSERTH
RHUDDLAN
ST. ASAPH
TREFNANT
BODFARI
DENBIGH
RHEWL
RUTHIN
EYARTH
NANTCLWYD
DERWEN
GWYDDELWERN
CORWEN
BONWM
HALT
CYNWYD
LLANDRILLO
LLANDDERFEL

DENBIGH

BLAENAU FFESTINIOG
DINAS
NORTH
TAN-Y-GRISIAU
FEST
CENTRAL
MANOD
TEIGL HALT
FESTINIOG
TAN-Y-BWLCH
DDUALLT
FESTINIOG
RLY.
MAENTWROG RD.
TRAWSFYNYDD
LAKE HALT
TRAWSFYNYDD
LLAFAR
HALT
BRYNCELYNOG
HALT
CWM PRYSOR
HALT
ARENIG
CAPEL CELYN HALT
TYDDYN
BRIDGE
HALT
FRONGOCH
Llandderfel
Tun.
BALA
Bala Lake
BALA JUNC.
LLANGOWER HALT
GLAN LLYN
LLANUWCHLLYN
LLYS HALT
GARNEDDWEN HALT
Aran Benllyn
DRWS-Y-NANT
Rhobell fawr
Aran Fawddwy
BONTNEWYDD
WNION HALT

MERIONETHSHIRE

TWENTY

5   4   3   Twenty four   2   1

Twenty one

A

B

Fifteen

C

D

E

F

G

Gds.
ANSDELL & FAIRHAVEN
NEW LONGTON & HUTTON
LYTHAM
LONGTON BRIDGE
PENWORTHAM (COP LANE)
PENWORTHAM Jc.
PRESTON JUNC.
BAMBER BRI.
HOGHTON
MILL HILL
CHERRY TREE
LOWER DARWEN
BAXENDEN
Summit
Kitson Wood Tun.
PORTSMOUTH
TODMORDEN
HESKETH BANK
HOOLE
FARINGTON
East Jc.
LOSTOCK HALL
LEYLAND
N.U. Jc.
Euxton Jc.
MIDGE HALL
PLEASINGTON
FENISCOWLES
WITHNELL
BRINSCALL
HOLLINS
DARWEN
SPRING VALE
Loco Sheds.
HASLINGDEN
RAWTEN-STALL
CLOUGH FOLD

CROSSENS
BANKS
HUNDRED END
WHITE BEAR
HEAPEY
FRIDAY STREET
CHORLEY
ENTWISTLE
TURTON & EDGEWORTH
Sough Tun.
HELMSHORE
EWOOD BRI.
NEWCHURCH TEADS
WATERFOOT
STACKS
FACIT
WHITWORTH

SOUTHPORT
CHAPEL STREET
HESKETH PARK
CHURCHTOWN
Roe Lane Jc.
MEOLS COP
KENSINGTON ROAD
BIRKDALE
AINSDALE
ST LUKES
BLOWICK
BESCAR LANE
NEW LANE
CROSTON
RUFFORD
BALSHAW LANE & EUXTON
COPPULL
ADLINGTON
BROMLEY CROSS
ASTLEY BRI.
HOLCOMBE BROOK
STUBBINS
RAMSBOTTOM
SUMMERSEAT
TOTTINGTON
SMITHY BR.
SHAWCLOUGH
WARDLEWORTH
HEAP BR.
WOOLFOLD
ROCHDALE
MILNROW

1 HOPE & PENYFFORDD
FRESHFIELD
ALTCAR & HILLHOUSE
FORMBY
ORMSKIRK
BURSCOUGH BRI.
HOSCAR
PARBOLD
APPLEY BRI.
BURSCOUGH JUNC.
AUGHTON PARK HALT
SKELMERSDALE
UPHOLLAND
GATHURST
Whelley Jc.
WIGAN
RED ROCK
BLACKROD
HORWICH
Standish Jc.
LOSTOCK JUNC.
BOLTON
DICCONSON LANE
BLACKRODE
RADCLIFFE
BLACK LANE
HEYWOOD
H.L.
EXCHANGE
BOLTON ST.
BRADLEY FOLD
RADCLIFFE BRIDGE
CASTLE-TON
BROADFIELD
BURY
KNOWSLEY STR.
THE OAKS
MIDDLETON
MIDDLETON JUNC.

TOWN GREEN & AUGHTON
HIGHTOWN
HALL ROAD
BLUNDELLSANDS & CROSBY
WATERLOO
SEAFORTH
NEW BRIGHTON
WALLASEY GROVE ROAD
WALLASEY VILLAGE
MORETON
BIDSTON
MEOLS
MANOR ROAD
LEASOWE
SEFTON
MAGHULL
OLD ROAN
AINTREE
KIRKBY
FAZACKERLEY
PRESTON RD.
LIVERPOOL
BUSHEY LANE Jc.
RAINFORD JUNC.
Randle Jc.
RAINFORD VILLAGE
GARSWOOD
CARR MILL
MOSS BANK
ST. CENTRAL
HAYDOCK
BRYN
PEMBERTON
ORRELL
RAINHILL
HINDLEY
DAISY HILL
PLODDER LANE
ATHERTON
HOWE BRI.
WALKDEN
FARNWORTH
KEARSLEY
PREST-WICH
WHITEFIELD
CLIFTON
JC. MILES PLATTING
HEATON PK.
CRUMPSALL
NEWTON HEATH
BOLTON
DEAN LANE
LONDON RD.

HESWALL
LEASOWE
NEW FERRY
BEBINGTON
ROCK FERRY
ST. MICHELS
GARSTON
WOODSIDE
BIRKENHEAD
HOYLAKE
WEST KIRBY
KIRBY PARK
CALDY
THURSTASTON
STORETON FOR BARNSTON
SPITAL
WOODSIDE
MOSSLEY HILL
CRESSINGTON
AIGBURTH
BRUNSWICK
EXCHANGE
LIME ST.
CENTRAL
EDGE HILL
WAVERTREE
BROAD GREEN
HUYTON
ROBY
PRESCOT
ECCLESTON PARK
ST. HELENS
THATTO HEATH
BREN RD.
TUE BROOK
SPEKE
HUYTON QUARRY
FARNWORTH & BOLD
SANKEY
WIDNES
WARRINGTON
DITTON
CLOCK FACE
ST. HELENS Jc.
COLLINS GREEN
EARLESTOWN
NEWTON-LE-WILLOWS
GOLBORNE
KENYON JUNC.
LOWTON
CULCHETH
LEIGH
TYLDESLEY
BARTON MOSS
PATRICROFT
ECCLES
SWINTON
PENDLETON
VICTORIA
EXCHANGE
SALFORD
MANCHESTER CENT.
TRAFFORD PK.
ORDSALL
HORLTON-CUM-HARDY
LEVENSHULME
ARDWICK
ASHBURY'S

CHILDWALL
GATEACRE
HUNTS CROSS
ALLERTON
DITTON
HALEBANK
DOCKS
RUNCORN
MOORE
Acton Grange Jc.
Old Main Line Jc.
THELWALL
Via.
PRESTON BROOK
(SEE SHEET NO. FORTY FIVE)
WIDNES E.L.
FIDLERS FERRY
ARPLEY
LATCHFORD
LYMM
HEATLEY
DUNHAM MASSEY
HALE
ALTRINCHAM
NORTHENDEN
HEALD GREEN
STYAL
ASHLEY
BAGULEY
WITHINGTON & WEST DIDSBURY
DIDSBURY
TIMPERLEY
BROADHEATH
PARTINGTON
GLAZE
Dam BROOK
PADGATE
Glazebrook Moss Jc.
GLAZEBURY
ASTLEY
FLIXTON
IRLAM
East
CADISHEAD
BROOKLANDS
HEATON MERSEY
HEATON CHAPEL
LEVENSHULME
BURNAGE
STOCKPORT
DAVENPORT
HAZEL GROVE
CHEADLE HULME
BRAMHALL
POYNTON
WILMSLOW
ADLINGTON

MOSTYN
TALACRE
HOLYWELL JUNC.
BAGILLT
FLINT
CAERWYS
NANNERCH
STAR CROSSING HALT
RHYDYMWYN
MOLD
RUTHIN
EYARTH
COED TALON
PADESWOOD & BUCKLEY
LLONG
CAERGWRLE CASTLE & WELLS
CEFN-Y-BEDD
GWERSYLLT & WHEATSHEAF
BRYMBO
COED POETH
MINERA
RHOSTYLLEN
LEGACY
RHOS
WYNN HALL SIDING
ACREFAIR
TREVOR
RHOSYMEDRE HALT
CEFN
Dee Viaduct
WHITEHURST HALT
CHIRK
Chirk Viaduct
TRENCH HALT
ELSON HALT
FRANKTON
WESTON-RHYN
GOBOWEN
Gobowen Jc.
PARK HALL HALT
Loco Sheds
OSWESTRY
Summit
TINKERS GREEN HALT
WHITTINGTON HIGH LEVEL
WHITTINGTON LOW LEVEL
REDNAL & WEST FELTON
LLANRHAIADR MOCHNANT
LLANSILIN ROAD
NANTMAWR
PORTHYWAEN
LLYNCLYS
BLODWELL JUNC.
PANT
STANWARDINE HALT
BASCHURCH
MAESBROOK
LLANYMYNECH JUNCTION
ELSON HALT
WERN LAS
KINNERLEY JUNC.
OLD WOODS HALT
HADNALL
LLANFECHAIN

HAWARDEN
HAWARDEN BRIDGE
SHOTTON
SANDYCROFT
QUEENSFERRY
SALTNEY FERRY
SALTNEY
CHESTER
NORTH GATE
GENERAL
BROUGHTON & BRETTON
HOPE (HI)
HOPE (ILL)
BUCKLEY
PENYFFORDD FOR LEESWOOD
HOPE VILLAGE
KINNERTON
BALDERTON
PULFORD SIDING
ROSSETT
GRESFORD FOR LLAY
WHEATSHEAF JUNCTION
GATEWEN
COLL EXCHANGE
GENERAL
CENTRAL
HIGHTOWN HALT
MARCHWIEL
CESSWICK HALT
JOHNSTOWN & HAFOD
RUABON
PICKHILL HALT
BANGOR-ON-DEE
CLOY HALT
OVERTON-ON-DEE
GRINDLEY BROOK HALT
WHITCHURCH
FENN'S BANK
BETTISFIELD
WELSHAMPTON
ELLESMERE
PREES
WEM
HODNET
WOLLERTON HALT
PEPLOW

BACHE
MICKLE TRAFFORD EAST
BLACON
LIVERPOOL RD
SAUGHALL
MOULDS WORTH
DELAMERE
WHITEGATE
Winsford Jc.
WINSFORD & OVER
OVER & WHARTON
WINSFORD
MIDDLEWICH
HOLMES CHAPEL
SANDBACH
BRUNSWICK STREET
ELSWORTH WHARF
NORTH RODE
CONGLETON
Upper Jct.
BIDDULPH
MOW COP & SCHOLAR GR.
CHELFORD
GOOSTREY
ALDERLEY EDGE
PRESTBURY
Gds.
HIBEL ROAD
MACCLESFIELD
CENTRAL
Summit
BOLLINGTON
KNUTSFORD
MOBBERLEY
WINNINGTON
HARTFORD & GREENBANK
LOSTOCK GRALAM
NORTHWICH
PLUMLEY
WEAVER Jc.
ACTON BRIDGE
CUDDINGTON
MANLEY
HARTFORD
HELSBY & ALVANLEY
HELSBY
FRODSHAM
Frodsham Jc.
North Jc.
INCE & ELTON
ELLESMERE PORT
CAPENHURST
DUNHAM HILL
MOLLINGTON

FLINT
HADLOW RD.
NESTON
PARKGATE
HESWALL HILLS
BROMBOROUGH
HOOTON
LITTLE SUTTON
EDSHAM
Halton Jc.
HALTON
WEST Jc.
HAWARDEN
SEALAND
CONNAH'S QUAY
BURTON POINT
MANCHESTER Line Jc.
SHREWSBURY Line Jc.
WILLASTON
NANTWICH
WORLESTON
CHRISTLETON Tun.
WAVERTON
Tattenhall Jc.
TATTENHALL RD.
TATTEN-HALL
BEESTON CASTLE & TARPORLEY
BROXTON
MALPAS
HANDLEY
CALVELEY
ROOKERY BRIDGE
SANDBACH
TTILEY HEATH
BETTLEY ROAD
WRENBURY
AUDLEM
ADDERLEY
NORTON-IN-HALES
MARKET DRAYTON
TERN HILL
WORLESTON COAL DEPOT
Works
CUMBERLAND WHARF
Chester Line Jc.
Loco Shed
N.S. Jc.
CREWE
RADWAY GREEN
ALSAGER
HALMEREND
AUDLEY & BIGNALL END
Diglake
Jamage Jc.
Market Drayton Jc.
HAREICASTLE
CHATTERLEY
LAWTON
KIDSGROVE
BLACK BULL
NEWCHAPEL & GOLDENHILL
PITTS HILL
FORD GRN.
BURSLEY
COBRIDGE
HANLEY
LONGPORT
STOKE
NEWCASTLE UNDER LYME
KEELE
MADELEY
SILVERDALE
LEYCETT
BOTTESLOW
ETRURIA
FENTON
MILTON
STOCKTON BROOK
TURNHILL
FORD GREEN
ENDON
NORTON BRIDGE
STAFFORD
TRENT VALLEY Jc.
Loco Shed
HAUGHTON
GNOSALL
STAFFORD COMMON
NORTON BRIDGE FOR ECCLESHALL
GREAT BRIDGEFORD
DOXFORD.
BARLASTON & TITTENSOR
STONE
STANDON BRIDGE
ASTON-BY-STONE
TRENTHAM
WHITMORE
PIPE GATE
Summit
TRENTHAM GARDENS
AUDLEM

PART OF FLINT

CHESHIRE

SHROPSHIRE

ERDINE HALT
ELLERDINE HALT
YORTON
HADNALL

Fourteen   Fifteen

1   2   3   Twenty eight   4   5

Row A

ASKRIGG, REDMIRE, WENSLEY, LEYBURN, CONSTABLE BURTON, JERVAULX, CRAKEHALL, AINDERBY, SCRUTON, Cordio Jcs., NORTHALLERTON, South J.c., LEEMING BAR, NEWBY WISKE, OTTERINGTON, Poppleton Jc., Bootham Jc., Severus Jc., Burton Lane Jc., Foss Islands Jc., North J.c., Gould, KIRBY MOORSIDE, NAWTON, HELMSLEY

ELSLACK-IN-CRAVEN, THORNTON-IN-CRAVEN, BARNOLDSWICK, EARBY

ASHTON UNDER LYNE, OLDHAM ROAD, OLDHAM ROAD, Pass., PARK PARADE, DUKINFIELD, STALYBRIDGE, Joint Pass., SOUTH, Crowrun Jc., DUKINFIELD & ASHTON, Audenshaw Jc., GUIDE BRIDGE, Ashton Moss Jc., Goods, HOOLEY HILL, Denton Jc.

MASHAM, PICKHILL, THIRSK TOWN, JUNCTION, SINDERBY, TOPCLIFFE, Halgate Bridge Jc., YORK, FOSS ISLAND (Goods), NUNNINGTON, HOVINGHAM SPA, Chaloners Whin Jc., COXWOLD, LAYERTHORPE, GILLING, SLINGSBY

TANFIELD, MELMERBY, BALDERSBY, SESSAY, PILMOOR, HUSTHWAITE GATE

Row B

FOULRIDGE, COLNE, NELSON, RIPON, BRAFFERTON, RASKELF, EASINGWOLD, ALNE, TOLLERTON, FLAXTON

PATELEY BRIDGE, CARDIGAN RD., LEEDS, (Goods), (Goods), WELLINGTON ST, Geldard, WELLINGTON, CITY, CENTRAL, DACRE, WORMALD GREEN, BOROUGHBRIDGE, COPGROVE, STRENSALL

GRASSINGTON & THRESHFIELD, ARMLEY, Wortley Jc., Canal Jc., HOLBECK H.L., Leeds Jc., Three Signal Bri. Jc., BIRSTWITH, RIPLEY VALLEY, NIDD BRIDGE, BENINGBROUGH, HAXBY, WARTHILL

Row C

BELL BUSK, GARGRAVE, Skipton N. Jc., SKIPTON, EMBSAY, BOLTON ABBEY, ADDINGHAM, RYLSTONE, Wortley W. Jct., WHITEHALL, COPLEY HILL, Engine Shed Jc., Wortley S. Jc., FARNLEY & WORTLEY, HUNSLET LANE, DARLEY, HAMPSTHWAITE, Bilton Road Jc., Dragon Jc., KNARESBOROUGH, STARBECK, HARROGATE, Goods, Loco Shed, GOLDSBOROUGH, HOPPERTON, CATTAL, HAMMERTON, WILSTROP (Goods), EARSWICK, YORK, Bootham Jc., Burton Lane Jc.

MID., BEN RHYDDING, BURLEY-IN-WHARFEDALE, Milner Wood Jc., POOL-IN-WHARFEDALE, COLLINGHAM BRIDGE, WEETON, Crimple Jc., Crimple Tun., PANNAL, SPOFFORTH, Wetherby W.Jc., Wetherby E.Jc., WETHERBY, Goods, THORP ARCH, COPMANTHORPE, POPPLETON, Poppleton Jc., Severus Jc., Holgate Bridge Jc., Chaloners Whin Jc., LAYERTHORPE, MURTON LANE, OSBALDWICK, DUNNINGTON (FOR KEXBY), ELVINGTON FOR SUTTON, Swing Bridge Jc., NABURN, WHELDRAKE

ELSLACK, THORNTON-IN-CRAVEN, EARBY, CONONLEY, STEETON & SILSDEN, ILKLEY, KILDWICK & CROSSHILLS, NEWTON KYME, COTTINGWITH, THORGANBY, SKIPWITH & NORTH DUFFIELD

Row D

KEIGHLEY SOUTH, INGROW WEST, OLDHAM CENTRAL, GLODWICK Rd., OAKWORTH, HAWORTH, OXENHOPE, DENHOLME, INGROW EAST, BINGLEY, Bingley Tun., SALTAIRE, CULLINGWORTH, FRIZING HALL, WILSDEN, MANNINGHAM, BRADFORD, LAISTER-DYKE, BAILDON, THACKLEY, SHIPLEY, IDLE, ECCLESHILL, BRAMLEY, ARMLEY, MARSH LANE, PUDSEY LOWTOWN, HUNSLET, Gds., Hunslet Bch Jc., Stourton Jc., GARFORTH, MICKLEFIELD, SOUTH MILFORD, Milford Jc., SHERBURN-IN-ELMET, Swing Bri., HAMBLETON, SELBY, Brayton N. Jc., Brayton E. Jc., MENTHORPE GATE, CLIFF COMMON, Le Earby, WISTOW, BUBWITH, RICCALL, CAWOOD, CHURCH FENTON, WOODLES-FORD, DUFFIELD, HEMINGBROUGH

MUMPS, LEES STREET, GLODWICK ROAD, MENSTON, OTLEY, GUISELEY, ARTHINGTON, Bramhope Tun., THORNER, Summit, YEADON, ESHOLT, BARDSEY, TADCASTER, BOLTON PERCY, ULLESKELF, ESCRICK, WRESSLE, BARMBY, DRAX ABBEY

SEE SHEET NO. FORTY TWO, HEADINGLEY, KIRKSTALL, LEEDS, Cross Gates Jc., SCHOLES, Loco Shed Jc., CROSSGATES, STUTTON SIDING, STANNINGLEY, MONK FRYSTON, LEDSTON, THORP GATES SIDING, BARLOW

THORNTON, QUEENSBURY, CLAYTON, GT. HORTON, HOLMFIELD, WHEATLEY, DUDLEY HILL, PUDSEY GILL, BIRKENSHAW, CHISLEWELL, BESTON, ROBIN HOOD, MORLEY, KIPPAX

Row E

STANSFIELD HALL, Hall RoydJc., Millwood Tun., EASTWOOD, Castle Hill Tun., Horstall Tun., TODMORDEN, WALSDEN, Summit Tun., LITTLEBOROUGH, Weasel Hall Tun., HEBDEN BRI., MYTHOLMROYD, SOWERBY BRI., LUDDENDEN FOOT, RIPPONDEN, WEST VALE, STAINLAND, SMITHY BRIDGE, LUDDENDEN, ST.PAULS, N. BRIDGE, WYKE, Wyke Jc., HALIFAX, Milner Royd, GREETLAND, ELLAND, Bradley Wood Jc., LOW MOOR, CLECKHEATON, HECKMONDWIKE, DEWSBURY, LIVERSEDGE, BRIGHOUSE, COOPER BRI., CLIFFE, HIGHTOWN, BIRSTALL, HEATON LODGE, SOOTHILL, BATLEY, OSSETT, HORBURY & OSSETT, ARDSLEY, METHLEY, CASTLEFORD, FERRYBRIDGE (S.&K.), MONKHILL, PONTEFRACT (L.Y.&G.N.), WHITLEY BRIDGE, Hensall Jc., Gowdall Jc., CARLTON TOWERS, Aire Jc., AIRMYN & RAWCLIFFE, RAWCLIFFE, SNAITH, SNAITH & POLLINGTON, HECK, BALNE, SKYEHOUSE

WATERLOO, WHEATLEY, EMBSAY, RYHILL, WAKEFIELD, NORMANTON, TANSHELF, BAGHILL, KNOTTINGLEY, TEMPLE HIRST, SHARLSTON, FEATHERSTONE, WOMERSLEY, BURTON SALMON, SNAITH

HILLHOUSE, DEIGHTON, KIRKHEATON, MIRFIELD, Springwood Jc., LONGWOOD, HUDDERSFIELD, GOLCAR, LOCKWOOD, BERRY BROW, FENAY BRI. & LEPTON, HORBURY MILLFIELD ROAD, Crigglestone Jc., CRIGGLESTONE, OAKENSHAW, CROFTON, HARE PARK, NOSTELL, ACKWORTH, Brackenhill Jc., KIRK SMEATON, NORTON, THORNE NORTH, THORNE SOUTH

LINTHWAITE (Gds.), SLAITHWAITE, NETHERTON, Robin Hood Tun., KIRKBURTON, Royston Jc., NOTTON & ROYSTON, HEMSWORTH, UPTON, Wrangbrook Jc., ASKERN, Joan Croft Jc., THORPE-IN-BALNE

Row F

WANDSWORTH, Rochdale L Jc., MILNROW, NEW HEY, SHAW & CROMPTON, ROYTON, ROYTON JUNC., MARSDEN, Standedge Tun., HEALEY HOUSE, MELTHAM, HONLEY, BROCKHOLES, STOCKSMOOR, THONGS BRI., SHEPLEY, Thurstonland Tun., DENBY DALE, HAIGH, CLAYTON WEST, SKELMANTHORPE, Cumberworth Tun., DARTON, STAINCROSS, MONK BRITTON, CUDWORTH, Adwick & Skellow Jc., PICKBURN & BRODSWORTH, CARCROFT, BRAMWITH, BARNBY DUN, Kirk Sandall Jc., KIRK SANDALL Jc., DONCASTER, Loco Shed, Bally Jc., Low Ellers Jc., Bessacar Jc., FINNINGLEY

DELPH, DIGGLE, DIGGLE, SADDLEWORTH, UPPERMILL, GREENFIELD, FRIEZLAND, Royal George Tun., MICKLEHURST (Goods), Scout Tunnel, STALEY & MILLBROOK, WOODHEAD, Woodhead Tun., HOLMFIRTH, Wellhouse Tun., HAZLEHEAD BRIDGE, DUNFORD BRIDGE, PENISTONE, Barnsley Jc., Thurgoland Tun., WORTLEY, THORNCLIFFE IRON WORKS, DODWORTH, SILKSTONE, SUMMER LANE, BARNSLEY, ROCKINGHAM COLLIERY, WOMBWELL, BIRDWELL, ELSECAR, WENTWORTH, CARLTON, WATH CENTRAL, Wath Rd. Jc., SWINTON, KILNHURST, MEXBORO, SWINTON, BOLTON ON DEARNE, HARLINGTON, SPROTBORO, WARMSWORTH, St. Catherine's Jc., LOVERSALL CARR Jc., ROSSINGTON, MISSON SIDING, BAWTRY

OLDHAM, LEES, GROTTON, GLODWICK RD., LEEK, MOSSLEY, BRI., DROYLSDEN, ASHTON, STALYBRIDGE, HYDE, GLOSSOP, BROADBOTTOM CENTRAL FOR MOTTRAM & CHARLESWORTH, WOODLEY, BREDBURY, ROMILEY, MARPLE, CROWDEN, WOODHOUSE, DEEPCAR, CLAPLETOWN, Tankersley Tun., DINTING VIA., HADFIELD, NEWTON FOR HYDE

Row G

STOCKPORT, DAVENPORT, ROSE HILL, HIGH LANE, MARPLE, HAYFIELD, BIRCH VALE, Hexthorpe Jc., Doncaster Avoiding Line Jc., Hexthorpe, ARKSEY, Kirk Sandall Jc., Bentley Jc., MARSH GATE (Gds), YORK ROAD, WHEATLEY PARK, Norton Jc., DONCASTER, Bay Jc., South Jc., CHERRY TREE LANE, Potteric Carr Jc., Low Ellers Jc., Bessaoar Jc., Black Carr Jc., Loversall Carr Jc., ECCLESFIELD, OUGHTY BRIDGE, WADSLEY BRIDGE, BRIGHTSIDE, WINCOBANK, HOLMES, TINSLEY, PARKGATE, ROTHERHAM (MASBORO), ROTHERHAM CENTRAL, Braithwell Jc., Northern Jc., CENTRAL HELLABY, TICKHILL & WADWORTH, MALTBY, RANSKILL, BAWTRY

Black Carr W. Jc., WARMSWORTH Jc., EDDINGTON, Black Carr E. Jc., S. Catherine's Jcs., NEEPSEND, SHEFFIELD VICTORIA, WHARF STREET, QUEENS RD. Gds., MIDLAND, WOODHOUSE, ATTERCLIFFE, DARNALL, WOODHOUSE MILL, Tinsley Jc., Treeton Jc., Southern Jc., CATCLIFFE, TREETON, THURCROFT, DINNINGTON & LAUGHTON, Dinnington Jc.

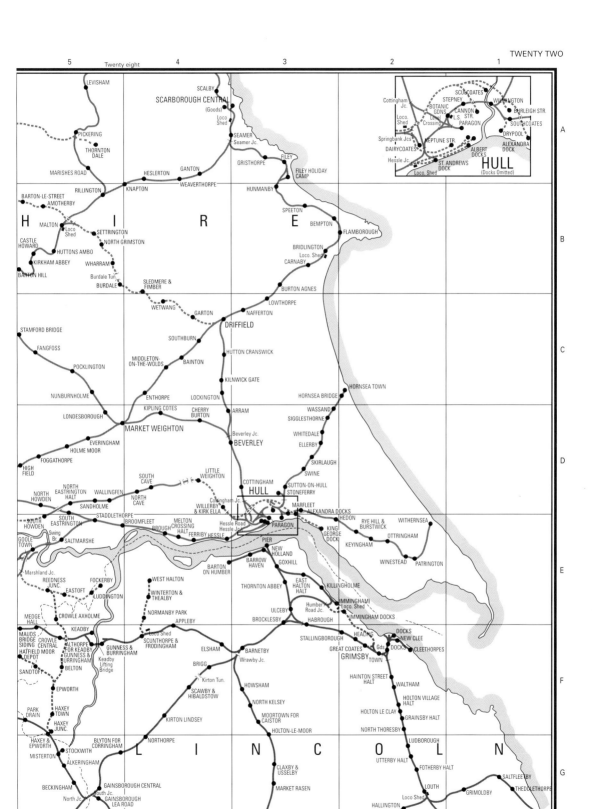

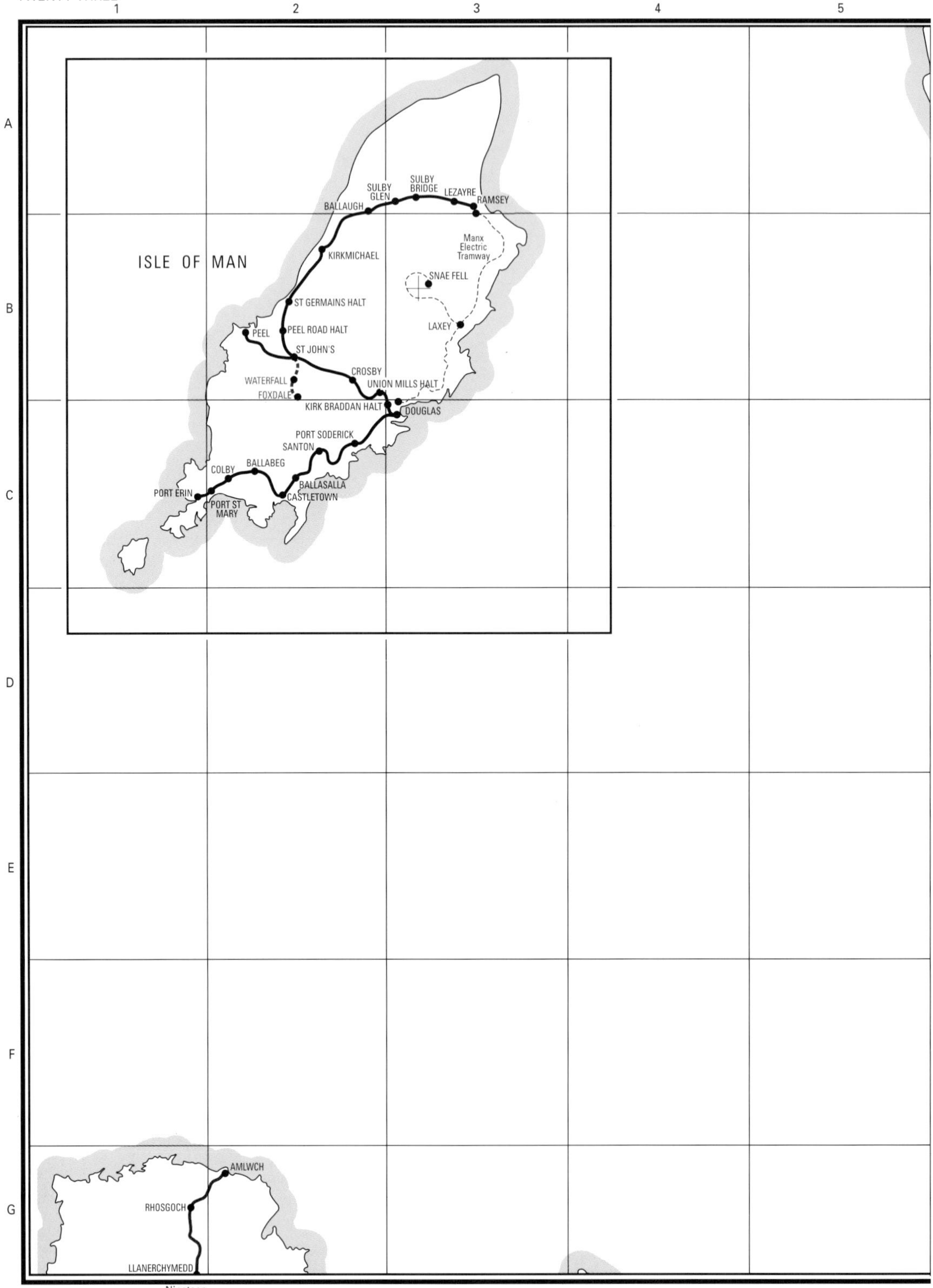
1
2
3
4
5
A
B
C
D
E
F
G
ISLE OF MAN
SULBY GLEN
SULBY BRIDGE
LEZAYRE
RAMSEY
BALLAUGH
KIRKMICHAEL
Manx Electric Tramway
SNAE FELL
ST GERMAINS HALT
PEEL ROAD HALT
PEEL
ST JOHN'S
LAXEY
CROSBY
UNION MILLS HALT
WATERFALL
FOXDALE
KIRK BRADDAN HALT
DOUGLAS
PORT SODERICK
SANTON
BALLABEG
COLBY
BALLASALLA
CASTLETOWN
PORT ERIN
PORT ST MARY
AMLWCH
RHOSGOCH
LLANERCHYMEDD

Nineteen

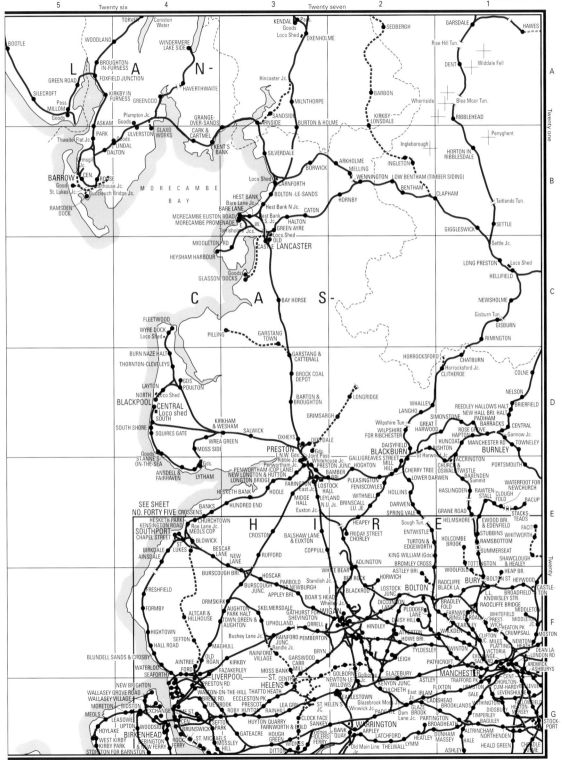

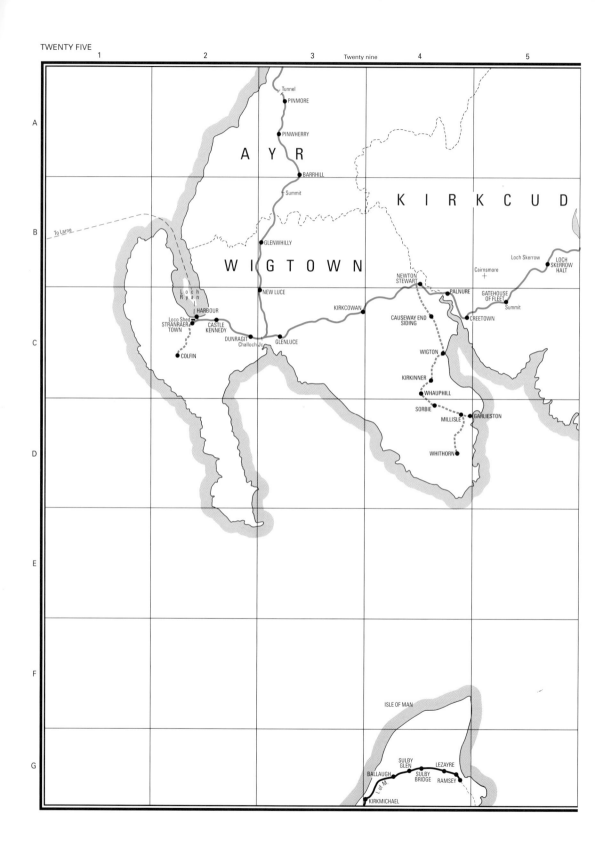

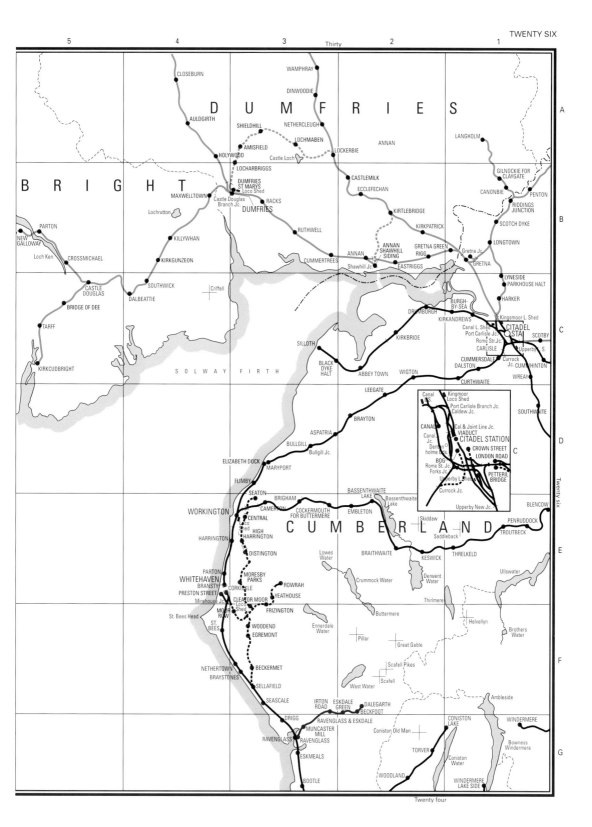

1   2   Thirty one   3   4   5

A

SAUGHTREE DEADWATER
STEELE ROAD
KIELDER FOREST
LEWIEFIELD HALT
PLASHETTS
EWESLEY
WIDDRINGTON
LONG WITTON
LONGHURST
ASHINGTON
NEWCASTLETON
FALSTONE THORNEYBURN
WOODBURN
SCOTSGAP
NORTH SEATON
PEGSWOOD
HEPSCOTT
MORPETH
NORTH
MIDDLETON
TARSET
BELLINGHAM
(NORTH TYNE)
KNOWESGATE
ANGERTON
CHOPPINGTON
BEDLINGTON
KERSHOPE FOOT
REEDSMOUTH
MELDON
STANNINGTON
BEBSIDE

N O R T H U M B E R L A N D
PLESSEY
WARK
CRAMLINGTON
BARRASFORD
PONTELAND
ANNITSFORD
CALLERTON
B
CHOLLERTON
KILLINGWORTH
FOREST
HUMSHAUGH
KENTON BANK
HALL
FOURSTONES
COXLODGE
BENTON
GILSLAND
WALL
LEMINGTON WEST GOSFORTH
NEWBURN SOUTH GOSFORTH
LONGBENTON
GREENHEAD
BARDON
MILL
HAYDON
BRIDGE
HEDDON-ON-THE-WALL
NORTH WYLAM
W. JESMOND JESMOND
HALTWHISTLE
HEXHAM
RYTON SCOTSWOOD
LOW ROW
Haltwhistle Tunnel
WYLAM
BLAYDON CENTRAL
CORBRIDGE Corbridge Tun.
PRUDHOE SWALWELL
BRAMPTON JUNC.
FEATHERSTONE PARK
RIDING MILL
STOCKSFIELD
BENSHAM
NEWCASTLE LOW FELL
COANWOOD
LINTZ
GREEN
ROWLANDS
GILL
LAMESLEY
HOW MILL
LAMBLEY
TANFIELD LEA
COLLIERY
BIRTLEY
HEADS NOOK
WETHERAL
WEST STANLEY
BEAMISH
PELTON
C
SLAGGYFORD
BLACKHILL
W. STANLEY (Goods)
CHESTER LE STREET
LEADGATE
CONSETT ANNFIELD PLAIN
KNITSLEY
PLAWSWORTH
ROWLEY

ARMATHWAITE
ALSTON
WASKERLEY
LANCHESTER
WITTON
GILBERT BEARPARK
Armathwaite Tun.
Baron Wood Tuns.
DURHAM
BLANCHLAND
ALDIN GRANGE SIDING
USHAW
MOOR
D
LAZONBY & KIRKOSWALD
WEATHER HILL
QUARRY
BRANDON Reilly
COLLIERY Mill
Jc.
CALTHWAITE
Lazonby Tun.
WEARHEAD
EASTGATE
STANHOPE
SUNNISIDE
DEPOTS & WATERHOUSES
SIDING
DEPOTS &
ST. JOHN'S CHAPEL
WESTGATE-
IN-WEARDALE
FROSTERLEY
TOW LAW
BRANCEPETH
PLUMPTON
LITTLE SALKELD
WOLSINGHAM
LANGWATHBY
HARPERLEY
CROOK WILLINGTON
SPENNYMOOR
D U R H A M
BEECHBURN HUNWICK
PENRITH FOR Waste Bank Tun.
ULLSWATER LAKE Culgaith Tun.
WITTON-LE-WEAR
BYERS GREEN
CULGAITH
NEW BIGGIN
ETHERLEY
BISHOP AUCKLAND
Eamont Bri. Jc.
CLIFTON MOOR TEMPLE
COUNDON
Eden SOWERBY
EVENWOOD
Valley Jc.
CLIBURN
BUTTERKNOWLE WEST
SHILDON
CLIFTON &
LONG MARTON
MIDDLETON -IN-TEESDALE
COCKFIELD FELL AUCKLAND
LOWTHER
MICKLETON
W E S T M O R L A N D
APPLEBY EAST
ROMALDKIRK
HEIGHINGTON
E
APPLEBY WEST
WINSTON FOR
STAINDROP
WARCOP
BARNARD
CASTLE
BROOMIELAW GAINFORD
Forcett Jc.
COTHERSTONE
Helm Tun.
LARTINGTON
PIERCEBRIDGE
SHAP
Stainmore
Summit
BOWES
FORCETT DEPOT
BARRAS
Shap Summit
CROSBY GARRETT
Belah Viaduct
MOULTON
F
KIRKBY STEPHEN WEST KIRKBY STEPHEN EAST
SCORTON
RAVENSTONEDALE
RICHMOND
Birkett Tun.
CATTERICK
TEBAY
BRIDGE
Wild Boar Fell High Seat
STAVELEY
Blease Fell
Great Shunner Fell
BURNESIDE
LOW GILL
GRAYRIGG
Y O R K
Pass
Aisgill Summit
G
KENDAL
Baugh Fell Shotlock Tun.
Moorcock Tun.
Gds.
OXENHOLME
SEDBERGH
GARSDALE
Mossdale Head Tun.
REDMIRE
LEYBURN CONSTABLE BURTON
HAWES
WENSLEY
Rise Hill Tun.
ASKRIGG
AYSGARTH
JERVAULX
BEDALE

Twenty six

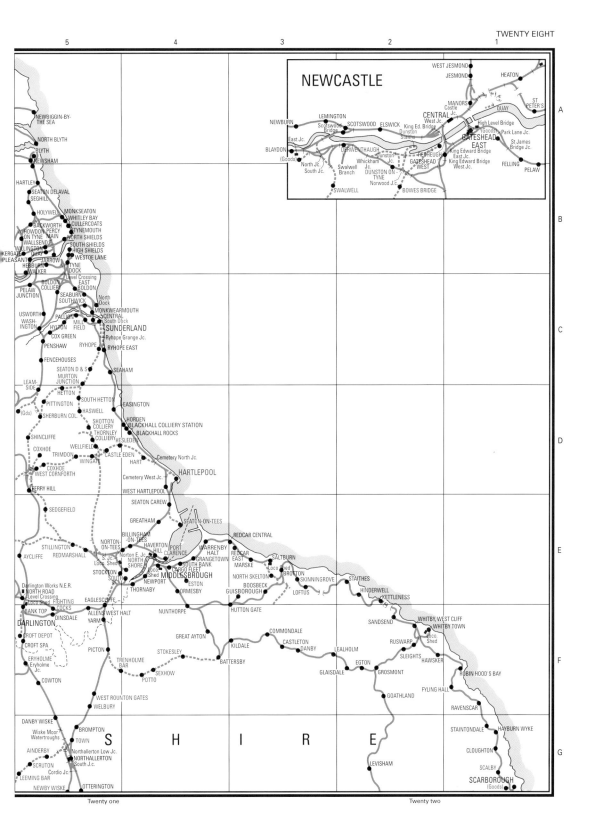

A

CRARAE

LOCHGOILHEAD
Loch Long
Summit
Ben Lomond
ROWARDENNAN
ABERFOYLE
DOUNE
GARTMORE
KIPPEN
GARGUNNOCK
PORT OF MENTEITH
Loch Goil
CARRICK CASTLE
BUCHLYVIE
WHISTLEFIELD
GARELOCHHEAD
DUM-BARTON
Loch Lomond
BALMAHA
S T I R L
CARDLINNTY
SHANDON
Gare Loch
DRYMEN
KILLEARN
DUMGOYNE
BARLFRON

B

ARDENTINNY
RHU
HELENSBURGH (UPPER)
Loco. Shed
BALLOCH PIER
BALLOCH CENTRAL
CALDARVAN
STRIL
KILMUN   BLAIRMORE   COVE
HELENSBURGH CENTRAL
CRAIGENDORAN
JAMESTOWN
BLANEFIELD
STRATHBLANE
Campsie Fells
KILSYTH
ARDNADAM
ALEXANDRIA & BONHILL
CAMPSIE GLEN
LENNOXTOWN
TWECHAIR
ORMIDALE
KIRN
DUNOON
GOUROCK   PRINCES PIER
GREENOCK CENTRAL
CARDROSS
RENTON
MILTON OF CAMPSIE
GARTSHORE
FORT MATILDA
DALREOCH
DUMBARTON CENTRAL
BALMORE   TORRANCE
KIRKINTILLOCH
Waterside Jc.
GREENOCK WEST
CARTSDYKE
DUMBARTON EAST
MILNGAVIE
Bridgend Jc.
LYNEDOCH STREET
INCH GRN.
DUMBUCK SIDING
HILLFOOT
SUMMERSTON
BOGSTON
WOODHALL
BOWLING
KILPATRICK
BEARSDEN
LENZIE JUNCTION FOR GARNGABER
OVERTON
PORT GLASGOW HALT
DALMUIR
MARYHILL   JUNCTION
BISHOPBRIGGS
SPRINGBURN PK
UPPER PORT GLASGOW
LANGBANK
CLYDEBANK
Milngavie Jc.
ROBROYSTON
STEPPS   ROGARNKIRK
INVERKIP
KILMACOLM
KILBOWIE
YOKER
SCOTSTOUNHILL
BUCHANAN ST.
BLAIRHILL

C

TIGHNABRUAICH
WEMYSS BAY
R E N F R E W   RENFREW
BISHOPTON
GEORGETOWN
SCOTSTOUN
NORTH
QUEEN ST.
ST. ROLLOX W.
SHETTLESTON
CARNTYNE
BARGEDDIE
PORT BANNATYNE
INNELLAN
LINWOOD
HOUSTON & CROSSLEE
Blackston
SCOTS RUN
GOVAN
IBROX
ELDERSLIE
CROOKSTON
CATHCART
RUTHERGLEN
MT VERNON
BROOMHOUSE
BRIDGE OF WEIR
PAISLEY
DYKEBAR
CROSSMYLOOF
CAMBUSLANG
CARMYLE
ROTHESAY
JOHNSTONE NORTH
JOHN-STONE HIGH
POTTERHILL
NITSHILL
GIFFNOCK
MUIREND
KIRKHILL
NEWTON
FIRTH OF CLYDE
BUTE
Hill of Stake
KILBARCHAN
MILLIKEN PARK
BARRHEAD   THORNLIEBANK
BURNSIDE
CLARKSTON & STAMPERLAND
BLANTYRE
HIGH BLANTYRE
LOCHWINNOCH
HOWWOOD
NEILSTON HIGH
PATTERTON
WHITE-CRAIGS
BUSBY
BOTH-WELL L.S.
LARGS
NEILSTON LOW   CALDWELL
NETHERTON DEPT
THORNTONHALL
LOCHSIDE
UPLAWMOOR
HAIRMYRES
EAST KILBRIDE
KILBIRNIE
BEITH NORTH
SEE SHEET NO: FORTY FOUR

D

LOCHRANZA
FAIRLIE PIER
FAIRLIE HIGH
GLENGARNOCK
BEITH TOWN
BARRMILL
Lugton Jc.
LUGTON
GIFFEN
DUNLOP
STRATHAVEN CENTRAL
L A
DALRY
Dalry Jc.
WEST KILBRIDE
STEWARTON

E

CORRIE
TOWN. NORTH.   SALTCOATS NORTH.
KILWINNING
CUNNINGHAMHEAD
ARDROSSAN
MONTGOMERIE PIER
Dubbs Jc.
KILMAURS
HILL STREET
WINTON PIER
IRVINE BOGSIDE
CROSSHOUSE
KILMARNOCK
DARVEL
NEWMILNS
SOUTH BEACH
SALTCOATS CENTRAL
RACECOURSE
IRVINE
SPRINGSIDE
Kaypark Jc.
HURLFORD
GALSTON
BARLEITH
STEVENSTON
ST MARNOCKS
GARROCHBURN
ARRAN
BRODICK
IRVINE HARBOUR
DREGHORN
GAILES   DRY-BRIDGE
GATEHEAD
Bellfield Jc.
RICCARTON & CRAIGIE
BARASSIE
TROON   Gds
Pass.
Lochgreen Jc.
MONKTON
MAUCHLINE
CATRINE
MUIRKIRK
Loco. Shed
LAMLASH
KING'S CROSS
PRESTWICK
Mossblown Jc.
TARBOLTON
Brackenhill Jc.
CRONBERRY
WHITING BAY
Falkland Jc.   L.C.
NEWTON-ON-AYR
TARBOLTON
AUCHINLECK
LUGAR
Logan Jc.
AUCHINCRUIVE
TRABBOCH
SKARES
CUMNOCK
AYR HARBOUR
Blackhouse Jc.
Hawkhill Jc.
OCHILTREE
CUMNOCK A & S
AYR
DRONGAN
Belston Jc.

F

HEADS OF AYR
ALLOWAY
Alloway Jc.
NEW CUMNOCK
DUNURE
GREENAN CASTLE
DALRYMPLE
Dalrymple Jc.
RANKINSTON
KNOWESIDE
HOLLYBUSH
HOLEHOUSE
A Y R S H I R E
CASSILLIS
PATNA
WATERSIDE
Blackcraig Hill
GLENSIDE
MAYBOLE
MAIDENS
TURNBERRY
KILKERRAN
DALMELLINGTON

G

DIPPLE SIDING
DAILLY
KILLOCHAN
GRANGESTON HALT
GIRVAN   Tunnel

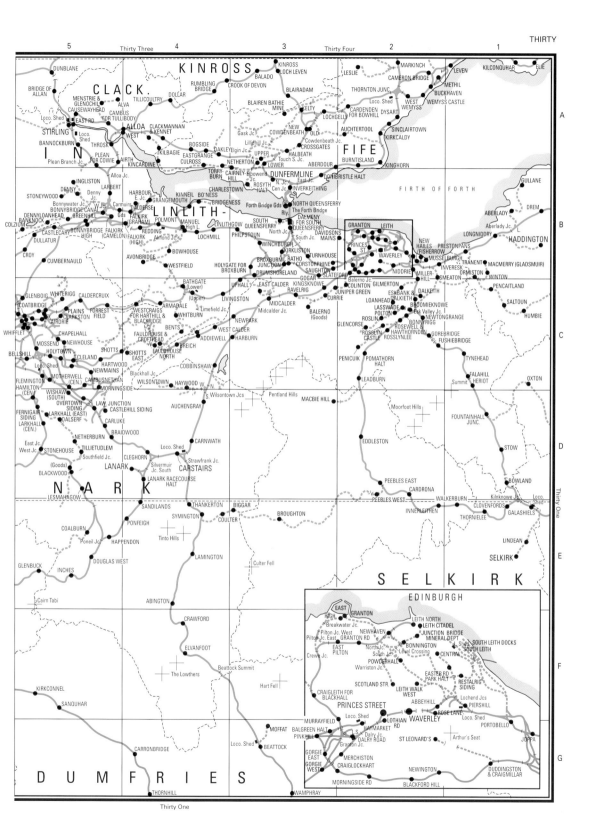

1 2 3 4 5

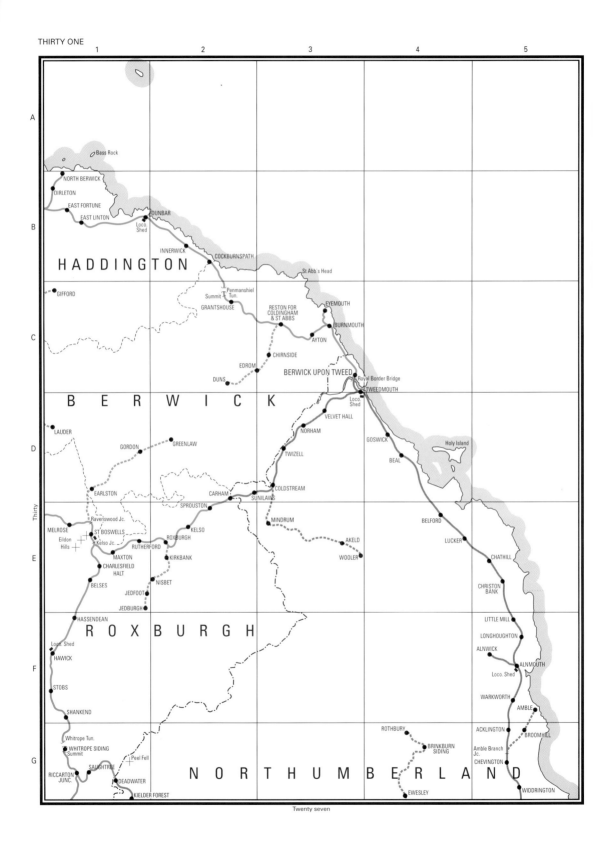

A

Bass Rock

NORTH BERWICK
DIRLETON
EAST FORTUNE
EAST LINTON
DUNBAR
Loco.
Shed

B

INNERWICK
COCKBURNSPATH

St Abb's Head

HADDINGTON

GIFFORD
Summit
Penmanshiel Tun.
GRANTSHOUSE
RESTON FOR
COLDINGHAM
& ST ABBS
EYEMOUTH
BURNMOUTH
AYTON
CHIRNSIDE

C

EDROM
DUNS
BERWICK UPON TWEED
Royal Border Bridge
TWEEDMOUTH
Loco.
Shed

BERWICK

LAUDER
GORDON
GREENLAW
VELVET HALL
NORHAM
TWIZELL
GOSWICK
BEAL
Holy Island

D

EARLSTON
CARHAM
SUNILAWS
COLDSTREAM
SPROUSTON
MINDRUM
BELFORD

Thirty

MELROSE
Ravenswood Jc.
ST BOSWELLS
Eildon
Hills
Kelso Jc.
RUTHERFORD
ROXBURGH
KELSO
MAXTON
KIRKBANK
CHARLESFIELD
HALT
BELSES
NISBET
JEDFOOT
JEDBURGH
AKELD
WOOLER
LUCKER
CHATHILL
CHRISTON
BANK

E

HASSENDEAN

ROXBURGH

Loco. Shed
HAWICK
STOBS
SHANKEND
LITTLE MILL
LONGHOUGHTON
ALNWICK
ALNMOUTH
Loco. Shed
WARKWORTH
AMBLE

F

Whitrope Tun.
WHITROPE SIDING
Summit
Peel Fell
SAUGHTREE
RICCARTON
JUNC.
DEADWATER
KIELDER FOREST
ROTHBURY
BRINKBURN
SIDING
Amble Branch
Jc.
ACKLINGTON
BROOMHILL
CHEVINGTON
WIDDRINGTON
EWESLEY

N O R T H U M B E R L A N D

G

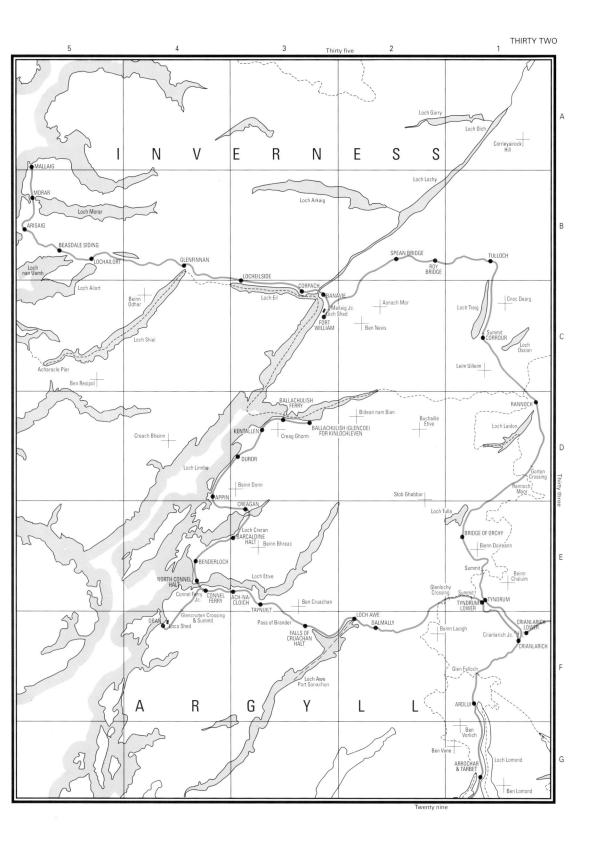

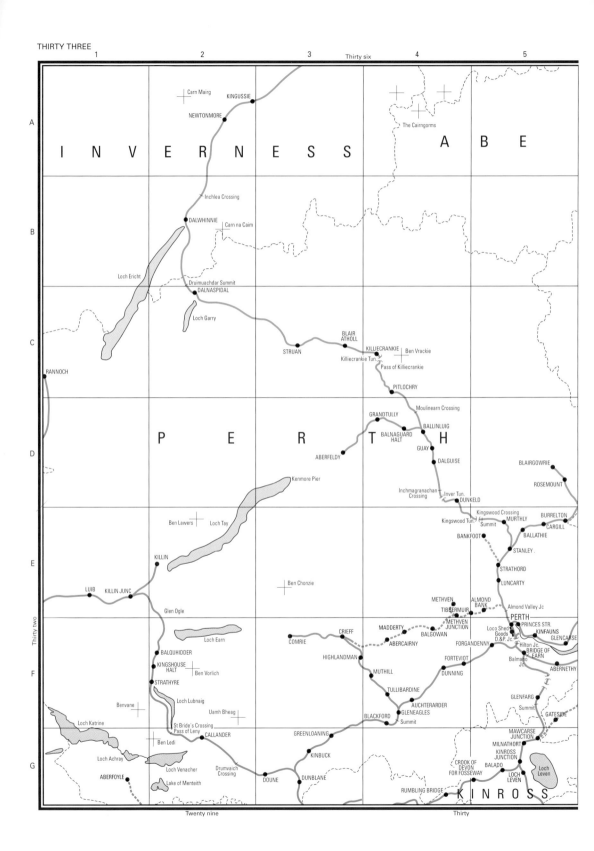

A

Carn Mairg
KINGUSSIE
NEWTONMORE

The Cairngorms

I N V E R N E S S   A B E

B

Inchlea Crossing
DALWHINNIE
Carn na Caim

Loch Ericht

Druimuachdar Summit
DALNASPIDAL

Loch Garry

C

BLAIR ATHOLL
KILLIECRANKIE   Ben Vrackie
STRUAN
Killiecrankie Tun.
Pass of Killiecrankie
RANNOCH

PITLOCHRY

Moulinearn Crossing
GRANDTULLY
BALLINLUIG
P   E   R   BALNAGUARD HALT   T   H
GUAY
ABERFELDY
DALGUISE
BLAIRGOWRIE

D

Kenmore Pier

ROSEMOUNT

Inchmagranachan Crossing
Inver Tun.
DUNKELD

Kingswood Crossing
Ben Lawers   Loch Tay
Kingswood Tun.
Summit
MURTHLY
BURRELTON
CARGILL
BALLATHIE
BANKFOOT
STANLEY

KILLIN
STRATHORD
LUNCARTY

E

LUIB
KILLIN JUNC
Glen Ogle
Ben Chonzie
METHVEN
ALMOND BANK
TIBBERMUIR
Almond Valley Jc
MADDERTY
METHVEN JUNCTION
PERTH
CRIEFF
BALGOWAN
Loco Shed
PRINCES STR.
COMRIE
ABERCAIRNY
FORGANDENNY
Goods
KINFAUNS
D.&P. Jc.
GLENCARSE
Loch Earn
HIGHLANDMAN
FORTEVIOT
Hilton Jc.
BALQUHIDDER
MUTHILL
DUNNING
BRIDGE OF EARN
KINGSHOUSE HALT   Ben Vorlich
Balmano Jc
ABERNETHY

F

STRATHYRE
TULLIBARDINE
Loch Lubnaig
GLENFARG
Benvane
Uamh Bheag
AUCHTERARDER
Summit
Loch Katrine
St Bride's Crossing
GLENEAGLES
GATESIDE
Pass of Leny
BLACKFORD
Summit
MAWCARSE JUNCTION
ABERFOYLE
CALLANDER
GREENLOANING
MILNATHORT
Ben Ledi
KINBUCK
KINROSS JUNCTION
Loch Achray
CROOK OF DEVON
BALADO
FOR FOSSEWAY
Loch Venacher
Drumvaich Crossing
DOUNE
DUNBLANE
LOCH LEVEN
Loch Leven

G

Lake of Menteith
RUMBLING BRIDGE
K I N R O S S

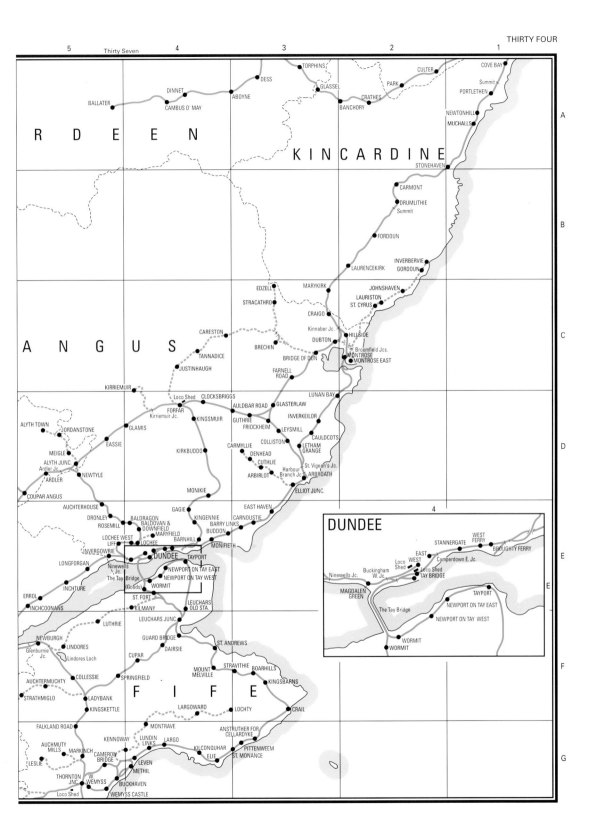

A

B

C

D

E

E

F

G

RDEEN

KINCARDINE

ANGUS

FIFE

DUNDEE

TORPHINS
DESS
GLASSEL
CULTER
COVE BAY
PARK
DINNET
ABOYNE
CRATHES
Summit
PORTLETHEN
BALLATER
CAMBUS O' MAY
BANCHORY
NEWTONHILL
MUCHALLS

STONEHAVEN

CARMONT
DRUMLITHIE
Summit
FORDOUN

INVERBERVIE
GORDOUN
LAURENCEKIRK

EDZELL
MARYKIRK
JOHNSHAVEN
LAURISTON
STRACATHRO
ST. CYRUS
CRAIGO
Kinnaber Jc.
HILLSIDE
CARESTON
DUBTON
BRECHIN
Broomfield Jcs.
TANNADICE
BRIDGE OF DUN
MONTROSE
JUSTINHAUGH
MONTROSE EAST
FARNELL
ROAD

KIRRIEMUIR
LUNAN BAY
Loco Shed
CLOCKSBRIGGS
GLASTERLAW
AULDBAR ROAD
FORFAR
INVERKEILOR
Kirriemuir Jc.
KINGSMUIR
GUTHRIE
ALYTH TOWN
FRIOCKHEIM
JORDANSTONE
GLAMIS
LEYSMILL
CAULDCOTS
MEIGLE
EASSIE
COLLISTON
LETHAM
ALYTH JUNC.
CARMYLLIE
GRANGE
Ardler Jc.
KIRKBUDDO
DENHEAD
St. Vigean's Jc.
ARDLER
NEWTYLE
CUTHLIE
Harbour
ARBIRLOT
Branch Jc.
ARBROATH
COUPAR ANGUS
MONIKIE
ELLIOT JUNC.

AUCHTERHOUSE
GAGIE
EAST HAVEN
DRONLEY
KINGENNIE
CARNOUSTIE
ROSEMILL
BALDRAGON
BARRY LINKS
BALDOVAN &
DOWNFIELD
MARYFIELD
BUDDON
LOCHEE WEST
BARNHILL
LIFF
LOCHEE
MONIFIETH
INVERGOWRIE
DUNDEE
TAYPORT
LONGFORGAN
Ninewells Jc.
NEWPORT ON TAY EAST
The Tay Bridge
NEWPORT ON TAY WEST
INCHTURE
(Goods)
WORMIT
ERROL
ST. FORT
INCHCOONANS
LEUCHARS
KILMANY
OLD STA.

LEUCHARS JUNC.
LUTHRIE
NEWBURGH
GUARD BRIDGE
LINDORES
DAIRSIE
ST. ANDREWS
Glenburnie
CUPAR
Jc.
Lindores Loch
STRAVITHIE
BOARHILLS
COLLESSIE
SPRINGFIELD
MOUNT
AUCHTERMUCHTY
MELVILLE
KINGSBARNS
STRATHMIGLO
LADYBANK
LARGOWARD
LOCHTY
CRAIL
KINGSKETTLE

FALKLAND ROAD
MONTRAVE
ANSTRUTHER FOR
CELLARDYKE
KENNOWAY
LUNDIN
LARGO
AUCHMUTY
LINKS
KILCONQUHAR
PITTENWEEM
MILLS
MARKINCH
ELIE
ST. MONANCE
CAMERON
LESLIE
BRIDGE
LEVEN
METHIL
THORNTON
W. WEMYSS
JNC.
BUCKHAVEN
Loco Shed
WEMYSS CASTLE

DUNDEE

4

WEST
STANNERGATE
FERRY
EAST
WEST
BROUGHTY FERRY
Loco
Camperdown E. Jc.
Shed
Buckingham
Ninewells Jc.
W. Jc.
Loco Shed
TAY BRIDGE
MAGDALEN
TAYPORT
GREEN
NEWPORT ON TAY EAST
The Tay Bridge
NEWPORT ON TAY WEST
WORMIT
WORMIT

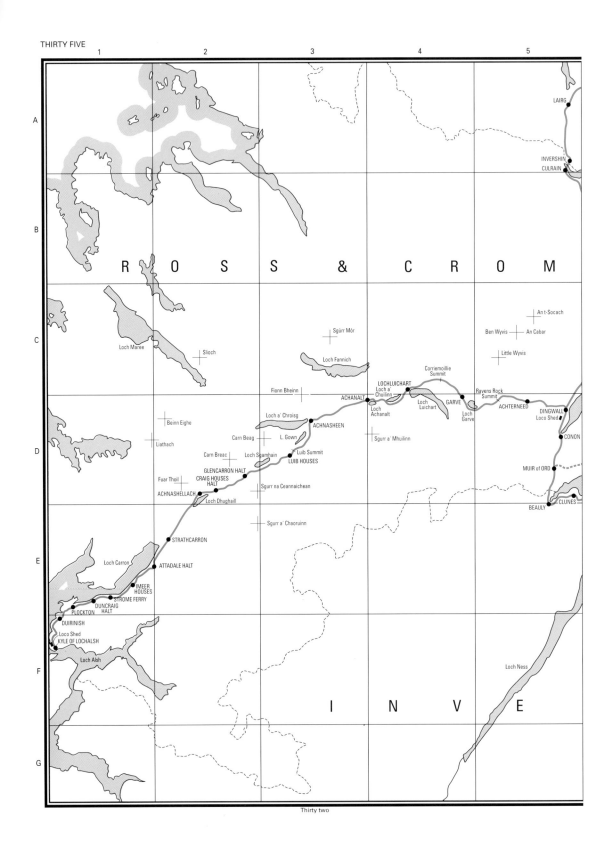

1   2   3   4   5

A

LAIRG

INVERSHIN
CULRAIN

B

R O S S   &   C R O M

An t-Socach

Sgùrr Mòr
Ben Wyvis ─┼─ An Cabar

C

Loch Maree
─┼─ Slioch
Little Wyvis

Loch Fannich

Corriemoillie
Summit

Fionn Bheinn ─┼─
LOCHLUICHART
Loch a'
Chuilinn
Ravens Rock
Summit

ACHANALT
Loch
Achanalt
Loch
Luichart   GARVE
ACHTERNEED

Loch a' Chroisg
Loch
Garve
DINGWALL
Loco Shed

─┼─ Beinn Eighe
ACHNASHEEN
CONON

Liathach
Carn Beag ─┼─   L. Gown
─┼─ Sgurr a' Mhuilinn

D

Carn Breac ─┼─   Loch Sgamhain
Luib Summit
LUIB HOUSES
MUIR of ORD

GLENCARRON HALT
Fuar Thoil   CRAIG HOUSES
HALT
CLUNES
ACHNASHELLACH ●
Loch Dhughaill
─┼─ Sgurr na Ceannaichean
BEAULY

─┼─ Sgurr a' Chaoruinn

STRATHCARRON

E

Loch Carron
ATTADALE HALT

IMEER
HOUSES
STROME FERRY
DUNCRAIG
PLOCKTON   HALT
DUIRINISH
Loco Shed
KYLE OF LOCHALSH
Loch Ness
Loch Alsh

F

I   N   V   E

G

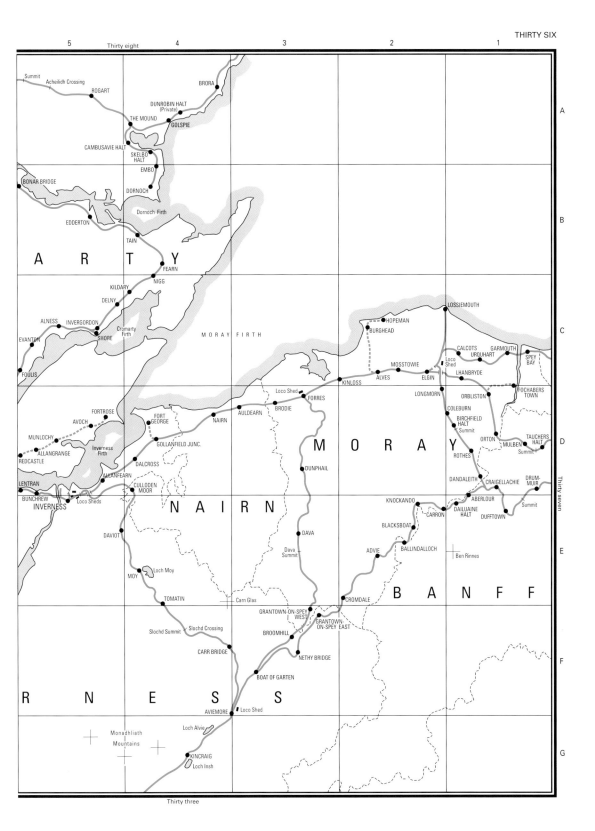

Summit
Acheilidh Crossing
ROGART
BRORA
DUNROBIN HALT
(Private)
THE MOUND
GOLSPIE
CAMBUSAVIE HALT
SKELBO
HALT
EMBO
BONAR BRIDGE
DORNOCH
EDDERTON
Dornoch Firth
TAIN
A R T Y
FEARN
NIGG
KILDARY
DELNY
LOSSIEMOUTH
ALNESS INVERGORDON
HOPEMAN
EVANTON
SHORE
BURGHEAD
Cromarty
Firth
M O R A Y   F I R T H
CALCOTS GARMOUTH
FOULIS
URQUHART
SPEY
BAY
Loco
Shed
MOSSTOWIE
LHANBRYDE
FORTROSE
KINLOSS ALVES ELGIN
FOCHABERS
TOWN
AVOCH
FORT
GEORGE
Loco Shed
FORRES
LONGMORN
ORBLISTON
MUNLOCHY
NAIRN AULDEARN
BRODIE
COLEBURN
ALLANGRANGE
GOLLANFIELD JUNC.
BIRCHFIELD
HALT
REDCASTLE
Inverness
Firth
M O R A Y
Summit
ORTON
TAUCHERS
HALT
DALCROSS
DANDALEITH
MULBEN
LENTRAN
ALLANFEARN
DUNPHAIL
ROTHES
Summit
DRUM-
MUIR
BUNCHREW
CULLODEN
MOOR
CRAIGELLACHIE
INVERNESS Loco Sheds
N A I R N
KNOCKANDO
ABERLOUR
Summit
DAVIOT
DAVA
BLACKSBOAT
CARRON
DAILUAINE
HALT DUFFTOWN
ADVIE BALLINDALLOCH
Ben Rinnes
MOY
Loch Moy
Dava
Summit
B A N F F
TOMATIN
Carn Glas
CROMDALE
GRANTOWN-ON-SPEY
WEST
GRANTOWN-
ON-SPEY EAST
Slochd Summit Slochd Crossing
BROOMHILL
CARR BRIDGE
NETHY BRIDGE
BOAT OF GARTEN
R N E S S
AVIEMORE Loco Shed
Monadhliath
Mountains
Loch Alvie
KINCRAIG
Loch Insh

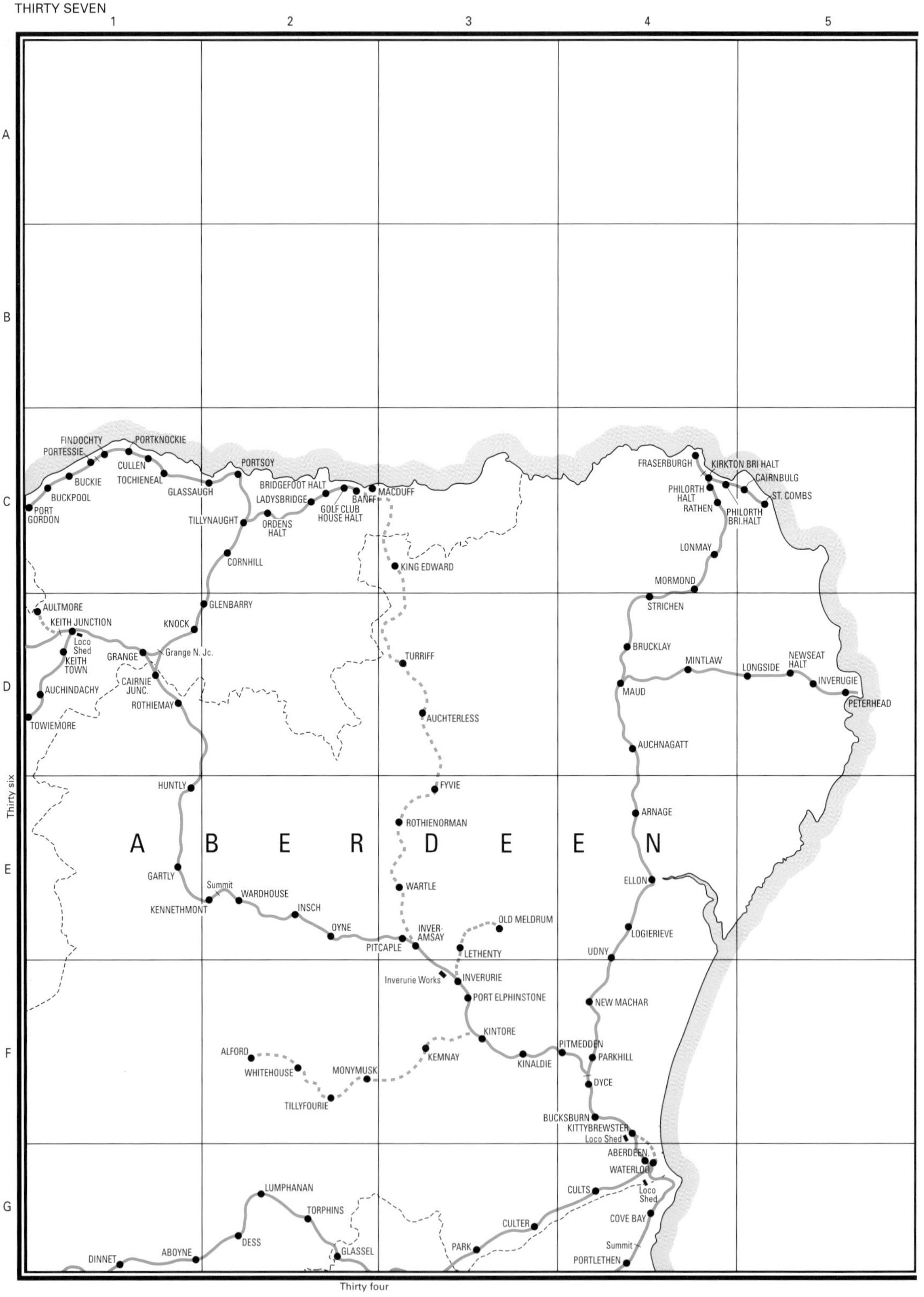

1   2   3   4   5

A

B

C

Thirty six

D

E

F

G

FINDOCHTY PORTKNOCKIE
PORTESSIE
BUCKIE CULLEN
BUCKPOOL TOCHIENEAL
PORT GLASSAUGH
GORDON
PORTSOY
BRIDGEFOOT HALT
LADYSBRIDGE
TILLYNAUGHT BANFF MACDUFF
GOLF CLUB
ORDENS HOUSE HALT
HALT
CORNHILL
KING EDWARD

FRASERBURGH KIRKTON BRI HALT
CAIRNBULG
PHILORTH
HALT ST. COMBS
RATHEN PHILORTH
BRI.HALT
LONMAY
MORMOND

AULTMORE
KEITH JUNCTION GLENBARRY
Loco KNOCK
Shed
KEITH GRANGE Grange N. Jc.
TOWN
AUCHINDACHY CAIRNIE
JUNC.
ROTHIEMAY
TOWIEMORE

STRICHEN

BRUCKLAY
MINTLAW NEWSEAT
TURRIFF LONGSIDE HALT
INVERUGIE
MAUD
PETERHEAD

AUCHTERLESS

AUCHNAGATT

HUNTLY

FYVIE
ROTHIENORMAN

ARNAGE

A B E R D E E N

GARTLY
Summit WARDHOUSE
KENNETHMONT INSCH
OYNE
PITCAPLE INVER-
AMSAY
LETHENTY

WARTLE

OLD MELDRUM

ELLON

LOGIERIEVE

UDNY

Inverurie Works INVERURIE
PORT ELPHINSTONE

NEW MACHAR

ALFORD KINTORE
WHITEHOUSE MONYMUSK KEMNAY
TILLYFOURIE KINALDIE

PITMEDDEN
PARKHILL

DYCE

BUCKSBURN
KITTYBREWSTER
Loco Shed
ABERDEEN
WATERLOO
LUMPHANAN CULTS Loco
TORPHINS Shed
CULTER COVE BAY
DINNET ABOYNE DESS GLASSEL PARK Summit
PORTLETHEN

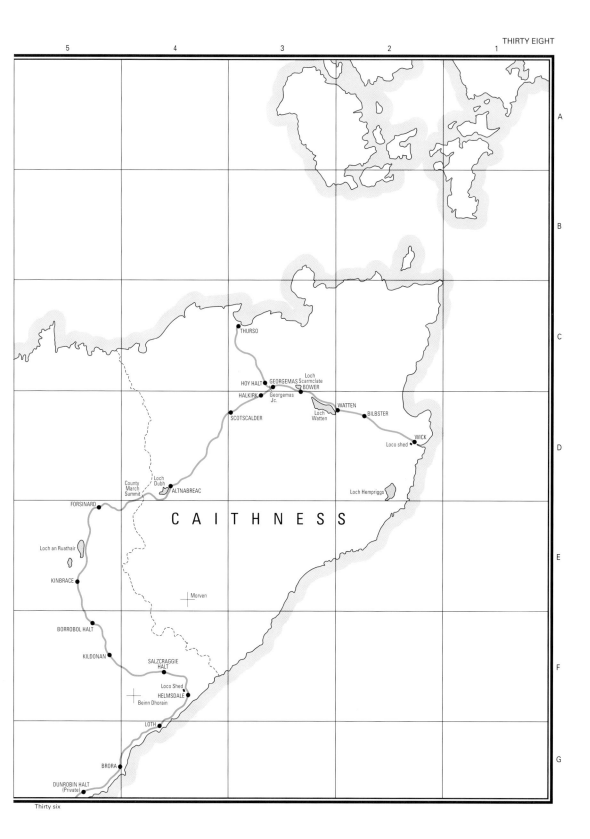

5   4   3   2   1

A

B

C

THURSO

Loch
Scarmclate
HOY HALT   GEORGEMAS
HALKIRK   BOWER
Georgemas
Jc.
SCOTSCALDER   WATTEN
Loch   BILBSTER
Watten
WICK
Loco shed

D

Loch
Dubh
County
March   ALTNABREAC
Summit
Loch Hempriggs
FORSINARD

C A I T H N E S S

Loch an Ruathair

E

KINBRACE
Morven

BORROBOL HALT

KILDONAN
SALZCRAGGIE
HALT

F

Loco Shed
HELMSDALE
Beinn Dhorain

LOTH

G

BRORA

DUNROBIN HALT
(Private)

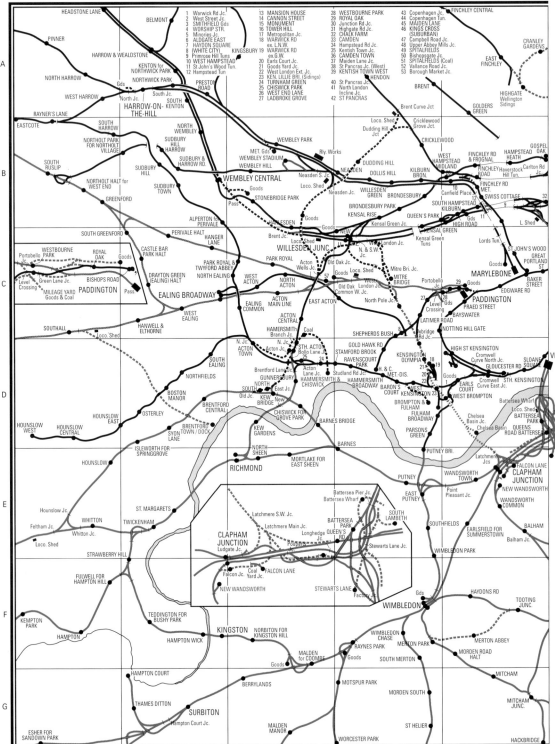

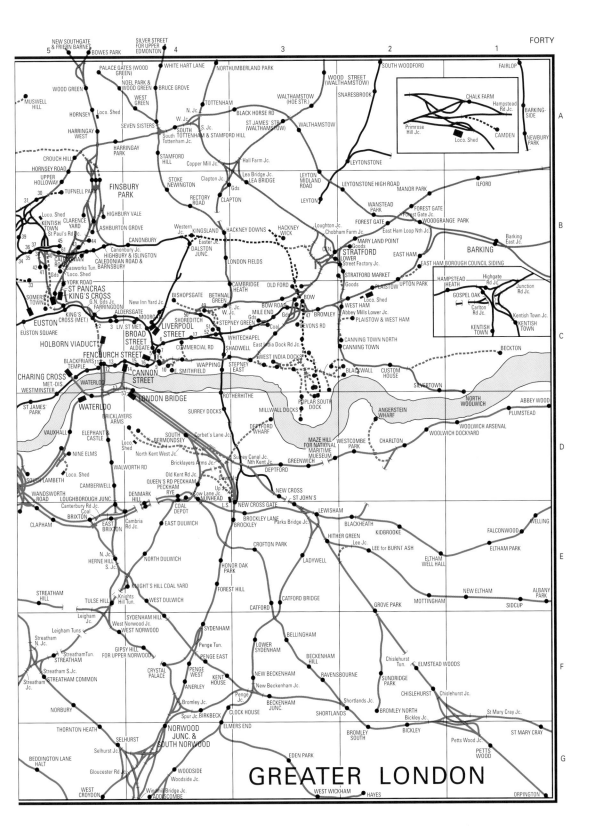

GREATER LONDON

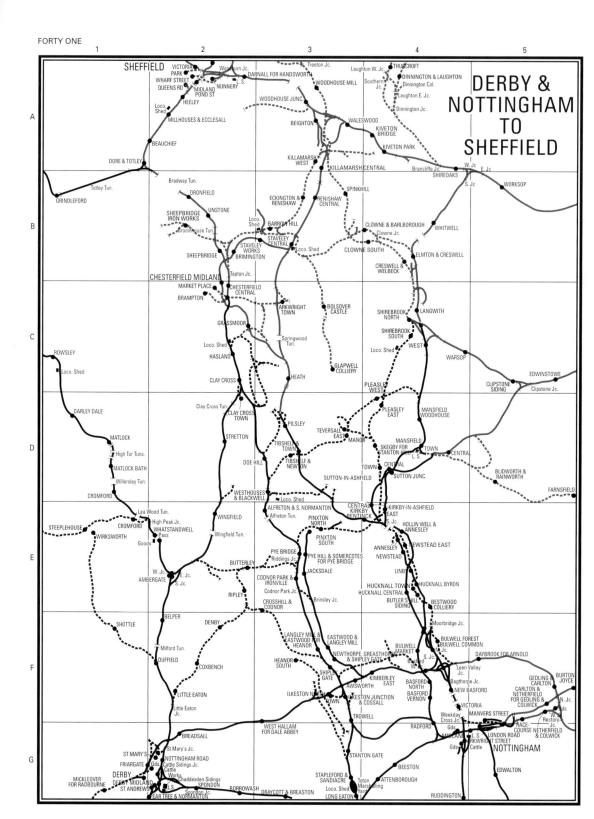

DERBY &
NOTTINGHAM
TO
SHEFFIELD

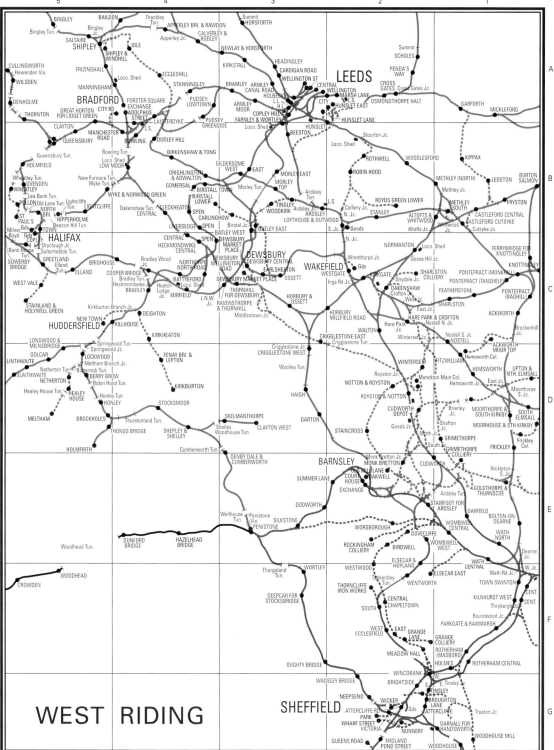

WEST RIDING

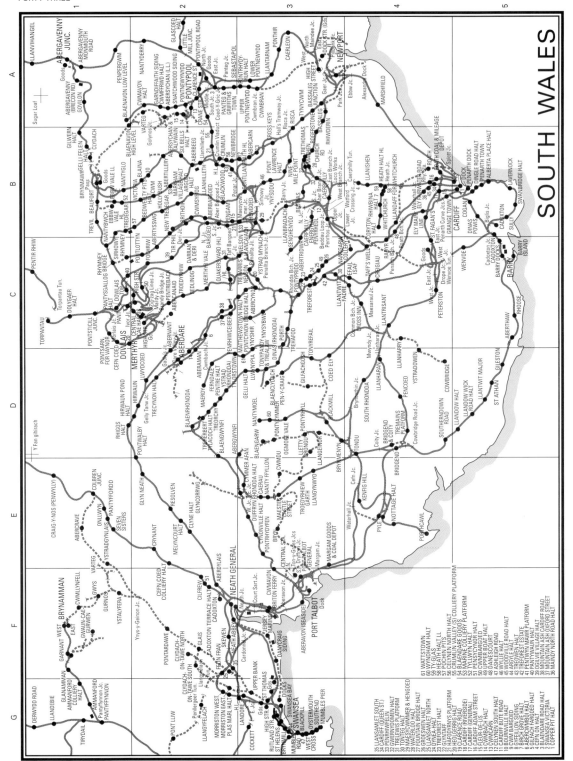

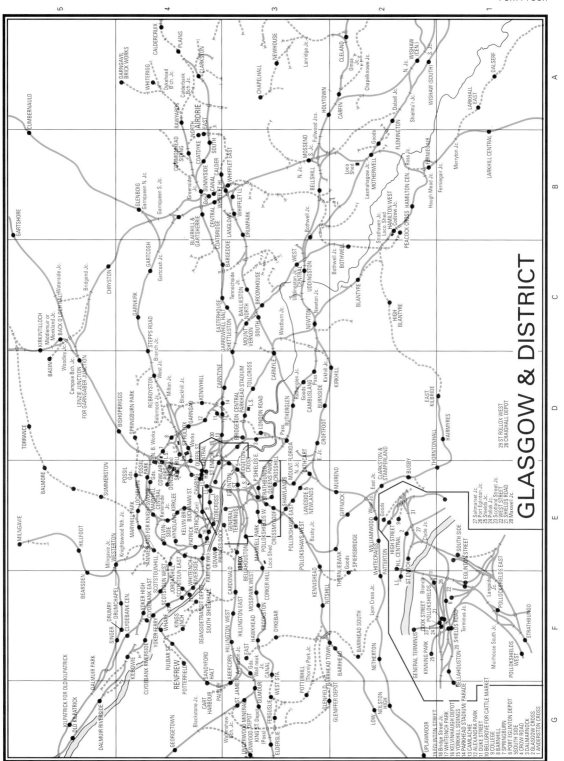

GLASGOW & DISTRICT

LIVERPOOL & MANCHESTER

1 WARWICK ROAD
2 RANELAGH for HALE
3 LITTLE LEVER
4 BLOWICK
5 ST LUKES
6 HINDLEY & AMBERS-
7 WOOD
8 HINDLEY SOUTH
9 HINDLEY GREEN
10 BICKERSHAW & ABRAM
11 ASHTON-IN-MAKERFIELD
12 PENDLETON
13 BIRKENHEAD NORTH
14 FARNWORTH & HALSHAW
15 MOORSIDE & WARDLEY
16 PENDLEBURY
17 CLUBMOOR
18 WINDSOR'S RD HALT
19 PENDLETON BRINDLE HEATH
20 IRLAMS-O'-TH'HEIGHT
21 PENDLETON BROAD ST
22 MANCHESTER DOCKS STA
23 CROSS LANE
24 ORDSALL LANE for SALFORD
25 MANCHESTER VICTORIA
26 MANCHESTER EXCHANGE
27 OLDHAM RD
28 DEANSGATE
29 CLAYTON BRIDGE
30 RESESCS
31 ANCOATS
32 DUCIE ST
33 DOCKS
34 MANCHESTER CENTRAL
35 GUIDE BRIDGE
36 GUILDE BRIDGE
37 HEATON NORRIS
38 MANCHESTER (OXFORD ROAD)

40 ALEXANDRA & LANGTON DOCK
41 MARSH LANE & STRAND ROAD
42 BOOTLE & ORIEL ROAD
43 BROOKE LANE & ALLERTON
44 ALLERTON
45 KIRKDALE
46 MANCHESTER (OXFORD ROAD)

47 HALEBANK for HALE
48 RAVENSHOME NORTH
49 WATERLOO ROAD
50 EDGE HILL
51 CANADA DOCK
52 CROWN ST
53 JAMES ST
54 LIVERPOOL CENTRAL
55 LIVERPOOL EXCHANGE
56 LITHERLAND & SEAFORTH
57 PARK LANE
58 NEW BRIGHTON

59 WAVERTREE & EDGE HILL
60 RAVENSHOME ROAD
61 WALLASEY VILLAGE
62 SEACOMBE
63 CANADA DOCK
64 CROWN ST
65 CATHCART STR
66 DOCKS
67 BIRKENHEAD STR
68 WOODSIDE
69 HAMILTON SQUARE
70 BIRKENHEAD PARK
71 WALTON JUNC.
72 CORNBROOK
73 CROXT STR
74 PEASLEY CROSS
75 PARK LANE

SOUTHPORT

NOTE: Liverpool Overhead Railway

MERSEY DOCKS LINES

INDEX TO PASSENGER STATIONS

Abbey & West Dereham 10A5/17F5
Abbey Wood 5A4/40D1
Abbeyhill. 30F2
Abbeydore 14F1
Abbeytown 26C2
Abbots Ripton 11B2
Aber 19D3
Aberaman 8B5/43D2
Aberavon (Seaside) 7B4/43F3
Aberayron 13D4
Aberbeeg 8B4/43C2
Aberbran Halt 14F4
Abercairny 33F4
Abercamlais Halt 14F4
Abercanaid 43C2
Abercarn 8B4/43B3
Abercrave 7A5/43E1
Abercwmboi Halt 43C2
Abercynon 8B5/43C3
Aberdare High Level 8B5/43D2
Aberdare Low Level 8B5/43D2
Aberdeen Waterloo 37G4
Aberdeen 37G4
Aberdour 30A3
Aberdovey 13B5
Aberdylais 7B4/43F2
Aberedw 14E3
Abererch 19F1
Aberfeldy 33D3
Aberffrwd 14C5
Aberfoyle 33G1
Abergavenny Brecon Road 8A3/43A1
Abergavenny Junction 8A3/43A1
Abergavenny Monmouth Road .8A3/43A1
Abergele 19D4
Abergwili 13G4
Abergwynfri 7B5/43D3
Abergynolwyn 13B5
Aberlady 30B1
Aberlour 36E1
Abermule 14B2
Abernant 8A5/43D2
Abernethy 33F5
Abersychan & Talywain 8A4/43A2
Abersychan Low Level 8A4/43A2
Abertafol Halt 13B5
Aberthaw 8D5/43C5
Abertillery 8A4/43B2
Abertridwr 8B5/43C3
Aberystwyth 13C5
Abingdon 10F4
Abington 30E4
Aboyne 34A3/37G1
Aby for Claythorpe 17A3
Accrington 24E1
Achanalt 35D3
Ach-na-Cloich 32D3
Achnasheen 35D3
Achnashellach 35D2
Achterneed 35D5
Acklington 31G5
Ackworth Moor Top 42C5
Ackworth 21E4/42C5
Acle 18E2
Acocks Green &
    South Yardley 9A5/15G5
Acrefair (HL/LL) 20F5
Acton Bridge 15A2/20D3/45D5
Acton Central 39C3

Acton Main Line 39C3
Acton Town 39D3
Adderbury for Deddington 10D4
Adderbury 10C4
Adderley Park 13C4
Adderley 15C2/24C2
Addiewell 30C4
Addingham 21C2
Addiscombe 40G4
Addlestone 5C2
Addlestrop 9D5
Adisham for Wingham 6C2
Adlington (Cheshire) . .15A3/20C1/45A5
Adlington (Lancs) 20A2/24F2/45D1
Admaston Halt 15E2
Advie 36E2
Afonwen 19F1
Ahilton .16G5
Ainderby 21A3/28G5
Ainsdale 20A4/24E1/45F1
Aintree 20B4/24F4/45F3
Airdrie East 44B4
Airdrie North 44B4
Airdrie South 44B4
Airdrie .30C5
Airmyn & Rawcliffe 21E5
Airth 30A5
Akeld 31E3
Akeman Street 10E3
Albany Park 5B4
Albert Docks (Hull) 22A1
Alberta Bridge Halt 43B5
Albion .13B2
Albrighton 15F3
Alcester .9B4
Aldeburgh 12C2
Aldeby 12A1/18F1
Alderley Edge 15A3/20D1/45A5
Aldermaston 4A3
Aldersgate 40C5
Aldershot 4B1
Aldgate East 40C4
Aldgate 40C4
Aldin Grange Siding 27D5
Aldridge 15F4
Aldrington Halt 5F3
Alexandra Docks 22A1/22D3
Alexandra Parade 44D4
Alexandria & Bonhill 29B3
Alford Halt 3C2/8F1
Alford Town 17A3
Alford 37F2
Alfreton & Normanton 16C4/41E3
Algarkirk & Sutterton 17D2
All Stretton Halt 14B1
Allanfearn 36D5
Allangrange 36D5
Allens West Halt 28F5
Allerton 45E4
Allhallows-on-Sea 6B4
Alloa West 30A4
Alloa 30A4
Alloway 29F3
Alltddu Halt 14D5
Almond Bank 33E5
Alne 21B4
Alness .36C5
Alnmouth 31F5
Alnwick 31F5

Alperton 39B2
Alphington Halt 2B3
Alresford (Essex) 12E4
Alresford (Hants) 4C3
Alrewas .15E5
Alsager 15C3/24E1
Alsop-en-le-Dale 15C5
Alston .27D2
Altcar & Hillhouse 20B4/24F4/45F2
Althorne 12G5
Althorne 6A4
Althorp Park 10B3
Althorpe for Keadby, Gunness &
    Burringham 22F5
Altnabreac 38D4
Altofts & Whitwood 21E3/42B5
Alton Towers 15C4
Alton 4C2
Altrincham &
    Bowdon 15A3/20C1/24G1/45B4
Alva 30A5
Alvechurch 9A4
Alverstone 4F3
Alves 36C2
Alvescot 10E5
Alyth Junction 34D5
Alyth Town 34D5
Ambergate 16C5/41E2
Amberley 5F1
Amble 31F5
Amersham & Chesham Bois . .10F1/11G1
Amesbury 4C5
Amisfield 26A3
Amlwch 19C1/23G2
Ammanford Colliery Halt . .7A4/43G1
Ammanford 7A4/43G1
Amotherby 22B5
Ampthill 10C1/11D1
Ancaster 16C1/17C1
Anderston Cross 44E4
Andover Junction 4C4
Andover Town 4C4
Andoversford & Dowdeswell 9E4
Andoversford Junction 9D4
Anerley .40F4
Angel Road 5A3
Angerstein Wharf 40D2
Angerton 27A4
Angmering 5F2
Annan Shawhill Siding 26B2
Annan .26B2
Annbank 29E4
Annesley 41E4
Annfield Plain 27C5
Anniesland for Knightswood 44E4
Annitsford 27B5
Ansdell & Fairhaven 20A4/24E4
Anstruther for Cellardyke 34G3
Apperley Bridge & Rawdon . .21D2/42A2
Appin 32D4
Appleby (Lincs) 22F4
Appleby East 27E2
Appleby West 27E2
Appledore 6E4
Appleford Halt 10F4
Appley Bridge 20B3/24F3/45D2
Apsley 10E1/11F1
Arbirlot 34D3
Arbroath 34D3

Arddleen Halt 14A2
Ardibgly 5E3
Ardleigh 12E4
Ardler 34D5
Ardley 10D4
Ardlui 32F1
Ardrossan Montgomerie Pier 29D3
Ardrossan North 29D3
Ardrossan South Beach 29D3
Ardrossan Town 29D3
Ardrossan Winton Pier 29D3
Ardwick 20B1/24F1/45A3
Arenig 19F4
Argoed Halt 8B4/43B2
Argyle Halt 43G3
Arisaig 32B5
Arkholme 24B2
Arksey 21F5
Arkwright Town 16B4/41C3
Arlesey & Henlow 11D2
Arley & Fillongley 16G5
Arley 9A2
Armadale 30C4
Armathwaite 27D1
Armitgae 15E5
Armley Canal Road 21D3/42A3
Armley Moor 21D3/42A3
Arnage .37E4
Arnside .24A3
Arram 22D4
Arrochar & Tarbert 32G1
Arthington 21D3
Arthog 13A5
Arundel .5F1
Ascot 4A1/5B1
Ascott-under-Wychwood 10D5
Asfordby 16E3
Ash Vale 4B1
Ash 4B1
Ashbourne 15C5
Ashburton Grove 40B5
Ashburton 2C4
Ashbury .1A5
Ashburys for Belle Vue .20B1/24F1/45A3
Ashby Magna 16G4
Ashby-de-la-Zouch 16E5
Ashchurch 9D3
Ashcott 3C2/8E2
Ashdon Halt 11D4
Ashey 4F3
Ashford (Kent) 6D4
Ashford (Middlesex) 5B2
Ashington 27A5
Ashleigh Road 43G3
Ashley & Weston 16G2
Ashley Heath Halt 3E5
Ashley Hill 3A2/8C1/9G1
Ashley 15A3/20C1/24G1/45B4
Ashperton 9C2
Ashtead .5C2
Ashton (Devon) 2C3
Ashton Gate Platform 3G1
Ashton under Lyme Charlestown . .21A2
Ashton under Lyme
    Oldham Road Goods 21A2
Ashton under Lyme Oldham Road . .21A2
Ashton under Lyme 21F1
Ashton-in-Makerfield 45D3
Ashton-under-Hill 9C4
Ashurst .5D4
Ashwater 1A5
Ashwell & Moden 11D2
Ashwell .16E2
Askam 24A5
Askern 21E5

Askrigg 21A127G3
Aslockton 16C2
Aspatria .26D3
Aspley Guise Halt 10C1
Astley Bridge 20B2/24F2/45C1
Astley 20B2/24F2/45C3
Aston Goods 13B4
Aston Rowant 10F3
Aston 13B4/15G4
Aston-by-Stone 15D3/24G1
Aswarby & Scredington 17D1
Atelney 3D1/8F3
Atherstone 16F5
Atherton Central 45C2
Atherton Hag Lane 45C2
Atherton 24F2
Attadale Halt 35E2
Attenborough 16D4/41G4
Attercliffe Road 42G4
Attercliffe 21G4/42G4
Attleborough 12A4/18F4
Attlebridge 18E3
Auchengray 30D4
Auchincruive 29F3
Auchindachy 37D1
Auchinleck 29F4
Auchmuty Mills 34G5
Auchnagatt 37D4
Auchterarder 33F4
Auchterhouse 34E5
Auchterless 37D3
Auchtermuchty 34F5
Auchterool 30A2
Audgirth 26A4
Audlem 15C2/24F2
Audley & Bignall End 15C3/24E1
Audley End 11E4
Aughton Park Halt . . .20B4/24F3/45E2
Auldbar Road 34D3
Auldearn 36D3
Aultmore 37D1
Authorpe 17A3
Aviemore 36F3
Avoch 36D5
Avonbridge 30B4
Avoncliff Halt 3B4
Avonmouth Central 8C2/9G1
Avonmouth Dock 8C2/9G1
Avonmouth Town 8C2/9G1
Avonmouth 3A2/8C2
Avonwick 2D4
Awre Junction 8A1/9E2
Awsworth 16C4/41F3
Axbridge 3B1/8E3
Axminster 2B1
Aycliffe .28E5
Aylesbury High Street 10E2
Aylesbury 10E2
Aylesford 6C5
Aylesham Halt 6C2
Aylsham North 18D3
Aylsham South 18D3
Aynho Park Platform 10D4
Aynho 10D4
Ayot Siding 11F2
Ayr Harbour 29F3
Ayr 29F3
Aysgarth 21A1/27G4
Ayton 31C3
Bache 20D4
Back o'Loch Halt 44C5
Backney Halt Siding 9D1
Backworth 28D5
Bacup 20A1/24E1
Badminton 9G3

Bagillt 20D5
Bagshot 4B1/5C1
Baguley 20C1/24G1/45B4
Bagworth & Ellistown 16E4
Baillieston 44C3
Bainton .22C4
Baker Street 39C5
Bakewell 15B5
Bala Junction 19F4
Bala 19F4
Balado 30A3/33G5
Balcombe 5E3
Baldersby 21A3
Baldock .11E2
Baldovan & Downfield 34E4
Baldragon 34E4
Balerno .30C3
Balfron .29A4
Balgowan 33F4
Balgreen Halt 30G3
Balham 5B3/39E5
Ballabeg 23C3
Ballachulish (Glencoe) for
    Kinlochleven 32D3
Ballachulish Ferry 32D3
Ballasalla 23C2
Ballater .34A5
Ballathie 33B5
Ballaugh 23A2/25G4
Ballingham 9D1
Ballinluig 33D4
Balloch Pier 29B3
Balloch .29B3
Balmore 29B5/44C5
Balnaguard Halt 33D4
Balne 21E5
Balquhidder 33F2
Balshaw Lane &
    Euxton 20A3/24E3/45D1
Bamber Bridge 20A3/24E3
Bamford .15A5
Bampton 7F5
Banavie .32C3
Banbury General 10C4
Banbury Merton Street 10C4
Banchory 34A2
Banff 37C2
Bangor 19D2
Bangor-on-Dee 20F4
Bank Hall 45F3
Bankfoot 33E5
Banknock 30B5
Banks 20A4/24E4
Bannockburn 30A5
Banstead 5C3
Baptist End Halt 13C1
Barassie .29E3
Barber's Bridge 9D2
Barbon 24A2
Barcaldine Halt 32E3
Barcombe Mills 5F4
Barcombe 5F4
Bardney .17B1
Bardon Hill 16E4
Bardsey .21D3
Bare Lane 24B3
Bargeddie 29C5/44C3
Bargoed 8B4/43B2
Barking 5A4/40B1
Barkingside 40A1
Barkston 16C1
Barlaston & Tittensor 15D3/24F1
Barleith .29E4
Barlow 21D5
Barmby .21E5

Barming 6C5
Barmouth Junction 13A5
Barmouth .13A5
Barnard Castle 27E4
Barnby Dun 21F5
Barnehurst 5B4
Barnes Bridge 39D3
Barnes 5B3/39E4
Barnetby .22F3
Barnham .12B5
Barnham Junction 5F1
Barnhill 34E4
Barnhill 44D4
Barnoldswick 21A1
Barnsley Court House 21F3/42E4
Barnsley Exchange 21F342E4
Barnsley Oakwell 42E4
Barnsley Old Mill Lane 42E4
Barnstaple Junction 7F3
Barnstaple Town 7F3
Barnstaple Victoria Road 7F3
Barnstone 16D2
Barnt Green 9A4
Barnwell Junction 11C3
Barnwell 10A1/16G1/17G1
Baron's Court 39D4
Barras 27F3
Barrasford 27B3
Barrhead South 44F2
Barrhead Town 44F2
Barrhead 29C4/44F2
Barrhill 25A3
Barrmill .29D3
Barrow & Soar & Quorn 16E3
Barrow Central 24B5
Barrow Haven 22E3
Barrow Hill 16A4/41B3
Barry Docks 8D4/43C5
Barry Island 8D4/43C5
Barry Links 34E3
Barry 8D4/43C5
Bartdon Mill 27A2
Bartlow 11D4
Barton & Broughton 24D3
Barton & Walton 15E5
Barton Hill 22B5
Barton on Humber 22E4
Barton-le-Street 22B5
Baschurch 14A1/20G4
Basford North 16C4/41F4
Basford Vernon 41F4
Basingstoke 4B2
Bason Bridge 3B1/8E3
Bassaleg Junction 43A3
Bassaleg 8C4/43A3
Bassenthwaite Lake 26E2
Bat & Ball 5C4
Bath Green Park 3A3/8D1
Bath Spa 3A3/8D1
Bathampton 3A3
Bathford Halt 3A4
Bathgate Lower 30C4
Bathgate Upper 30C4
Batley East 21E3/42B3
Batley West 21E3/42B3
Battersby 28F4
Battersea Park 39D5
Battersea Wharf 39D5
Battle 6F5
Battlesbridge 6A5/11G5
Battyeford 42C2
Baxenden 24E1
Bay Horse 24C3
Bayford 11F2
Baynards .5D2

Bayswater 39C5
Beaconsfield & Jordans 5A1/10F1
Beal 31D4
Bealings .12D3
Beamish .27C5
Bearley 9B5
Bearpark .27D5
Bearsden 29B4/44F5
Bearsted & Thurnham 6C5
Beasdale Siding 32B5
Beattock .30F3
Beauchief 16A5/41A2
Beaufort 8A4/43B1
Beaulieu Road 4E4
Beauly 35E5
Beaver's Hill Halt 7D2
Bebington &
   New Ferry 20C4/24G4/45F4
Bebside 27A5
Beccles 12A2/18G2
Beckenham Hill 40F3
Beckenham Junction 40F3
Beckermet 26F3
Beckford .9C4
Beckingham 22G5
Beckton 5B4/40C1
Becontree 5A4
Bedale 21A3/27G5
Beddington Lane Halt 40G5
Bedford Midland Road 10C1/11D1
Bedford St Johns 11D1
Bedhampton Halt 4E2
Bedlington 27A5
Bedlinog 8B5/43C2
Bedminster 3G1
Bedwas 8B4/43A5
Bedwellty Pits Halt 8A4/43B2
Bedworth 16G5
Bedwyn 4A5
Beechburn 27D5
Beeston Castle & Tarporley . . .15B1/24E3
Beeston 16D4/41G4
Beeston 21D4/42B3
Beighton 16A4/41A3
Beith North 29D3
Beith Town 29D3
Bekesbourne 6C2
Belford 31E4
Belgrave & Birstall 16E4
Bellahouston 44B3
Bellbusk .21C1
Belle Vue 20C1/24G1/45A3
Bellgrove for Cattle Market 44D4
Bellingham (North Tyne) 27A3
Bellingham 40F3
Bellshill 30C5/44B3
Belmont (Middlesex) 5A2/39A2
Belmont (Surrey) 5C3
Belper 16C5/41F2
Belses 31E1
Belton & Borough 18F1
Belton 22F5
Beltring & Branbridges Halt 5D5
Beluncle Halt 6B5
Belvedere .5B4
Bempton .22B3
Ben Rhydding 21C2
Benderloch 32E4
Benfleet for Canvey Island 6A5
Beningborough 21C4
Bentham .24B2
Bentley 12D4
Bentley 4C1
Benton 27B5
Bents 30C4

Benwick 10A3/17G3
Bere Alston 1D5
Bere Ferrers 1D5
Berkeley Road 8B1/9F2
Berkeley 8B1/9F2
Berkhamsted 10E1
Berkswell & Balsall Common 9A5
Berney Arms Halt 18F1
Berrington & Eye 9B1
Berrington 15F1
Berry Brow 21E2/42D1
Berwick upon Tweed 31C3
Berwick 5F4
Berwyn 20F5
Bescar Lane 20A4/24E4/45F1
Bescot Junction 13A3/15F4
Besses o'th'Barns 45B2
Bestwood Colliery 16C4/41E4
Beswick 45A3
Betchworth 5C2
Bethesda .19D2
Bethnal Green 40C4
Bettisfield 15D1/24F3
Betwys-y-Coed 19E4
Beverley .22D4
Bewdley 9A3
Bexhill Central 6F5
Bexhill West 6F5
Bexley 5B4
Bexleyheath 5B4
Bicester London Road 10D3
Bicester North 10D4
Bickershaw & Abram 45C2
Bickley 40G2
Biddulph 15B3/24E1
Bideford 7F3
Bidford-on-Avon 9B5
Bidston 20C4/24G4/45G4
Biggar 30E3
Biggleswade 11D2
Bilbster 38D2
Billacombe 2D5
Billericay 5A5/11G5
Billing 10B2
Billingborough & Horbling 17D1
Billingham on Tees 28E4
Billingshurst 5E2
Bilson Junction 8A1/9E2
Bilsthorpe 16B3
Bilston Central 13A2/15F4
Bilston West 13A1
Binegar 3B3/8E1
Bingham .16C3
Bingley 21D2/42A1
Binton 9B5
Birch Vale 15A4/21G1
Birches & Bilbrook Halt 15F3
Birchfield Halt 36D1
Birchgrove Halt 43B4
Birchington-on-Sea 6B3
Birdbrook 11D5
Birdingbury 10A4
Birdwell 21F3/42E4
Birkbeck .40F4
Birkdale 20A4/24E1/45F1
Birkenhead Cathcart 45F4
Birkenhead Central 45F5
Birkenhead Docks 45F4
Birkenhead Green Lane 45F5
Birkenhead Hamilton Square 45F5
Birkenhead North 45F4
Birkenhead Park 45F5
Birkenhead Shore Road 45F5
Birkenhead Woodside 20C4/24G4
Birkenhead Woodside 45F5

Birkenshaw & Tong 21D2/42B2
Birmingham Camp Hill 13C4
Birmingham Central 13C3
Birmingham Curzon Street 13C4
Birmingham Lawley Street 13C4
Birmingham Moor Street 13C4
Birmingham New Street . . .13C4/15G4
Birmingham Snow Hill . . .13C4/15G4
Birstall Lower 43B4
Birstall Town 43B4
Birstall 21E2/42B2
Birtley 27C5
Birtwith .21C3
Bishop Auckland 27E5
Bishop's Lydeard 8F4
Bishop's Nympton & Molland 7F5
Bishop's Waltham 4D3
Bishopbriggs 29C5/44D4
Bishops Stortford 11E3
Bishopsgate 40C4
Bishopstone 5F4
Bishopton 29C4
Bittaford Platform 2D5
Bitterley Siding 9A1
Bitterne .4E4
Bitton 3A3/8D1
Blaby 16F4
Black Bank 10A4/17G4
Black Bull 15C3/24E1
Black Dog Siding 3A5
Black Dyke Halt 26C3
Black Horse Drove Siding 17G4
Black Horse Road 40A3
Black Mill 7C5/43D3
Black Rock Halt 19F2
Blackburn Galligreaves Street 24E2
Blackburn 24D2
Blackford Hill 30G2
Blackford 33F4
Blackhall Colliery Station 28D4
Blackhall Rocks 28D4
Blackheath 5B4/40E2
Blackpill 43G3
Blackpool Central 24D4
Blackpool North 24D4
Blackpool South Shore 24D4
Blackpool South 24D4
Blackrod 20B2/24F2/45C2
Blacksboat 36E2
Blackthorn 10D3
Blackwall 5B4/40C2
Blackwater 4B1
Blackwater (IoW) 4F3
Blackwell 9A4
Blackwood 30D5
Blackwood 8B4/43B2
Blacon .20D4
Blaenau Ffestiniog Central 19F3
Blaenavon High Level 8A4/43A1
Blaenavon Low Level 8A4/43A1
Blaenclydach 8B5/43D3
Blaendare Goods 43B2
Blaendare Road Halt 43A2
Blaengarw 7B5/43D3
Blaengwynfi 43D2
Blaenrhondda 7B5/43E2
Blaina 8A4/43B2
Blair Atholl 33C3
Blairadam 30A3
Blairebathie Mine 30A3
Blairgowrie 33D5
Blairhill & Gartsherrie 29C5/44B4
Blaisdon Siding 8A1/9E2
Blake Hall 11G4
Blake Street 15F5

Blakesley 10C3
Blanchland 27D4
Blandford Forum 3E4
Blanefield 29B4
Blankney & Metheringham . .16B1/17B1
Blantyre 29C5/44C2
Blaydon 27C5/28A3
Bleadon & Uphill 3B1/8D3
Bleasby 16C3
Bledlow 10E2
Bledlow Bridge Halt 10F3
Blencow 26E1
Bletchington 10E4
Bletchley 10D2
Blidworth & Rainworth 16B3/41D5
Blisworth 10B3
Blockley 9C5
Blodwell Junction 14A2/20G4
Blowers Green 13B1
Blowick 20A4/24E4/45F1
Bloxham 10C4
Bloxwich 15F4
Blue Anchor 8E5
Bluestone Siding 18D3
Blundellsands & Crosby .20B4/24F4/45F3
Blunham 11D1
Bluntisham 11B3
Blyth 28A5
Blythe Bridge 15C4
Blyton for Corringham 22G5
Bo'ness 30B4
Boarhills 34F3
Boat of Garten 36F3
Bodfari .19D5
Bodiam for Staplecross 6E5
Bodmin General 1D3
Bodmin North 1D3
Bodmin Road 1D3
Bodorgan 19D1
Bognor Regis 5G1
Bogside 30A4
Bogston 29B3
Boldon Colliery 28C5
Bolham Halt 2A3
Bollington 15A3/20D1/45A5
Bolsover Castle 16B4/41C3
Bolton Abbey 21C1
Bolton Crook Street 45C2
Bolton Percy 21D4
Bolton Trinity Street . . .20B2/24F2/45B2
Bolton-le-Sands 24B3
Bolton-on-Dearne 21F4/42E5
Boltopn Craddock Lane 45B2
Bonar Bridge 36D5
Boncath 13F3
Bonnington 30F2
Bonnybridge Canal 30B5
Bonnybridge High 30B5
Bonnyrigg 30C2
Bontnewydd 14A5/19G3
Bonwm Halt 19F5
Bookham 5C2
Boosbeck 28E3
Bootle Oriel Road 45F3
Bootle 24A5/26G3
Bordesley 13C4/15G5
Bordon .4C1
Boroughbridge 21B4
Borrobol Halt 38F5
Borrowash 16D4/41G2
Borth 13C5
Borwick 24B3
Boscombe 3F5
Bosham .4E1
Bosley 15B3/24D1

Boston .17C3
Boston Manor 39D
Botanic Gardens (Hull) 22A2
Bothwell 29C5/44C2
Botley 4E3
Bottesford 16D2
Bottisham & Lode 11C4
Boughrood & Llyswen 14F3
Boughton Halt 9B3
Boughton 16B3
Bourne End 5A1/10G2
Bourne .17E1
Bournemouth Central 3F5
Bournemouth West 3F5
Bournville Halt 43B2
Bournville 9A4
Bourton-on-the-Water 9D5
Bovey 2C4
Bow Brickhill Halt 10D2
Bow Road 40C3
Bow Street 13C5
Bow 2B4
Bow 40C3
Bowbridge Crossing Halt 9E3
Bower .38C3
Bowes .27F4
Bowes Bridge 28B2
Bowes Park 5A3/40A5
Bowhouse 30B4
Bowland 30D1
Bowling 29B4
Bowling 3A4
Boxford .4A4
Boxhill & Burford Bridge 5C2
Boyces Bridge 17F4
Box 3A4
Bracebridge Siding 16B1
Brackley Central 10C3
Brackley Town 10C3
Bracknell 4A1
Bradfield 12E4
Bradford Adolphus Street 21D2/42B2
Bradford City Road 21D2/42A2
Bradford Exchange 21D2/42A2
Bradford Forster Square 21D2/42A2
Bradford Peverell & Stratton Halt 3F3
Bradford-on-Avon 3B4
Brading .4F3
Bradley Fold 20B2/24F1/45B2
Bradnop 15C4
Bradwell 10C2
Brafferton 221B4
Braidwood 30D5
Braintree & Bocking 11E5
Braithwaite 26E2
Bramber 5F2
Bramford 12D4
Bramhall Moor Lane 45A4
Bramhall 15A3/20C1/45A4
Bramley & Wonersh 5D1
Bramley for Silchester 4B2
Bramley 21D3/42A3
Brampford Speke Halt 2B3
Brampton (Suffolk) 12B2
Brampton Junction 27C1
Bramwith 21F5
Brancepeth 27D5
Brandon & wolston 10A5
Brandon Colliery 27D5
Brandon 10A5/17G5
Branksome 3F5
Bransford Road 9B3
Branston for Heighington . . .16B1/17B1
Branston Sidings 15E5
Brasted .5C4
Braughing 11E3

Braunston & Willoughby 10B4
Braunston London Road 10B4
Braunton 7F3
Braystones 26F3
Brayton 26D4
Breadsall 16D5/41G2
Breamore 4D5
Brean Road Halt 8E3
Brechin 34C3
Breck Road 20C4/24G4/45F3
Brecon Free Street 14F3
Brecon Mount Street 13F3
Brecon Watton 14G3
Bredbury 21G1/45A3
Bredon 9C3
Breich 30C4
Breidden 14A2
Brent (Devon) 2D4
Brent (London) 39A4
Brent Knoll 3B1/8E3
Brentford Central 5B2/39D2
Brentford Town/Dock 39D2
Brentor 1C5
Brentwood & Warley 5A5
Bretby Colliery 126E5
Brettell Lane 15G3
Bricket Wood 11G1
Bricklayers Arms 40D4
Bridestowe 2B5
Bridge of Allan 30A5
Bridge of Dun 34C3
Bridge of Earn 33F5
Bridge of Orchy 32E1
Bridge of Weir 29C3
Bridgefoot Halt 37C2
Bridgend & Coity 43D4
Bridgend 7C5/43D4
Bridgeness 30B4
Bridgeton Central 44D3
Bridgeton Cross D3
Bridgnorth 15F2
Bridgwater North 3C1/8F3
Bridgwater 3C1/8F3
Bridlington 22B3
Bridport 3F1
Brierfield .24D1
Brierley Hill 15G3
Brigg 22F4
Brigham 26E3
Brighouse 21E2/42C2
Brightlingsea 12F4
Brighton Kemp Town 5F3
Brighton Lewes Road 5F3
Brighton London Road 5F3
Brighton 5F3
Brightside 21G3/42G4
Brill & Ludgershall 10E3
Brimington 16A5/41B2
Brimley Halt 2C4
Brimscombe 9F3
Brimscombe Bridge Halt 9F3
Brimsdown for
    Enfield Highway 5A4/11G3
Brinkburn Siding 31G4
Brinklow .10A4
Brinkworth 9G4
Brinscall 20A2/24E2
Brislington 3A2/8D1
Bristol Avonside Wharf 3G1
Bristol Canon's Marsh 3G1
Bristol Pylle Hill 3G1
Bristol St Philip's Marsh 3G1
Bristol St Philip's 3G1
Bristol Temple Meads 3G1/8C2
Brithdir 8B4/43B2

Briton Ferry 7B4/43F3
Brixham 2D3
Brixton Road 2E5
Brixton 5B3/40E5
Brixworth 10A2
Brize Norton & Brampton 10E5
Broad Clyst 2B3
Broad Green 45E3
Broadbottom for Mottram &
    Charlesworth 21G1
Broadfield 20B1/24F1/45A2
Broadheath (Altrincham) 45B4
Broadstairs 6B2
Broadstone 3F5
Broadway .9C4
Brock Coal Depot 24D3
Brockenhurst 4E4
Brockholes 21F2/42D1
Brocklesby 22E3
Brockley Lane 40E3
Brockley .40E3
Brockweir Halt 8B2/9E1
Brodie 36C3
Bromborough 20C4/45F5
Bromfield .9A1
Bromford Bridge Racecourse 15G5
Bromham & Rowde 3B5
Bromley Cross 20A2/24F2/45B1
Bromley North 5B4/40F2
Bromley South 5B4/40G2
Bromley .40C3
Brompton & Fulham 39D4
Brompton 28G5
Bromsgrove 9A4
Bromyard .9B2
Brondesbury Park 39B4
Brondesbury 39B4
Bronwydd Arms 13G4
Brookland Halt 6E4
Brooklands 20C1/24G1/45B3
Brookmans Park 11G2
Brooksby .16E3
Brookwood for Bisley Camp 5C1
Broom Junction 9B4
Broome 14C1
Broomfleet 22E5
Broomhill 31G5
Broomielaw 27E4
Brora 36A4/38G5
Brotton 28E3
Brough 22E4
Broughton & Bretton 20D4
Broughton Astley 16G4
Broughton Gifford Halt 3B4
Broughton Lane 42G4
Broughton 30E3
Broughton-in-Furness 24A5
Broughty Ferry 34E4
Broxbourne & Doddesdon 11F3
Broxburn Junction 30B3
Broxton 15C1/24E3
Bruce Grove 40A4
Brucklay .37D4
Brundall Gardens Halt 18F2
Brundall .18F2
Bruton 3C3/8F1
Brymbo 20E4
Bryn for Ashton-in-Makerfield
    . . . . .20B3/24F3/45D3
Bryn Teify 13F4
Bryn 7B5/43E3
Brynamman East 7A4/43F1
Brynamman West 7A4/43F1
Bryncelynog Halt 19F3
Brynglas .13B5

Bryngwyn Halt 14A2
Brynmawr 8A4/43B1
Brynmenyn 7C5/43D3
Brynmill .43G3
Bubwith .21C5
Buchlyvie 29A4
Buckden .11C2
Buckenham 18F2
Buckfastleigh 2D4
Buckhaven 30A2/34G5
Buckie 37C1
Buckingham 10D3
Buckleigh .2D5
Bucknall & Northwood 15C3
Bucknell .14D1
Buckpool .37C1
Bucksburn 37F4
Bude 1A4
Bugle 1D2
Buildwas .15F2
Builth Road High Level 14E3
Builth Road Low Level 14E3
Builth Wells 14E3
Bulford 4C5
Bulford Camp 4C5
Bulgill 26D3
Bullo Cross Halt 8A1/9E2
Bullo Pill 8A1/9E2
Bulwell Common 16C4/41F4
Bulwell Forest 16C4/41F4
Bulwell Market 16C4/41F4
Bunchrew 36D5
Bungay 12A2/18G2
Buntingford 11E3
Burdale 22B5
Bures 12E5
Burgess Hill 5E3
Burgh 26C1
Burghclere 4B3
Burghead 36C2
Burgh-le-Marsh 17B4
Burleigh Street 22A1
Burlescombe 8G5
Burley-in-Wharfedale 21C2
Burlish Halt 9A3
Burmarsh Road Halt (RHDR) 6E3
Burn Halt .2A3
Burn Naze Halt 24D4
Burnage .45A3
Burneside 27G1
Burngullow 1D2
Burnham Market 18D5
Burnham on Crouch 6A4/12G5
Burnham 5A1/10G1
Burnham-on-Sea 3B1/8E3
Burnley Barracks 24D1
Burnley Central 24D1
Burnley Manchester Road 24D1
Burnmouth 31C3
Burnside 29C5/44D3
Burnt House 10A3/17G3
Burnt Mill 11F3
Burntisland 30A2
Burrator Halt 2C5
Burrelton 33E5
Burry Port 7B2
Burscough Bridge 20B4/24F3/45E1
Burscough Junction 20B4/24F3/45E1
Bursledon 4E3
Burslem 15C3/24E1
Burston 12B3
Burton & Holme 24A3
Burton Agnes 22B3
Burton Joyce 16C3
Burton Joyce 16C3/41F4

Burton Latimer for Isham 10A2
Burton on Trent Dallow Lane Wharf 15D5
Burton on Trent Horninglow Wharf 15D5
Burton on Trent Moor Street Wharf .15D5
Burton on Trent Shobnall Wharf . . .15D5
Burton on Trent 15D5
Burton Point 20D4/45F5
Burton Salmon 21D4
Burton Salmon 21E4/42B5
Burwarton 15G2
Burwell 11C4
Bury Bolton Street 20B1/24F1/45B1
Bury Knowsley Street . .20B1/24F1/45B2
Bury St Edmunds 12C5
Busby 29C5/44E2
Bush Hill Park 11G3
Bushbury .15F3
Bushey & Oxhey 5A2/11G1
Butler's Hill 16C4/41E4
Butterknowle 27E4
Butterley 16C5/41E2
Buttington 14A2
Buxted 5E4
Buxton Lammas 18E3
Buxton 15A4
Buxworth .15A4
Byers Green 27D5
Byfield 10B4
Bynea 7B3
Cadeleigh .2A3
Cadishead 20C2/24G2/45C3
Cadoxton Terrace Halt 43F2
Cadoxton .43F2
Cadoxton 8D4/43B5
Caerau 7B5/43E3
Caergwrle Castle & Wesll 20E4
Caerleon 8B3/43A3
Caernarvon 19D2
Caerphill 8C4/43B3
Caersws 14C3
Caerwys 20D5
Cairnbulg 37C5
Cairneyhill 30A3
Cairnie Junction 37D1
Caister Camp Halt 18E1
Caister-on-Sea 18E1
Calcots 36C1
Calder 44B4
Caldercruix 30C5/44A4
Caldicot Halt 8C2/9F1
Caldon Low 15C4
Caldwell .29D4
Caledonian Road & Barnsbury 40B5
Caledonian Road (Goods) 40B5
California Halt 18E1
Callander .33G2
Callerton .27B5
Callington for Stoke Climsland 1C5
Calne 3A5
Calstock 1C5
Calthwaite 27D1
Calveley 15B1/24E3
Calverley & Rodley 21D2/42A2
Calvert 10D3
Cam 8B1/9F2
Camberley for Yorktown &
    Sandhurst 4B1
Camberwell 40D5
Cambourne 1E5
Cambridge Brooklands Avenue 11C3
Cambridge Heath 40C4
Cambridge Mill Road Wharf 11C3
Cambridge Tenison Road Siding . .11C3
Cambridge 11C3
Cambus for Tullibody 30A5

Cambus O'May 34A4
Cambusavie Halt 36A4
Cambuslang 29C5/44D3
Camden Town 40B5
Camelford 1B3
Cameron Bridge 30A2/34G5
Camerton 26E3
Camlachie 44D4
Campsie Glen 29B5
Canley Halt 10A5
Canning Town 40C2
Canning Town North 40C2
Cannock .15E4
Canonbie .26B1
Canonbury 40B4
Canterbury East 6C3
Canterbury West 6C3
Cantley 18F2
Capel Bangor 13C5
Capel Celyn Halt 19F4
Capel 12D4
Capenhurst 20D4/45F5
Car & Cartmel 24B4
Caradog Falls Halt 14D5
Carbean Siding 1D2
Carbis Bay 1E4
Carbis Siding 1D2
Carcroft & Adwick-le-Street 21F4
Cardenden for Bowhill 30A2
Cardiff Adam Street 43B4
Cardiff Bute Road 43B5
Cardiff General 43B4
Cardiff Queen Street 43B4
Cardiff Riverside 43B4
Cardigan .13E2
Cardington 11D1
Cardonald 44F3
Cardrona .30D2
Cardross .29B3
Careston .34C4
Carfin 44A2
Cargill 33E5
Cargo Fleet 28E4
Carham 31D2
Carlinghow 42B3
Carlisle Bog 26C5
Carlisle Canal 26C4
Carlisle Citadel 26C1
Carlisle Crown Street 26C5
Carlisle London Road 26C5
Carlisle Petteril Bridge 26C5
Carlisle Viaduct 26C5
Carlton & Netherfield for
    Gedling & Colwick 16C3/41F4
Carlton Towers 21E5
Carlton-on-Trent 16B2
Carluke 30D5
Carmarthen Junction 7A2/13G4
Carmarthen Town 13G4
Carmont .34B2
Carmyle 29C5/44D3
Carmyllie .34D3
Carn Brea 1E5
Carnaby .22B3
Carnforth .24B3
Carno 14B4
Carnoustie 34E3
Carntyne 29C5/44D3
Carnwath .30D4
Carpenders Park for
    Oxhey Golf Club 5A2
Carr Bridge 36F4
Carr Mill 20B3/24F3/45D3
Carreghofa Halt 14A2
Carrog 20F5

Carron 36E1
Carshalton Beeches 5C3
Carshalton 5C3
Carstairs .30D4
Cart Harbour 44G4
Carters Siding 3E5
Carterton 10E5
Cartsdyke 29B3
Cashes Green Halt 9E3
Cassilis 29F3
Castle Ashby & Earl's Barton 10B2
Castle Bar Park Halt 39C2
Castle Bromwich 15G5
Castle Bytham 16E1/17E1
Castle Caereinion 14B2
Castle Cary 3C3/8F1
Castle Donington & Shardlow 16D4
Castle Eden 28D5
Castle Howard 22B5
Castle Kennedy 25C2
Castlecary 30B5
Castleford Central 21E4/42B5
Castleford Cutsyke 21E4/42B5
Castlehill Siding 30D5
Castlemilk 26B2
Castlethorpe 10C2
Castleton 20B1/24F1/45A1
Castleton .28F3
Castletown 23C2
Castor 10A1/17F1
Caterham .5C3
Catfield 18E2
Catford Bridge 40E3
Catford 40E3
Cathcart 29C5/44E3
Caton 24B3
Catrine 29E5
Cattal 21C4
Cattedown 1D5
Catterick Bridge 27F5
Cattistock Halt 3E2
Caulcots .34D3
Causeland Halt 1D4
Causewayend Siding 25C4
Causewayhead 30A5
Cavendish 11D5
Cawood 21D5
Cawston .18E3
Caythorpe 16C1
Cefn Coed 8A5/43C1
Cefn Coed Colliery Halt 43E2
Cefn On Halt 43B4
Cefn Tilla Halt 8B3
Cefn 20F4
Cefn-y-Bedd 20E4
Celynen North Halt 43B2
Celynen South Halt 43B3
Cemmes Road 14B5
Chacewater 1W1
Chadderton 45A2
Chadwell Heath for Becontree 5A4
Chalcombe Road Platform 10C4
Chalfont & Latimer 10F1/11G1
Chalford 9F3
Chalk Farm 39B5
Chalkwell .6A4
Challow 10F5
Chandlers Ford 4D4
Chapel-en-le-Frith Central 15A4
Chapel-en-le-Frith South 15A4
Chapelhall 30C5/44A3
Chapelton .7F3
Chapeltown Central 21F3/42F4
Chapeltown South 21F3/42F4
Chappel & Wakes Colne 12E5

Chard Central 2A1/3E1
Chard Junction 3E1
Chard Town 3E1
Charfield 8B1/9F2
Charing 6C4
Charlbury .10D5
Charlesfield Halt 31E1
Charlestown 30B3
Charlton 5B4/40D2
Charlton Kings 9D4
Charlton Mackrell 3D2/8F2
Charlton Marshall Halt 3E4
Chartham .6C3
Charwelton 10B4
Chassen Road 45B3
Chatburn 24D1
Chatham .6B5
Chathill 31E5
Chatteris Dock 17G3
Chatteris 10A3/17G3
Chatterley 15C3/24E1
Cheadle Hulme . .15A3/20C1/24G1/45A4
Cheadle .15C4
Cheam 5C3
Checker House 16A3
Cheddar 3B2/8E2
Cheddington 10E1
Cheddleton 15C4
Chedworth 9E4
Chelford 15A3/20D1/45B5
Chellaston & Swarkestone 16D5
Chelmsford 11F5
Chelsea Basin 39D5
Chelsfield 5C4
Cheltenham Racecourse 9D4
Cheltenham Spa Lansdown 9D3
Cheltenham Spa Malvern Road 9D4
Cheltenham Spa St James 9D4
Chepstow 8B2/9F1
Chequeherbert for Hulton 45C2
Cherry Burton 22D4
Cherry Tree 20A2/24E2
Chesham 10F1
Cheshunt 11G3
Chessington North 5C2
Chessington South 5C2
Chester General 20D4
Chester Liverpool Road 20D4
Chester Northgate 20D4
Chester Road 15F5
Chesterfield Brampton 16B541C2
Chesterfield Central 16B5/41C2
Chesterfield Market Place 16B541C2
Chesterfield Midland 16B5/41C2
Chester-le-Street 27C5
Chetnole Halt 3E2
Chettisham 11B4
Chevening Halt 5C4
Chevington 31G5
Chichester 4E1
Chigwell 5A4/11G3
Chilcompton 3B3/8E1
Chilham .6C3
Chilsworthy Halt 1C5
Chiltern Green for Luton Hoo 11F1
Chilvers Coton 16G5
Chilworth & Albury 5D1
Chingford 5A4/11G3
Chinley .15A4
Chinnor 10F3
Chippenham 3A4
Chipping Campden 9C5
Chipping Norton 10D5
Chipping Sodbury 8C1/9G2
Chipstead 5C3

Chirk 20F4
Chirnside 31C3
Chiseldon Camp Halt 9G5
Chiseldon 9G5
Chislehurst 5B4/40F2
Chiswick for Grove Park 39D3
Chiswick Park 39D3
Chittening Platform 8C2/99G1
Chollerton 27B3
Cholsey & Moulsford 10G4
Choppington 27A5
Chorley Friday Street . .20A3/24E2/45D1
Chorley 20A3/24E2/45D1
Chorleywood & Chenies 5A1/10F1
Chorlton-cum-Hardy . .20C1/24G1/45B3
Christ's Hospital (West Horsham) . . .5E2
Christchurch for Southbourne-on-Sea 4F5
Christian Malford Halt 3A5
Christon Bank 31E5
Christow .2B4
Chudleigh 2C3
Chudleigh Knighton Halt 2C4
Church & Oswaldtwistle 24E1
Church Fenton 21D4
Church Road 8B4/43B3
Church Stretton 14B1/15F1
Churchbury 5A3/11G3
Churchdown 9D3
Churchill & Blakedown 9A3
Churchtown 20A4/24E4/45F1
Churn Halt 10G4
Churston .2D3
Chwilog .19F1
Cilfrew 7B4/43F2
Ciliau-Aeron 13E4
Cinderford Town 8A1/9E2
Cinderford Whimsey 8A1/9E2
Cirencester Town 9F4
Cirencester Watermoor 9F4
Clackmannan & Kennet 30A4
Clacton-on-Sea & Holland-on-Sea . .12F3
Clandon for Newlands Corner 5C2
Clapham (Yorks) 24B1
Clapham Junction 5B3/39E5
Clapham 40E5
Clapton .40B4
Clarbeston Road 13G1
Clare 11D5
Clarence Road 43B4
Clarence Yard 40B5
Clarkston & Stamperland . . .29C5/44E2
Clarkston 30C5/44A4
Clatford .4C4
Claverdon 9B5
Claxby & Usselby 22G3
Clay Cross Town 16B5/41D2
Clay Cross 16B5/41C2
Claydon 10D3
Claydon 12D4
Claygate for Claremont 5C2
Claypole 16C2
Clayton Bridge 45A3
Clayton West 21F3/542D3
Clayton 21D2/42B1
Clearbrook Halt 2D5
Cleator Moor 26F3
Cleckheaton Central 21E2/42B2
Cleckheaton Spen 21E2/42B2
Clee Hill .9A1
Cleethorpes 22F2
Cleeve 9D3
Cleghorn 30D4
Cleland 30C5/44A2
Clenchwarton 17E4
Cleobury Mortimer 9A2

Clevedon 3A1/8D3
Cliburn .27E1
Cliff Common 21C5
Cliffe Park Halt 15B4
Cliffe 6B5
Clifton & Lowther 27E1
Clifton Bridge 3A2/8C2/3G1
Clifton Down 3F1
Clifton Junction 20B1/24F1/45B2
Clifton Moor 27E1
Clifton .15C5
Clifton-on-Trent 16B2
Clipston & Oxendon 10A3/16G3
Clipstone Siding 16B3/41C5
Clitheroe 24D1
Clock Face 20C3/24G3/45D4
Clock House 40F4
Clockbriggs 34D4
Closeburn 26A4
Clough Fold 20A1/24E1
Cloughton 28G1
Clovenfords 30E1
Clowne & Barlborough 16A4/41B4
Clowne South 16A4/41B4
Cloy Halt 20F4
Clubmoor 45F3
Clunes .35D5
Clutton 3B3/8D1
Clydach 8A4/43B1
Clydach-on-Tawe North 7B4
Clydach-on-Tawe South 7B4
Clydebank Central 29C4/44F4
Clydebank Riverside 29C4/44F4
Clynderwen 13G2
Clyne Halt 43E2
Coal Pit Heath 8C19G2
Coalbrookdale 15F2
Coalburn 30E5
Coaley Junction 8B1/9E2
Coalport 15F2
Coalville East 16E4
Coalville Town 16E4
Coanwood 27C2
Coatbridge Canal 44B4
Coatbridge Central 44B4
Coatbridge Sunnyside 44B4
Coatbridge 30C5
Cobbinshow 30C4
Cobham & Stoke D'Abernon 5C2
Cobridge 15C3/24E1
Cockburnspath 31B2
Cockermouth for Buttermere 26E3
Cockett 7B3/43G3
Cockfield Fell 27E4
Cockfield 12C5
Codford .3C5
Codnor Park & Ironville 16C4/41E3
Codsall .15F3
Coed Ely 43D3
Coed Poeth 20E5
Coed Talon 20E4
Cogan 8C4/43B5
Cogar 30B3
Colbren Junction 7A5/43E1
Colby 23C2
Colchester 12E4
Coldham 17F3
Coldharbour Halt 2A2
Coldstream 31D3
Cole Green 11F2
Cole 3C3/8F1
Coleburn 36D1
Coleford 8A1/9E1
Coleshill 15F5
Colfin 25C2

Colinton 30C2
College 44D3
Collessie 34F5
Collingbourne 4B5
Collingham Bridge 21C4
Collingham 16B2
Collington Halt 6F5
Colliston 34D3
Colnbrook 5B1/10G1
Colne 21B1/24D1
Coltishall 18E3
Colwall 9C2
Colwich 15E4
Colwyn Bay 19D4
Colyford 2B1
Colyton 2B1
Colzium 30B5
Combe Halt 10E5
Combpyne 2B1
Commercial Road 40C4
Commins Coch Halt 14B4
Commondale 28F3
Commonhead Siding 44B4
Compton 10G4
Comrie 33F3
Condover 15F1
Congleton Brunswick
   Street Wharf 15B3/24D1
Congleton 15B3/24E1
Congresbury 3A1/8D3
Coningsby 17C2
Conisborough 21F4
Coniston 26G1
Connah's Quay 20D4
Connel Ferry 32E4
Conon 35D5
Cononley 21C1
Consall 15C4
Constable Burton 21A2/27G5
Conway 19D3
Conwil 13G4
Cooden Beach 6F5
Cookham 5A1/10G2
Cooksbridge 5F4
Coole Pilate Halt 15C2
Coombe Junction Halt 1D4
Coombe Road 5C3
Cooper Bridge 21E2/42C2
Copgrove 21B3
Copley Hill 21C2/42A3
Copmanthorpe 21C5
Copper Pit Halt 43G2
Copplestone 2A4
Coppull 20A3/24E3/45D1
Corbridge 27C4
Corby & Weldon 16G2
Corby Glen 16D1/17E1
Corfe Castle 3G5
Corfe Mullen Halt 3F5
Corkerhill 44E3
Cornhill 37C2
Cornwood 2D45
Corpach 32C3
Corpusty & Saxthorpe 18D4
Corrour 32C1
Corsham 3A4
Corton 12A1/18F1
Corwen 19F5
Coryton 1C5
Cosford 15F3
Cosham 4E2
Costorphine 30B3
Cotham 16C2
Cotherstone 27E4
Cottam 16A2

Cottesmore 16E1
Cottingham 22D3
Cottingworth 21D5
Coulsdon North 5C3
Coulsdon South 5C3
Coulter 30E4
Cound Halt 15F1
Coundon Road 10A5
Coundon 27E5
Counter Drain 17E2
Countesthorpe 16F3
County School 18E4
Coupar Angus 34D5
Court Sart 43F3
Cove Bay 34A1/37G4
Cove Halt 7G5
Coventry 10A5
Cowbit 17E2
Cowbridge 8C5/43D4
Cowden 5D4
Cowdenbeath New 30A3
Cowdenbeath Old 30A3
Cowes 4F3
Cowlairs 44E4
Cowley 5BA2/10G1
Cowton 28F5
Cox Green 28C5
Coxbank Halt 15C2
Coxbench 16C5/41F2
Coxhoe Bridge 28D5
Coxhoe 28D5
Coxlodge 27B5
Coxwold 21A4
Cradley Heath 15G4
Cradoc 14F3
Craigellachie 36D1
Craigendoran 29B3
Craighall Depot 44E4
Craig Houses Halt 35D2
Craigleith for Blackhall 30F2
Craiglockart 30G2
Craigo 34C3
Craig-y-Nos (Penwyllt) 7A5/43E1
Crail 34F3
Cramlington 27B5
Cranbrook 6D5
Cranford 10A1
Cranleigh for Eswhurst 5D2
Cranley Gardens 39A5
Cranmore 3C3/8E1
Crathes 34A2
Craven Arms & Stokesey 14C1
Crawford 30F4
Crawley 5D3
Cray 14G4
Crayford 5B4
Credenhill 14F1
Crediton 2B4
Creech St Michael 8F3
Creekmoor Halt 3F5
Creetown 25C4
Creigiau 8C5/43C4
Cressage 15F1
Cressing 11F5
Cressington & Grassendale . . .20C4/45F4
Cresswell 15D4
Creswell & Welbeck 16A4/41B4
Crewe Cumberland Wharf . . .15B2/24E2
Crewe 15C2/24E2
Crewkerne 3E1
Crews Hill 11G2
Crianlarich Lower 32F1
Crianlarich 32F1
Criccieth 19F2
Cricklade 9F5

Cricklewood 5A3/39B4
Crieff 33F3
Criggion Quarry 14A2
Crigglestone East 21E3/42C3
Crigglestone West 2121E3/42D3
Croft Depot 28F5
Croft Spa 28F5
Croft 16F4
Croftfoot 44D2
Crofton Park 40E3
Cromdale 36E2
Cromer Beach 18D3
Cromer High 18D3
Cromford (Goods) 16C5/41E1
Cromford 16B541D1
Cronberry 29F5
Crook of Devon 30A3/33G5
Crook 27D5
Crookston 44F3
Cropredy 10C4
Crosby 23B2
Cross Gates 21D3/42A4
Cross Hands Halt 8C2/9G1
Cross Hands 7A3
Cross Inn 8C5/43C4
Cross Keys 8B4/43B3
Cross Lane 45B3
Crossens 20A4/24E4/45F1
Crossgates 30A3
Crosshill 44E3
Crosshouse 29E4
Crossmichael 26B5
Crossmyloof 44E3
Croston 20A3/24E3/45E1
Crouch Hill 40A5
Crow Park 16B2
Crow Road 44E4
Crowborough & Jarvis Brook 5E5
Crowcombe 8F4
Crowden 21F2/45F5
Crowhurst 6F5
Crowle Axholme 22E5
Crowle Central 22F5
Crowthorne 4B1
Croxley Green 5A2/11G1
Croy 30B5
Crumlin High Level 8B4/43B2
Crumlin Low Level 8B4/43B2
Crumlin Valley(s) Colliery Platform .43B2
Crumpsall 20B1/24F1/45A2
Crymmych Arms 13F2
Crynant 43E2
Crystal Palace 5B3/40F4
Cupar 34F4
Cuddington 15B2/24D2/45D5
Cudworth Depot 42D4
Cuffley & Goff's Oak 11G2
Culcheth 20C2/24G2/45C3
Culgaith 27E1
Culham 10F4
Culkerton 9F3
Cullen 37C1
Cullercoats 28D5
Cullingworth 21D2/42A1
Culloden Moor 36D4
Cullompton 2A2
Culmstock 2A2/8G5
Culrain 35A5
Culross 30A4
Culter 34A2/37G3
Cults 37G4
Culworth 10C4
Cumbernauld 30B5/44B5
Cummersdale 26C1
Cummertrees 26B3

Cumnock (A&C) 29F5
Cumnock 29F5
Cumwhinton 26C1
Cunninghamhead 29D3
Currie 30C3
Curthwaite 26C1
Custom House 40C2
Cuthlie .34D3
Cutnall Green 9A3
Cuxton 6B5
Cwm Avon 7B4/43F3
Cwmbargoed 43C2
Cwm Blawd for Pontyberem 7A3
Cwm Prysor Halt 19F4
Cwm 8A4/43B2
Cwmavon (Mon) 43A2
Cwmbach Halt 43D2
Cwmbran 8B3/43A3
Cwmcarn 43B3
Cwmcarn 43B3
Cwmffrwyd 43A2
Cwmllynfell 7A4/43F1
Cwmsyfiog 43B2
Cwm-y-Glo 19E2
Cyfronydd 14B3
Cymdu 7B5/43B3
Cymmawr 7A3
Cymmer Afan 7B5/43E3
Cynfal Halt 13B5
Cynghordy 14F5
Cynheidre 7A3
Cynwyd 19F5
Dacre 21B2
Dagenham Dock 5A4
Dagenham East 5A4
Dagenham Heathway 5A4
Daggons Road 3E5
Dailly 29G3
Dailuaine Halt 36E1
Dairsie .34F4
Dairycoates 22A2
Daisy Bank & Bradley 13A1/15F4
Daisy Hill 20B2/24F2/45C2
Daisyfield 24D2
Dalcross 36D4
Dalderse 30B5
Dalegarth 26F2
Dalguise 33D4
Dalkeith 30C2
Dalmally 32F2
Dalmarnock 44D3
Dalmellington 29G4
Dalmeny for South Queensferry . . .30B3
Dalmuir Park 44G5
Dalmuir Riverside 29C4/44G5
Dalnaspidal 32C2
Dalreoch 29B3
Dalry Road 30G2
Dalry 29D3
Dalrymple 29F3
Dalserf 30D5/44A1
Dalston Junction 40B4
Dalston .26C1
Dalwhinnie 33B2
Danby Wiske 28G5
Danby 28F3
Dandaleith 36D1
Dane Road 45B3
Danescourt 43B4
Danygraig Siding 7B4/43F3
Danzey for Tanworth 9A5
Darby End Halt 13C1
Darfield 21F4/42E5
Darlaston 13A2
Darley Dale 16B5/41D1

Darley 21C2
Darlington Bank Top 28F5
Darlington North Road 28E5
Darnall for
   Handsworth . .16A5/21G4/41A2/42G5
Darngavil Brick Works 44A4
Darran & Deri 8B4/43C2
Darsham 12B2
Dartford .5B5
Darton 21F3/42D3
Darvel 29E5
Darwen 20A2/24E2
Datchet 5B110G1
Daunstey 9G4
Dava 36E3
Davenport 15A3/21G1/45A4
Daventry 10B3
Davidsons Main 30B2
Daviot 36E5
Dawley & Stirchley 15F2
Dawlish .2C3
Dawlish Warren 2C3
Daybrook for Arnold 16C3/41F4
Deadwater 27A1/31G1
Deal 6C2
Dean 4D5
Deanside Transit Depot 44F4
Debden .5A4
Deepcar for Stocksbridge 21F3/42F3
Deepdale 24D3
Deepdene 5C2
Deepfields & Coseley 13A1/15F4
Defford .9C3
Deganwy 19C3
Deighton 21E2/42C2
Delabole 1B3
Delamere 15B1/24D3
Delny 36C5
Delph 21F1
Denaby .21F4
Denbigh 19D5
Denby Dale & Cumberworth .21F2/42E3
Denby 16C5/41F2
Denham for Harefield 5A1/10G1
Denham Golf Club Platform . . .5A110G1
Denhead 34D3
Denholme 21D2/42A1
Denmark Hill 40D4
Denny Ingliston 30B5
Denny Stoneywood 30B5
Denny 30B5
Dennyloanhead 30B5
Denstone 15C5
Dent 24A1
Denton Halt 20C1
Denton Siding 16D2
Denton 21G1/45A3
Denver 10A4/17F4
Deptford Wharf 40D3
Deptford 40D3
Derby Friargate 16D5/41G2
Derby Midland 16D5/41G2
Derby Nottingham Road 16D5/41G2
Derby Road 12D3
Derby St Andrew's 16D5/41G2
Derby St Mary's 16D5/41G2
Dereham 18E4
Derry Ormond 13E5
Dersingham 17D5
Derwen .19E5
Derwenthaugh 28B2
Derwydd Road 7A3/13G5/43G1
Desborough & Rothwell 10A2/16G2
Desford .16F4
Dess 34A3/37G2

Devil's Bridge 14C5
Devizes 3B5
Devonport Albert Road 1A1
Devonport King's Road 1A1
Devonport 1D5
Devons Road 40C3
Dewsbury Central 21E3/42C3
Dewsbury Market Place 21E3/42C3
Dewsbury Wellington Road . .21E3/42C3
Didcot 10F4
Didsbury 45A4
Digby 17C1
Diggle 21F1
Dilton Marsh Halt 3B4
Dinas (Rhondda) 8B5/43D3
Dinas Powis 8D4/43B5
Dingestow 8A2/9E1
Dingle Road Halt 43B5
Dingwall 35D5
Dinmore .9B1
Dinnet 34A4/37G1
Dinninton & Laughton .16A4/21G5/41A4
Dinsdale 28F5
Dinting .21G1
Dinton 3C5
Dinwoodie 26A3
Dipple Siding 29G2
Dirleton .31B1
Disley 15A4
Diss 12B4
Distinton 26E3
Ditchingham 12A2/18G2
Ditton Priors 15G1
Ditton 15A1/20C3/24G3/45E4
Docking .17D5
Dockyard Halt 1A1
Doddington & Harby 16B2
Dodworth 21F3/42E3
Doe Hill 16B4/41D3
Dogdyke 17C2
Dolau 14D3
Doldowlod 14D4
Doleham Halt 6E4
Dolgaer Halt 8A5//43C1
Dolgarrog 19D3
Dolgoch 13B5
Dollar 30A4
Dollgelley 14A5
Dollis Hill 39B4
Dolwddelen 19E3
Dolwen .14C3
Dolyhir .14E2
Doncaster Cherry Tree Lane 21G2
Doncaster Marsh Gate 21G2
Doncaster York Road 21G2
Doncaster 21F4/21G2
Donington Road 17D2
Donington-on-Bain 17A2
Donisthorpe 16E5
Donnington 15E2
Donyatt Halt 3E1
Dorchester South 3F3
Dorchester West 3F3
Dore & Totley 41A1
Dorking North 5C2
Dorking Town 5C2
Dormans 5D4
Dornoch 36B4
Dorrington 14B1/15F1
Dorton Halt 10E3
Doseley Halt 15F2
Doublebois 1D4
Douglas West 30E5
Douglas .23C3

Doune 33G3
Dousland 2C5
Dove Holes 15A4
Dovecliffe 42E4
Dover Marine 6D2
Dover Priory 6D2
Dover Town Yard 6D2
Dovercourt Bay 12E3
Dovey Junction 14B5
Dowlais Cae Harris 8A5/43C2
Dowlais Central 8A5/43C2
Dowlais High Street 8A5/43C2
Dowlais Top 8A5/43C1
Dowlais 8A5
Downfield Crossing Halt 9E3
Downton 4D5
Drax Abbey 21E5
Drax Hales 21E5
Draycott & Breaston 16D4/41G3
Draycott 3B2/8E2
Drayton for Costessy 18E3
Drayton Green Halt 39C2
Drayton 4E1/5F1
Dreghorn 29E3
Drem 30B1
Driffield 22C4
Drigg 26G3
Drighlington & Adwalton 42B2
Droitwich Spa 9B3
Dronfield 16A5/41B2
Drongan 29F4
Dronley 34E5
Droxford 4D3
Droylsden 21F1/45A3
Drum Park 44B3
Drumbirgh 26C2
Drumchapel 44F4
Drumlithie 34B2
Drummuir 36D1
Drumry 44F4
Drumshoreland 30B3
Drws-y-Nant 14A5/19G4
Drybridge 29E3
Drypool (Hull) 22A1
Dryssllwyn 7A3/13G5
Dubton 34C3
Dudbridge 9E3
Dudding Hill 39B4
Duddingston & Craigmillar 30G1
Dudley Castle 13B1
Dudley Hill 21D2/42B2
Dudley Port High Level 13B2/15F4
Dudley Port Low Level 13B2/15F4
Dudley Town 13B1
Dudley 13B1/15G4
Dufftown 36E1
Duirinish 35F1
Duke Street 44D4
Dukinfield 21A2
Dullatur 30B5
Dullingham 11C4
Dulverton 7F5
Dumbarton Central 29B3
Dumbarton East 29B4
Dumbuck Siding 29B4
Dumfries St Mary's 26B3
Dumfries 26B3
Dumgoyne 29B4
Dumpton Park for East Ramsgate . . .6B2
Dunball 3C1/8E3
Dunbar 31B1
Dunblane 30A5/33G3
Dunbridge 4D4
Dunchurch 10A4
Duncraig Halt 35E1

Dundee East 34E4
Dundee Tay Bridge 34E4
Dundee West 34E4
Dunfermline Lower 30A3
Dunfermline Upper 30A3
Dunford Bridge 21F2/42E2
Dungeness (RHDR) 6E3
Dunham Hill 15A1/20D3
Dunham Massey .15A2/20C2/24G2/45B4
Dunham 18E5
Dunkeld 33D4
Dunlop 29D4
Dunmere Halt 1C3
Dunmow 11E4
Dunning 33F4
Dunnington for Kexby 21C5
Dunphail 36D3
Dunragit 25C2
Dunrobin Castle 36A4/38G5
Duns 31C2
Dunsbear 1A5
Dunsford Halt 2B4
Dunsland Cross 1A5
Dunstable North 10D1/11E1
Dunstable Town 10D1/11E1
Dunstall Park 15F3
Dunster 8E5
Dunston on Tyne 28B2
Dunton Green 5C4
Dunure 29F3
Dunvant 7B3
Durham 27D5
Duror 32D3
Durrington on Sea 5F2
Dursley 8B1/9F2
Durston 3D1/8F3
Dyce 37F4
Dyffryn Ardudwy 13A5/19G2
Dykebar 29C4/44F3
Dymchurch (RHDR) 6E3
Dymock 9D2
Dynea Halt C3
Dysart 30A2
Dyserth 19D5
Eaglescliffe 28E5
Ealing Broadway 5B2/39C2
Ealing Common 39C3
Earby 21C1
Eardington 15G2
Eardisley 14E2
Earith Bridge 11B3
Earlestown 20C3/24G2/45D3
Earley 4A2
Earls Colne 12E5
Earls Court 39D5
Earlsfield for Summerstown . . .5B3/39E5
Earlston 31D1
Earlswood Lakes 9A5
Earlswood 5D3
Easington 28D5
Easingwold 21B4
Eassie 34D5
East Acton 39C3
East Anstey 7F5
East Barkwith 17A2
East Boldon 28C5
East Brixton 40E5
East Budleigh 2B2
East Calder 30C3
East Croydon 5C3
East Didsbury 45B4
East Dulwich 40E4
East Farleigh 6C5
East Finchley 9A5
East Fortune 31B1

East Garston 4A4/10G5
East Halton Halt 22E3
East Ham Borough Council Siding . .40B2
East Ham 40B2
East Haven 34E3
East Kilbride 29D5/44D1
East Langton 16G3
East Leake 16D4
East Linton 31B1
East Norton 16F2
East Pilton 30F3
East Putney 39E4
East Road Park Halt 30F2
East Rudham 18D5
East Smithfield 40C4
East Tilbury 5B5
East Ville 17C3
East Winch 17E5
East Worthing Halt 5F2
Eastbourne 5G5
Eastbury Halt 4A4/10G5
Eastcote 39B1
Eastgate 27D3
Eastgrange 30A4
Eastleigh 4D3
Eastoft 22E5
Easton Court for Little Hereford . . .9A1
Easton 3G3
Eastriggs 26B2
Eastwood & Langley Mill 16D4/41F3
Eastwood 21E1
Ebbw Vale High Level 8A4/43B1
Ebbw Vale Low Level 8A4/43B1
Ebley Crossing Halt 9E3
Ecclefechan 26B2
Eccles Road 12A4/18G4
Eccles 45B3
Ecclesfield East 21G3/42F4
Ecclesfield West 21G3/42F4
Eccleshill 21D2/42A2
Eccleston Park 20C3/24G3/45E3
Eckington & Renishaw 41B3
Eckington 9C3
Edale 15A5
Edderton 36B5
Eddleston 30D2
Eden Park 5B3/40G3
Edge Hill Goods 45F4
Edge Hill 45F4
Edgware Road 39C5
Edinburgh Haymarket 30G2
Edinburgh Lothian Road 30G2
Edinburgh Princes Street 30F2
Edinburgh Scotland Street . . . . . .3)F2
Edinburgh St Leonards 30G2
Edinburgh Waverley 30G2
Edington Burtley 3C1/8E3
Edlington 21G2
Edmondthorpe & Wymondham . . .16E2
Edrom 31C2
Edwalton 16D3/41G5
Edwinstowe 16B3/41C5
Edzell 34C3
Efail Isaf 8C5/43C4
Effingham Junction 5C2
Eggesford 2A5/7G4
Egginton 16D5
Egham for Englefield Green 5B1
Eglinton Street (Goods) 44F2
Eglinton Street 44F1
Egloskerry 1B4
Egremont 26F3
Egton 28F2
Elderslie 29C4/44G3
Elephant & Castle 40D5

Elgin 36C2
Elie 30A1/34G4
Elland 21E2/42C1
Ellenbrook for Boothstown 45B2
Ellerby 22D3
Ellerdine Halt 15E2
Ellesmere Port 20D4/45E5
Ellesmere .20F4
Ellingham 12A2/18G2
Elliot Junction 34D3
Ellon 37E4
Elm Park 5A4
Elmbridge .17F4
Elmers End 5B3/40G4
Elmesthorpe for Barwell &
    Earl Shilton 16F4
Elms Bridge Halt 8A3
Elmstead Woods 40F2
Elmswell .12C4
Elmton & Creswell 16A4/41B4
Elsecar East 21F3/42F4
Elsenham .11E4
Elsham 22F4
Elson Halt 20F4
Elsted 4D1
Elstree & Borehamwood 5A211G2
Elswick 28A2
Eltham Park 40E1
Eltham Well Hall 5B4/40E2
Elton & Orston 16C2
Elvanfoot .30F4
Elvington for Sutton 21C5
Ely Fairwater Road 43B4
Ely Main Lin 43B4
Ely 11B4
Embleton .26E2
Embo 36B4
Embsay 21C1
Emerson Park Halt 5A5
Emneth 17F4
Emsworth 4E2
Enderby 16F4
Endon 15C3
Enfield Chase 11G2
Enfield Lock for Enfield Wash 11G3
Enfield Town 5A311G3
Enthorpe .22C4
Entwistle 20A2/24E2/45B1
Epping 11G3
Epsom Downs 5C3
Epsom 5C2
Epworth 22F5
Erdidge 5D5
Erdington 15F5
Erith 5B4
Errol 34E5
Erwood 14F3
Eryholme .28F5
Esher for Sandown Park 5B2/39G1
Eskbank & Dalkeith 30C2
Eskmeals .26G3
Essendine 16E1/17E1
Eston 28E4
Etchingham 6E5
Etherley 27E5
Ettingshall Road & Bilston 15F4
Ettington .10C5
Etwall 16D5
Evanton 36C5
Evenwood 27E5
Evercreech junction 3C3/8F1
Evercreech New 3C3/8E1
Everingham 22D5
Evershot 3E2
Evesham North 9C4

Evesham South 9C4
Ewell East .5C3
Ewell West .5C3
Ewesley 27A4/31G4
Ewood Bridge & Ednefield . . .20A1/24E1
Exeter Central 2B3
Exeter St Davids 2B3
Exeter St Thomas 2B3
Exminster .2B3
Exning Road Halt 11C4
Eyarth 19E5/20E5
Eydon Road Platform 10C4
Eye Green for Crowland 17F2
Eye 12B3
Eyemouth 31C3
Eynsford 5C5
Eynsham .10E4
Eythorne 6C2
Facit 20A1/24E1/45A1
Failsworth 45A2
Fairbourne 13A5
Fairfield for Droylsden 45A3
Fairford 9F5
Fairlie High 29D2
Fairlie Pier 29D2
Fairlop 5A4/40A1
Fakenham East 18D5
Fakenham West 18D5
Falahill 30C1
Falcon Lane, Clapham Junction . . .39E5
Falconwood 40E1
Falkirk Camelon 30B5
Falkirk Grahamstown 30B4
Falkirk High 30B4
Falkland Road 34G5
Fallowfield for Withington &
    Didsbury 20C1/24G1/45A3
Falls of Cruachan Halt 32F3
Falmer 5F3
Falmouth 1F1
Falstone 27A2
Fambridge 12G5
Fambridge .6A5
Fangfoss 22C5
Fareham 4E3
Faringdon 10F5
Farington 20A3/24E3
Farley Halt 15F2
Farlington .4E2
Farnborough 4B1
Farnborough North 4B1
Farncombe 5D1
Farnell Road 34C3
Farnham 4C1
Farningham Road &
    Sutton-at-Hone 5B5
Farnley & Wortley 21C2/42A3
Farnsfield 16B3/41D5
Farnworth &
    Bold 15A1/20C3/24G3/45D4
Farnworth &
    Halshaw Moor 20B2/24F1/45B2
Farnworth (Widnes) 45D4
Farringdon 40C5
Farringdon .4C2
Farrington Gurney Halt 3B3/8D1
Farthinghoe 10C4
Fauldhouse & Crofthead 30C4
Fauldhouse North 30C4
Faversham .6C4
Fawkham for Hartley & Longfield . . .5B5
Fawley (Hants) 4E4
Fawley 9D1
Faygate 5D3
Fazackerley 20B4/24F4/45F3

Fearn 36B4
Featherstone Park 27C2
Featherstone 21E4/42C5
Febce Houses 28C5
Feguslie 44G3
Felin Fach .13E5
Felin Foel .7B3
Felin Fran 7B4/43F2
Felindyffryn Halt 13D5
Felixstowe Beach 12E3
Felixstowe Dock 12E3
Felixstowe Town 12E3
Felling 28A1
Felmingham 18D3
Felsted 11E4
Feltham 5B2
Fen Ditton Halt 11C3
Fenay Bridge & Lepton 21E2/42D2
Fencehouses 28C5
Feniscowles 20A2/24E2
Fenn's Bank 15D1/24F3
Fenny Bentley 15C5
Fenny Compton West 10B4
Fenny Compton 10B4
Fenny Stratford 10D2
Fenton 15C3/24F1
Fenton Manor 15C3/24F1
Ferndale 8B5/43D2
Fernhill Heath 9B3
Ferniegair 30D5/44B2
Ferriby 22E4
Ferry Hill .28D5
Ferry 17E3
Ferrybridge for Knottingley . .21E4/42C5
Ferryside 7A2
Festiniog .19F3
Ffairfach .13G5
Fidlers Ferry &
    Penketh 15A1/20C3/24G3/45D4
Fighting Cocks 28F5
Filey Holiday Camp 22A3
Filey 22A3
Filleigh 7F4
Filton Junction 3A2/9G2
Finchley Central 5A3/39A5
Finchley Road & Frognal 39B5
Finchley Road (goods) 39B5
Finchley Road 39B5
Findochty .37C1
Finedon 10A2
Finmere 10D3
Finningham 12C4
Finningley 21F5
Finsbury Park 5A3/40B5
Finstock Halt 10E5
Firsby 17B3
Fishbourne Halt 4E1
Fisherrow .30B2
Fishersgate Halt 5F3
Fishguard & Goodwick 13F1
Fishguard Harbour 13F1
Fishponds 3A2/8C2/9G2
Fiskerton .16C3
Fittleworth .5E1
Fitzwilliam 42D1
Five Mile House 17B1
Five Ways .15E4
Fladbury 9C4
Flamborough 22B2
Flax Bourton 3A2/8D2
Flaxton 21B5
Flecknoe .10B4
Fledborough 16B2
Fleet (Lincs) 17E3
Fleet 4B1

Fleetwood 24C4
Flemington 30C5/44A2
Fletton 10A2/17G2
Fleur-de-Lis 43B3
Flimby .26D3
Flint 20D5
Flitwick 10D1/11E1
Flixton 20C2/24G145B3
Flordon 12A3/18F3
Fochabers Town 36C1
Fochriw 8A5/43C2
Fockerby 22E5
Foggathorpe 22D5
Foleshill 10A5
Foley Park Halt 9A3
Folkestone Central 6D2
Folkestone Harbour 6D2
Folkestone Junction 6D2
Forcett Depot 27F5
Ford & Crossgates 14A1
Ford (Devon) 1D5
Ford 5F1
Ford Green 15C3/24E1
Forden .14B2
Fordham 11B4
Fordingbridge 4D5
Fordoun 34B2
Forest Gate (Goods) 40B2
Forest Gate 40B2
Forest Hall 27B5
Forest Hill 40E4
Forest Row for Ashdown Forest . .5D4
Forfar .34D4
Forgandenny 33F5
Formby 20B4/24F4/45G2
Forncett 12A3/18G3
Forres .36C3
Forrest Field 30C5
Forsinard 38E5
Fort Brockhurst 4E3
Fort George 36D4
Fort Matilda 29B3
Fort William 32C3
Fortevoit 33F4
Fortrose 36D5
Forty Hill 11G3
Foryd Pier 19C5
Foss Cross 9E4
Fotherby Halt 17A3/22G2
Foulis .36C5
Foulridge 21B1
Foulsham 18E4
Fountain Bridge Halt 43B3
Fountainhall Junction 30D1
Four Crosses 14A2
Four Oaks Halt 9D2
Four Oaks 15F5
Fourstones 27B3
Fowey 1D3
Foxdale 23B2
Foxfield 24A5
Foxton 11D3
Framlingham 12C3
Frankton 20F4
Fransham 18E5
Frant 5D5
Fraserburgh 37C4
Fratton .4E2
Frecester 9E2
Frefeinon 14F3
Fremington 7F3
French Drove & Gedney Hill . . .17F3
Freshfield 20B4/24F4/45G2
Freshford 3B3
Frickley Colliery 42D5

Frickley 21F4/42D5
Friden .15B5
Friezland 21F1
Frimley 4B1/5C1
Frinton on Sea 12E3
Friockheim 34D3
Frisby .16E3
Fritwell & Somerton 10D4
Frizinghall 21D2/42A1
Frodsham 15A1/20D3/45D5
Frome 3C3/8E1
Frongoch 19F4
Frosterley 27D4
Fryston 21E4/42B5
Fulbourne 11C4
Fullerton 4C4
Fulwell & Westbury 10D3
Fulwell for Hampton Hill 5B2/39F1
Furness Vale 15A4
Furze Platt 10G2
Fushiebridge 30C2
Fyling Hall 28F1
Fyvie 37E3
Gaerwen 19D2
Gagie 34E4
Gailes .29E3
Gainford 27E5
Gainsborough Central 16A2/22G5
Gainsborough Lea Road 16A2/22G5
Galashiels 30E1
Galston 29E4
Gamlingay 11D2
Ganton 22A4
Gara Bridge 2D4
Garelochhead 29A3
Garforth 21D4/42A5
Gargrave 21C1
Gargunnock 29A5
Garlieston 25D4
Garmouth 36C1
Garnant 7A4/43F1
Garndiffaith Halt 43A2
Garneddwen Halt 19G4
Garnkirk 29C5/44C4
Garrochburn 29R4
Garrowhill Halt 44C3
Garsdale 24A1/27G2
Garstand & Catterall 24D3
Garstang Town 24C3
Garston Docks 45E4
Garston 20C4/45F4
Garswood 20B3/24F3/45D3
Garth 14E4
Gartly .37E1
Gartmore 29A4
Garton 22C4
Gartshore 29B5/44B5
Garve .35D4
Gateacre for Woolton . .20C4/24G3/45E4
Gatehead 29E4
Gatehouse of Fleet 25C5
Gateshead East 2881
Gateshead East 28A1
Gateshead West 2881
Gateshead West 28B12
Gateside 33F5
Gathurst for
    Shevington 20B3/24F3/45D2
Gatley for Cheadle 45A4
Gatwick Airport 5D3
Gayton Road 17E5
Gedling & Carlton 16C3/41F4
Gedney 17E3
Geldeston 12A2/18G2
Gelli Felen Halt 43B1

Georgemas Junction 38C3
Georgetown 29C4/44G4
Gerrards Cross 5A1/10F2
Gidea Park & Squirrels Heath 5A4
Giffen .29D3
Giffnock 29C5/44E2
Gifford 31C1
Giggleswick 24B1
Gildersome East 21E3/42B3
Gildersome West 21E3/42B3
Gileston 8D5/43D5
Gilfach Fargoed Halt 43B2
Gilfach Goch 8B5/43D3
Gilling .21A5
Gillingham (Dorset) 3D4
Gillingham 6B5
Gilmerton 30C2
Gilnockie for Claygate 26B1
Gilsland 27B2
Gilwern Halt 8A4/43B1
Gipsy Hill for Upper Norwood . . .40F4
Girvan .29G2
Gisburn 24C1
Glais 7B4/43F2
Glaisdale 28F2
Glamis .34D4
Glan Conway 19D4
Glan Llyn 19F4
Glanamman 7A4/43F1
Glandyfi 14B5
Glanrafon 13C5
Glanrhyd 14G5
Glan-yr-Afon Halt 14C4
Glapwell Colliery 16B4/41C3
Glasbury-on-Wye 14F2
Glascoed Halt 43A2
Glasgow Buchanan Street . .29C5/44E4
Glasgow Central (HL/LL) 29C5/44E4
Glasgow Cook Street 44F2
Glasgow Cross 44E4
Glasgow General Terminus 44E3
Glasgow
    Queen Street (HL/LL) 29C5/44E4
Glasgow South Side 44E1
Glasgow St Enoch 29C5/44E4
Glassaugh 37C2
Glassel 34A3/37G2
Glasson Docks 24C3
Glasterlaw 34D3
Glastonbury & Street 3C2/8E2
Glazebrook 20C2/24G2/45C3
Glazebury 20B2/24G2/45C3
Glemsford 12D5
Glen Parva 16F4
Glenbarry 37D2
Glenboig 30C5/44B4
Glencarron Halt 35D2
Glencarse 33F5
Glencorse 30C2
Glendon & Rushton 10A2/16G2
Gleneagles 33F4
Glenfarg 33F5
Glenfield 16F4
Glenfield 44G3
Glenfinnan 32B4
Glengarnock 29D3
Gleniffer Depot 44G2
Glenluce 25C3
Glenside 29F3
Glenwhilly 25B3
Glodwick Road 21F1
Glogue .13F3
Glossop Central 21G1
Gloucester Central 9E3
Gloucester Eastgate 9E3

Gloucester Road 39D5
Glyn Neath 7A5/43E2
Glyncorrwg 43E2
Glynde 5F4
Glyndyfrdwy 20F5
Glyntaff .43C3
Gnosall 15E3
Goathland 28F2
Gobowen .20F4
Godalming 5D1
Godley Junction 21G1
Godmanchester 11B2
Godstone .5D3
Godwn's Depot 10E1/11F1
Gogarth Halt 13B5
Golant Halt 1D3
Golborne North 45D3
Golborne South 20B2/24F2/45D3
Golcar 21E2/42D1
Golden Grove 13G5
Golders Green 39A5
Goldhawk Road 39D4
Goldsborough 21C4
Goldthorpe & Thurnscoe 42E5
Golf Club House Halt 37C2
Gollanfield Junction 36D4
Gomersal 21E2/42B2
Gomshall & Shere 5D1
Goodmayes 5A4
Goodrington Sands Halt 2D3
Goole Town 22E5
Goonavern Halt 1D1
Goonbell Halt 1E1
Goostrey 15B3/24D1
Gordon Hill 11G2
Gordon 31D1
Gordoun .34B2
Gorebridge 30C2
Gorgie East 30G3
Gorgie West 30G3
Goring & Streatley 10G3
Goring-by-Sea 5F2
Gorleston Links Halt 18F1
Gorleston-on-Sea 18F1
Gorseinon .7B3
Gorton for Openshaw 45A3
Gosberton 17D2
Gosford Green 10A5
Gospel Oak 39B5
Gosport 4E3
Goswick .31D4
Gotham 16D4
Gotherington Halt 9D4
Goudhurst 6D5
Gourock .29B3
Govan 44E4
Govilon 8A4/43A1
Gowerton North 7B3
Gowerton South 7B3
Goxhill 22E3
Grafham .11B1
Grafton & Burbage 4B5
Grageston Halt 29G2
Grain 6B4
Grainsby Halt 22F2
Grampound Road 1E2
Grandtully 33D4
Grane Road 20A1/24E1
Grange Colliery 42F4
Grange Court 8A1/9E2
Grange Hill 5A4
Grange Lane 42F4
Grange Park 11G2
Grange Road for Crawley Down &
  Turners Hill 5D3

Grange 37D1
Grangemouth Harbour 30B4
Grangemouth 30B4
Grange-over-Sands 24B3
Grangetown 28E4
Grangetown 8C4/43B4
Gransthouse 31C2
Grantham Gonerby Siding 16D1
Grantham 16D1
Granton East 30F2
Granton High 30F2
Granton Road 30F2
Grantown on Spey East 36F3
Grantown on Spey West 36F3
Grassington & Threshfield 21B1
Grassmoor 16B5/41C2
Grateley 4C5
Gravelly hill 15G5
Graveney Siding 6C3
Gravesend Central 5B5
Gravesend West 5B5
Grays 5B5
Great Ayrton 28F4
Great Barr 13B3/15F4
Great Bentley 12E4
Great Bridge North 13B2
Great Bridge South 13B2
Great Bridgeford 15D3/24G1
Great Chesterford 11D3
Great Coates 22F2
Great Glen 16F3
Great Harwood 24D1
Great Horton for Lidget Green21D2/42A1
Great Lavern 9C3
Great Linford 10C2
Great Longstone for Ashford 15B5
Great Missenden 10F2
Great Ormesby 18E1
Great Ponton 16D1
Great Portland Street 39C5
Great Shefford 4A4/10G5
Greatham 28E4
Greatstone-on-Sea Halt 6C3
Green Bank Halt 15F2
Green Road 24A5
Greenan Castle 29F3
Greenfield 21F1
Greenford 5A2/39B1
Greengairs 30C5/44A5
Greenhead 27B2
Greenhill .30B5
Greenhithe 5B5
Greenlaw .31D2
Greenloaning 33G3
Greenock Central 29B3
Greenock Princes Pier 29B3
Greenock West 29B3
Greenodd 24A4
Greenway Halt 9D2
Greenwich 5B4/40D3
Greetland 21E2/42C1
Grerigg 27G1
Gresford for Llay 20E4
Gresley 16E5
Gretna Green 26B1
Gretton Halt 9D4
Gretton 16F2
Griffiths Crossing 19D2
Grimes Hill & Wythall 9A5
Grimethorpe Colliery 42E5
Grimethorpe 21F4/42D5
Grimoldby 17A3/22G1
Grimsargh 24D2
Grimsby Docks 22F2
Grimsby Town 22F2

Grimston .16E3
Grimstone & Frampton 3F3
Grindleford 41B1
Grindley Brook Halt 15C1/20F3
Gristhorpe 22A3
Groesffordd Halt 14G3
Groeslon .19E2
Groeswen .43C3
Groombridge 5D4
Grosmont 28F2
Grotton & Springhead 21F1
Grove Ferry & Upstreet 6C2
Grove Park 5B4/40E2
Guardbridge 34F4
Guay 33D4
Guestwick 18D4
Guide Bridge 21F1/45A3
Guildford .5C1
Guisborough 28E3
Guiseley 21D2
Gullane 30B1
Gulston Siding 7A4
Gunheath Siding 1D2
Gunnersbury 39D3
Gunness & Burringham 22F5
Gunnislake 1C5
Gunton 18D3
Gurnos 7A4/43F1
Guthrie 34D3
Guyhirne .17F3
Gwernydomen Halt 43B3
Gwersyllt .20E4
Gwinear Road 1E4
Gwyddelwern 19F5
Gwys 7A4/43F1
Gyfeillon Siding 43C3
Habrough .22E3
Hackbridge 39G5
Hackney Downs 5A4/40B4
Hackney Wick 40B3
Haddenham 10E3
Haddenham 11B3
Haddington 30B1
Haddiscoe 12A1/18F1
Hadfield 21G1
Hadham 11F3
Hadleigh .12D4
Hadley Wood 11G2
Hadley 15E2
Hadlow Road for Willaston . . .20D4/45F5
Hadnall 24G3
Hadnock Halt 8A2/9E1
Hafodryrnys Platform 43A2
Hagley Road 13C3
Hagley 9A3
Haigh 21F3/42D3
Hailsham 5F5
Hainton Street Halt 22F2
Hairmyres 29D5/44D1
Halbeath .30A3
Halberton Halt 2A3
Hale for Altrincham &
  Bowdon 15A3/20C1/24G1/45B4
Halebank for Hale 15A1/45E4
Halesowen 9A4/15G4
Halesworth 12B2
Halifax North Bridge 21E2/42B1
Halifax St Paul's 21E2/42B1
Halifax Town 21E2/42B1
Halkirk 38D3
Hall Green 9A5/15G5
Hall Road 20B4/24F4/45F2
Hallaton 16F2
Hallatrow 3B3/8D1
Halling 6C5

Hallington 17A2/22G2
Halliwell .45C2
Halmerend 15C3/24E1
Halstead .11E5
Halton Holgate 17B3
Halton 15A1/20D3/45D5
Halton 24B3
Haltwhistle 27B2
Halwill for Beaworthy 1A5
Ham Green Halt 3A2
Ham Mill Crossing Halt 9F3
Ham Street & Orlestone 6D4
Hamble Halt 4E3
Hambleton 21D5
Hamilton Central 30D544B2
Hamilton West 44B2
Hammeron 21C4
Hammersmith & Chiswick 39D3
Hammersmith 39D4
Hammerwich 15E4
Hampden Park for Willingdon 5F5
Hampole .21F4
Hampstead Heath 39B5
Hampstead Norris 4A3/10G4
Hampton Court 5B2/39G2
Hampton Loade 15G2
Hampton Wick 39F2
Hampton 5B2/39F1
Hampton-in-Arden 9A5/15G5
Hamworthy Junction 3F5
Hamworthy 3F5
Handforth 15A3/20C1/45A4
Handsworth & Smethwick 13B2
Hanger Lane 39C2
Hanley 15C3/24E1
Hanwell & Elthorne 5B2/39C2
Hanwood 14A1
Happendon 30E5
Hapton 24D1
Harborne 9A4/13C3
Harburn .30C3
Harby & Stathern 16D2
Hardingham 18F4
Hardwick Road Siding 17E5
Hare Park & Crofton 21E3/42C4
Harecastle 15C3/24E1
Haresfield .9E3
Harker 26C1
Harlech .19F2
Harlesden 39B3
Harleston 12A3/18G3
Harling Road 12A4/18G4
Harlington 10D1/11E1
Harlington 21F4
Harlow 11F3
Harold Wood 5B5
Harpenden Central 11F1
Harpenden East 11F1
Harperley 27D4
Harrietsham 6C4
Harringay Park 40A5
Harringay West 40A5
Harrington 26E3
Harrogate 21C3
Harrow & Wealdstone 5A2/39A2
Harrow-on-the-Hill 5A2/39A2
Harston .11D3
Hart 28D4
Hartfield .5D4
Hartford & Greenbank .15A2/20D2/45C5
Hartford 15B2/24D2/45C5
Hartington 15B5
Hartlebury 9A3
Hartlepool 28D4
Hartley 28B5

Harts Hill 15G4
Hartwood 30C5
Harvington 9C4
Harwich Town 12E3
Hasland .41C2
Haslemere 4C1/5D1
Haslingden 24E1
Hassendean 31F1
Hassocks .5F3
Hassop .15B5
Hastings .6F5
Haswell .28D5
Hatch End 5A2
Hatch 3D1/8G3
Hatfield Moor 22F5
Hatfield Peverel 11F5
Hatfield .11F2
Hatherleigh 1A5
Hathern .16E4
Hathersage 15A5
Hatton 9B5
Haughley 12C4
Haughton 15E3/24G1
Havant 4E2
Havenhouse 17B4
Haverfordwest 7C2
Haverhill North 11D5
Haverhill South 11D5
Haverthwaite 24A4
Haverton Hill 28E4
Hawarden 20D4
Hawarden Bridge 20D4
Hawes 24A1/27G3
Hawick 31F1
Hawkesbury Lane 16G5
Hawkhead 44F3
Hawkhurst 6E5
Hawkmoor Halt 2C4
Hawkser .28F2
Haworth .21D1
Haxby 21C5
Haxey & Epworth 22F5
Haxey Junction 22F5
Haxey Town 22F5
Hayburn Wyke 28G1
Haydock Park 45D3
Haydon Bridge 27B3
Haydon Square 40C4
Haydons Road 39F5
Hayes & Harlington 5B2
Hayes 5C4/40G2
Hayfield 15A4/21G1
Hayle 1E4
Hayles Abbey Halt 9D4
Hayling Island 4E2
Hay-on-Wye 14F2
Haywards Heath 5E3
Haywood 30C4
Hazel Grove 15A3/21G1/45A4
Hazelhead Bridge 21F2/42E2
Hazelwell .9A4
Heacham 17D5
Headcorn .6D5
Headingley 21D3/42A3
Heads Nook 27C1
Heads of Ayr 29F3
Headstone Lane 39A1
Heald Green 15A3/20C1/24G1/45A4
Healey House 21F2/42D1
Healing .22F2
Heanor South 41F3
Heapey 20A2/24E2/45D1
Heath Halt (High Level) 43B4
Heath Halt (Low Level) 43B4
Heath Park Depot 10E1/11F1

Heath 16B4/41C3
Heather & Ibstock 16E5
Heathfield 2C4
Heathfield 5E5
Heatley &
    Warburton 15A2/20C2/24G2/45C4
Heaton Chapel & Heaton Moor . . .45A3
Heaton Mersey 20C1/24G1/45A4
Heaton Norris 45A3
Heaton Park 20B1/24F1/45B2
Heaton 28A1
Hebburn .28D5
Hebden Bridge 21E1
Heck 21E5
Heckington 17C2
Heckmondwike Central 21E2/42C2
Hednesford 15E4
Hedon 22E3
Heeley 16A5/41A2
Heighington 27E5
Hele & Bradninch 2A3
Helensburgh Central 29B3
Helensburgh Upper 29B3
Hellaby .21G4
Hellesdon 18E3
Hellifield 24C1
Hellingly .5F5
Helmdon for Sulgrave 10C4
Helmsdale 38F4
Helmshore 20A1/24E1
Helmsley 21A5
Helpringham 17D1
Helpston .17F1
Helsby & Alvanley 15A1/20D3/45E5
Helsby 15A1/20D3/45E5
Helston 1F5
Hemel Hempstead &
    Boxmoor 10E1/11F1
Hemel Hempstead
    Midland Road 10E1/11F1
Heminbrough 21D5
Hemsby .18E1
Hemsworth Colliery 42D5
Hemsworth 21E3/42D5
Hemyock 2A2/8G4
Henbury 8C2/9G1
Hendford Halt 3D2
Hendon 5A3/39A4
Henfield .5F2
Hengoed 8B4/43B3
Heniarth .14D3
Henley-in-Arden 9B5
Henley-on-Thames 10G2
Henllan .13F4
Henlow Camp 11E1
Hensall .21E5
Henstridge 3D3/8F1
Henwick .9B3
Heogerrig Halt 43C1
Hepscott 27A5
Hereford Barrs Court 9C1
Hereford Barton 9C1
Hereford Moorfields 9C1
Heriot 30C1
Hermitage 4A3
Herne Bay 6B2
Herne Hill 5B3/40E5
Hersham .5C2
Hertford East 11F2
Hertford North 11F2
Hertingfordbury 11F2
Heskeden 28D5
Hesketh Bank 20A3/24E3
Hesketh Park 20A4/24E4/45F1
Heslerton 22A4

Hessay 21C4
Hessle 22E4
Hest Bank 24B3
Heswall Hills 20C4/45F4
Heswall 20C5
Hethersett 18F3
Hetton 28D5
Hever 5D4
Hew Hadley Halt 15E2
Hexham 27B3
Heyford 10D4
Heysham Harbour 24C4
Heytesbury 3C4
Heywood 20B1/24F1/45A2
Hgh Street 44D4
High Barnet 5A3/11G2
High Blantyre 29C5/44C2
High Brooms 5D5
High Halstrow Halt 6B5
High Harrington 26E3
High Lane 15A4/21G1
High Shields 28D5
High Street Halt 13C1
High Street Kensingon 39D5
High Wycombe 10F2
Higham Ferrers 10A1
Higham 11C5
Higham 6B5
Highams Park & Hale End 5A4
Highbridge & Burnham-on-Sea . .3B1/8E3
Highbridge East 3B1/8E3
Highbury & Islington 40B5
Highbury Vale 40B5
Highclere 4B3
Higher Poynton 15A4
Highfield 22D5
Highgate Wellington Sidings . . .5A3/39A5
Highlandman 33F3
Highley 15G2
Hightown 20B4/24F4/45F2
Highworth 9F5
Hildenborough 5D5
Hilgay 10A4/17F4
Hill End 11F2
Hillfoot 29B4/44E5
Hillington East 44F3
Hillington for Sandringham 17E5
Hillington West 44F3
Hillside 34C2
Hillside (Lancs) 45F1
Hilsea Halt 4E2
Himley 15G3
Hinchley Wood 5C2
Hinckley 16F4
Hinderwell 28E2
Hindley & Amberswood 45C2
Hindley Green 45C2
Hindley North 45C2
Hindley South 45C2
Hindley 20B2/24F2
Hindlow 15B5
Hindolvestone 18D4
Hinton Admiral 4F5
Hinton 9C4
Hipperholme 42B1
Hirwaun 8A5/43D2
Hirwaun Pond Halt 43D2
Histon 11C3
Hitchin 11E2
Hither Green 40E3
Hockley 13C3/15G4
Hockley 6A5
Hodnet 15D2/24G2
Hoghton 20A2/24E2
Holbeach 17E3

Holbeck High Level 21C2/42A3
Holbeck Low Level 21C2/42A3
Holcombe Brook 20A1/24E1/45B1
Hole .1A5
Holland Road Halt 5F3
Hollingbourne 6C5
Hollins 20A2/24E2
Hollinswood 15E2
Hollinwell & Annesley 41E4
Hollinwood 45A2
Hollybush 29F4
Hollybush 8A4/43B2
Holme Hale 18F5
Holme Lacy 9C1
Holme Moor 22D5
Holme 10A2/17G2
Holmes Chapel 15B3/24D1
Holmfield 21D2/42B1
Holmfirth 21F2/42D1
Holmsley 4E5
Holmwood 5D2
Holsworthy 1A4
Holt Junction 3B4
Holt 18D4
Holton le Clay 22F2
Holton Village Halt 22F2
Holton-le-Moor 22F3
Holwell Junction 16E3
Holygate for Broxburn 30B3
Holyhead 19B2
Holytown 30C5/44A3
Holywell Junction 20D5
Holywell 28D5
Holywood 26A4
Homersfield 12A3/18G3
Honeybourne 9C5
Honing 18D2
Honington 16C1
Honiton 2B2
Honley 21F2/42D1
Honor Oak Park 40E4
Hook Norton 10D5
Hook 4B2
Hoole 20A3/24E3
Hooton 20D4/45F5
Hope & Pen-y-Ffordd 20E4
Hope (HL) 20E4
Hope (LL) 20E4
Hope for Castleton & Bradwell 15A5
Hope Village 20E4
Hopeman 36C2
Hopperton 21C4
Hopton Heath 14C1
Hopton-on-Sea 18F1
Horam 5F5
Horbury & Ossett 42C3
Horbury Millfield Road 21E3/42C4
Horden 28D4
Horeb 7A3
Horfield 3A2
Horley 5D3
Hornby 24B2
Horncastle 17B2
Hornchurch 5A5
Hornsea Bridge 22C2
Hornsea Town 22C2
Hornsey 40A5
Horrabridge 1C5
Horringford 4F3
Horrocksford 24D1
Horsebridge 4C4
Horsehay & Dawley 15F2
Horsforth 21D3/42A3
Horsham 5E2
Horsley for Ockham & Ripley 5C2

Horsmonden 6D5
Horspath Halt 10E4
Horsted Keynes 5E3
Horton in Ribblesdale 24B1
Horwich 20B2/24F2/45C1
Hoscar 20B3/24F3/45E1
Hothfield Halt 6D4
Hough Green for
   Ditton 15A1/20C3/24G3/45E4
Hougham 16C1
Hounslow Central 39D1
Hounslow East 5B2/39D1
Hounslow West 5B2/39D1
Hounslow 5B2/39E1
Houston & Crosslee 29C4
Hove .5F3
Hovingham Spa 21A5
How Mill 27C1
Howdon on Tyne 28D5
Howe Bridge 20B2/24F2/45C2
Howsham 22F3
Howwood 29C4
Hoy Halt 38C3
Hoylake 20C5/24G5
Hubbert's Bridge 17C2
Hucknall Byron 16C4/41E4
Hucknall Central 16C4/41E4
Hucknall Town 16C4/41E4
Huddersfield Hillhouse 21E2/42C2
Huddersfield Newtown 21E2/42C1
Huddersfield 21E2/42C1
Hugglescoate 16E4
Hull Cannon Street 22A1
Hull Paragon 22A1
Hullavington 9G3
Humbie 30C1
Humshaugh 27B3
Huncoat 24D1
Hundred End 20A4/24E3
Hungerford 4A4
Hunmanby 22B3
Hunnington 9A4/15G4
Hunslet East 42A4
Hunslet Lane 42A4
Hunslet 21D3/42A4
Hunstanton 17D5
Hunt's Cross 20C4/45E4
Huntingdon East 11B2
Huntingdon North 11B2
Huntly 37E1
Hunwick 27D5
Hurlford 29E4
Hurst Green Halt 5C4
Hurstbourne 4B4
Husthwaite Gate 21B4
Hutton Cranswick 22C4
Hutton Gate 28F3
Huttons Ambo 22B5
Huyton 20C3/24G3/45E4
Huyton Quarry 20C3/24G3/45E4
Hyde Central 21G1
Hyde North 21G1
Hyde Road 45A3
Hykeham 16B1
Hylton 28C5
Hyndland 44E4
Hythe (Hants) 4E4
Hythe (RHDR) 6D3
Hythe (Kent) 12E4
Ibrox 29C4/44E3
Ide 2B3
Idle 21D2/42A2
Idmiston Halt 4C5
Ifield 5D3
Ilford 5A4/40B1

Ilfracombe 7E3
Ilkeston Junction & Cossall . .16C4/41F3
Ilkeston North 16C4/41F3
Ilkeston Town 16C4/41F3
Ilkley .21C2
Ilmer Halt 10E2
Ilminster 3D1/8G3
Ilton Halt 3D1/8G3
Imeer Houses 35E1
Immingham Docks 22E2
Immingham 22E3
Ince & Elton 15A1/20D3/45E5
Ince 45D2
Inch Green 29B3
Inchcoonans 34E5
Inches 30E5
Inchture 34E5
Ingatestone 11G4
Ingham 12B5
Ingleton 24B2
Ingrator Halt 2C5
Ingrow East 21D1
Ingrow West 21D1
Innerleithen 30E2
Innerwick 31B2
Insch .37E2
Instow .7F3
Inveramsay 37E3
Inverbervie 34B2
Inveresk 30B2
Invergordon 36C5
Invergowrie 34E5
Inverkeilor 34D3
Inverkeithing 30B3
Inverkip 29C2
Inverness 36E5
Invershin 35A5
Inverugie 37D5
Inverurie 37F3
Ipstones 15C4
Ipswich 12D4
Irchester 10B1
Irlam for Cadishead . . .20C2/24G2/45C3
Irlams-o'-th'-Height 45B2
Iron Acton 8C1/9G2
Iron Bridge & Broseley 15F2
Irthlingborough 10A1
Irton Road 26F3
Irvine Bogside Racecourse 29E3
Irvine Harbour 29E3
Irvine 29E3
Isfield .5F4
Isleham 11B4
Isleworth 39D2
Islip .10E4
Itchen Abbas 4C3
Iver 5B1/10G1
Ivybridge 2D5
Jackfield Halt 15F2
Jacksdale 16C4/41E3
Jamestown 29B3
Jarrow 28D5
Jedburgh 31E1
Jedfoot 31E1
Jefferstone Lane (RHDR) 6E3
Jersey Marine 7B4/43F3
Jervaulx 21A2/27G5
Jesmond 27B5/28A1
John o'Gaunt 16E2
Johnshaven 34C2
Johnston 7C1
Johnstone High 29C4
Johnstone North 29C4
Johnstown & Haffod 20F4
Jones' Drove 10A3/17G3

Joppa 30G1
Jordanhill 44F4
Jordanston Halt 13F1
Jordanstone 34D5
Junction Bridge Mineral Depot 30F2
Junction Road 6E5
Juniper Green 30C3
Justinhaugh 34C4
Keadby 22F5
Kearsley 20B1/24F1/45B2
Kearsney for River & Ewell 6D2
Keele 15C3/24F1
Keighley South 21D1
Keighley 21D1
Keinton Mandeville 3C2
Keith Junction 37D1
Keith Town 37D1
Kelmarsh 10A2
Kelmscott & Langford 9E5
Kelso .31E2
Kelvedon 12F5
Kelvin Bridge 44E4
Kelvinhaugh Depot 44E4
Kelvinside 44E4
Kely .30A3
Kemble Junction 9F4
Kemnay 37F3
Kempston Hardwick Halt . . .10C1/11D1
Kemsing 5C5
Kemsley Halt 6B4
Kendal 24A3
Kenfig Hill 7C5/43E4
Kenilworth 10A5
Kenley .5C3
Kennethmont 37E2
Kennett 11C5
Kennishead 44F3
Kennoway 34G5
Kensal Green 39B4
Kensal Rise 39B4
Kensington
  Lillie Bridge Sidings 39D4
Kensington Olympia 39D4
Kent House 40F4
Kent's Bank 24B4
Kentallen 32D3
Kentish Town West 40B5
Kentish Town 5A3/40B5
Kenton Bank 27B5
Kenton for Northwick Park 39A2
Kenyon Junction 20C2/24G2/45C3
Kerne Bridge 8A2/9D1
Kerry 14C2
Kershope Foot 27A1
Keswick 26E2
Ketley Town Halt 15E2
Ketley 15E2
Kettering 10A2
Kettleness 28E2
Ketton & Collyweston 16F1/17F1
Kew Bridge North 39D3
Kew Bridge South 39D3
Kew Bridge 39D3
Kew Gardens 39D3
Keyham 1D5
Keynigham 22E2
Keynsham & Somersdale 3A3/8D1
Kibworth 16F3
Kidbrooke 5B4/40E2
Kidderminster 9A3
Kidlington 10E4
Kidsgrove Central 15C3/24E1
Kidsgrove Liverpool Road . . .15C3/24E1
Kidwelly Flats Halt 7A2
Kidwelly 7A2

Kielder Forest 27A231G1
Kilbagie 30A4
Kilbarchan 29C4
Kilbirnie 29D3
Kilbowie 44F4
Kilburn High Road 39B5
Kilburn 39B4
Kilconquhar 30A1/34G4
Kildale 28F3
Kildary 36C4
Kildonan 38F5
Kildwick & Crosshills 21C1
Kilgerran 13F3
Kilgetty 7D3
Kilkerran 29G3
Killamarsh Central 16A4/41A3
Killamarsh West 16A4/41A3
Killay .7B3
Killearn 29B4
Killiecrankie 33C4
Killin Junction 33E1
Killin .33E2
Killingholme 22E3
Killingworth 27B5
Killochan 29G3
Killywhan 26B4
Kilmacolm 29C3
Kilmany 34E4
Kilmarnock High Street 29E4
Kilmarnock 29E4
Kilmaurs 29E4
Kilnhurst Central 21F4/42F5
Kilnhurst West 21F4/42F5
Kilnwick Gate 22C4
Kilpatrick for Old Kilpatrick .29B4/44G5
Kilsby & Crick 10A4
Kilsyth 29B5
Kilwinning 29D3
Kimberley East 16C4/41F4
Kimberley Park 18F4
Kimbolton 11B1
Kinaldie 37F3
Kinbrace 38E5
Kinbuck 33G3
Kincardine 30A4
Kincraig 36G4
Kineton 10B5
Kinfauns 33F5
King Edward 37C3
King George Dock (Hull) 22E3
King Tor Halt 2C5
King's Cross Suburban 40B5
King's Langley & Abbots Langley . .11G1
King's Lynn 17E4
King's Norton 9A4
King's Nympton 7F4
King's Sutton 10C4
King's Worthy 4C3
Kingennie 34E4
Kingham 9D5
Kinghorn 30A2
Kings Heath 9A4/15G4
Kings Inch 44F4
Kingsbarns 34F3
Kingsbridge 2E4
Kingsbury 15F5
Kingsbury (London) 39A3
Kingscliffe 10A1/16F1/17F1
Kingscote 5D3
Kingshouse Halt 33F2
Kingskerswell 2D3
Kingskettle 34F5
Kingsland 14D1
Kingsland 40B4
Kingsley & Froghall 15C4

Kingsley Halt 4C1
Kingsmuir 34D4
Kingston Crossing Halt 10F3
Kingston 5B2/39F2
Kingston-on-Sea 5F3
Kingswear 2D3
Kingswood & Burgh Heath 5C3
Kington .14E2
Kingussie 33A2
Kinloss .36C2
Kinneil .30B4
Kinnerley Junction 14A1/20G4
Kinnersley 14E1
Kinnerton 20E4
Kinning Park 44F2
Kinross Junction 30A3/33G5
Kintbury 4A4
Kintore .37F3
Kipling Cotes 22D4
Kippax 21D4/42B5
Kippen .29A5
Kirby Cross 12E3
Kirby Moorside 21A5
Kirby Muxloe 16F4
Kirby Park 20C5/24G5
Kirk Braddan Halt 23C2
Kirk Smeaton 21E4
Kirkandrews 26C1
Kirkbank 31E2
Kirkbride 26C2
Kirkbuddo 34D4
Kirkburton 21E2/42D2
Kirkcaldy 30A2
Kirkby Bentinck 41E4
Kirkby Lonsdale 24A2
Kirkby Stephen East 27F2
Kirkby Stephen West 27F2
Kirkby .24A5
Kirkby-in-Ashfield Central . . .16C4/41E4
Kirkby-in-Ashfield East 16C4/41E4
Kirkcowan 25C3
Kirkdale 45F3
Kirkgunzeon 26B4
Kirkham & Wesham 24D3
Kirkham Abbey 22B5
Kirkheaton 21E2/42C2
Kirkhill 29C5/44D2
Kirkiconnel 30F5
Kirkinner 25C4
Kirkintilloch Basin 44C5
Kirkintilloch 29B5/44C5
Kirklee .44E4
Kirklington 16B3
Kirkmichael 23B2/25G4
Kirkpatrick 26B2
Kirkstall 12D342A3
Kirkton Bridge Halt 37C4
Kirliston 30B3
Kirriemuir 34C4
Kirtlebridge 26B2
Kirton Lindsey 22F4
Kirton .17D2
Kittybrewster 37F4
Kiveton Bridge 16A4/41A4
Kiveton Park 16A4/41A4
Knapton 22B4
Knaresborough 21C3
Knebworth 11E2
Knighton 14D2
Knights Hill Coal Yard 40E4
Knightwick 9B2
Knitsley 27C5
Knock .37D1
Knockando 36E2
Knockholt 5C4

Knottingley 21E4/42C1
Knotty Ash & Stanley 45E3
Knowesgate 27A4
Knoweside 29F3
Knowle & Dorridge 9A5
Knowle Halt 4E3
Knucklas 14D2
Knutsford 15A2/20D2/45B5
Kyle of Lochalsh 35F1
Lacock Halt 3A4
Ladbroke Grove 39C4
Lade Halt 6C3
Ladmanlow (Harpur Hill) 15B4
Ladybank 34F5
Ladysbridge 37C2
Ladywell 40E3
Laindon 5A5
Lairg 35A5
Laisterdyke 21D2/42A2
Lakenheath 10A5/17G5
Lambley 27C2
Lambourne 4A4/10G5
Lamesley 27C5
Lamington 30E4
Lampeter 13E5
Lamphey 7D2
Lamport 10A2
Lanark .30D4
Lanark Racecourse halt 30D4
Lancaster Castle 24C3
Lancaster Green Ayre 24B3
Lanchester 27D5
Lancing 5F2
Lando Platform 7B2
Landore 7B4/43G3
Langbank 29C4
Langford & Ulting 12F5
Langho 24D2
Langley Green & Rood End . .13C2/15G4
Langley Mill & Eastwood for Heanor 41F3
Langley 5B110G1
Langloan 44B3
Langolm 26A1
Langport East 3D1/8F3
Langport West 3D1/8F3
Langrick 17C2
Langside & Newlands 44E3
Langston 4E2
Langwith 16B4/41C4
Langwithby 27D1
Langworth 16A1/17A1
Lapford 2A4
Lapworth 9A5
Larbert .30B5
Largo 34G4
Largoward 34F4
Largs 29C2
Larkhall Central 30D5/44B1
Larkhall East 30D5/44A1
Lartington 27E4
Lasswade 30C2
Latchford 15A2/20C2/24G2/45C4
Latchley Halt 1C5
Latimer Road 39C4
Lauder .31D1
Launceston North 1B4
Launceston South 1B4
Launton 10D3
Laurencekirk 34B2
Lauriston 34C2
Lavant .4E1
Lavenham 12D5
Lavernock 8D4/43B5
Laverton Halt 9C4
Lavington Halt 3B5

Law Junction 30D5
Lawley Bank 15E2
Lawrence Hill 3G1
Lawton 15C3/24E1
Laxey 23B3
Layerthorpe 21C5
Layton .24D4
Lazonby & Kirkoswald 27D1
Lea Bridge 40B3
Lea Green 20C3/24G3/45D3
Lea Hall 15G5
Leadburn 30C2
Leadenham 16C1
Leadgate 27C5
Leagrave 10D1/11E1
Lealhom 28F3
Leamington Spa Avenue 10B5
Leamington Spa General 10B5
Leamside 28D5
Leasowe 20C5/24G4
Leatherhead 5C2
Leaton 14A1/15E1
Lechlade 9F5
Leckhampton 9D4
Ledbury Town Halt 9C2
Ledbury 9C2
Ledsham 20D4/45F5
Ledston 21D4/42B5
Lee for Burnt Ash 5B4/40E2
Leebotwood 14B1/15F1
Leeds Cardigan Road 21B1/42A3
Leeds Central 21B2/42A3
Leeds City 21B2/42A3
Leeds Marsh Lane 21D3/42A3
Leeds Wellington 21B2/42A3
Leeds Wellington Street 21B2/42A3
Leegate 26D4
Leek 15B4
Leeming Bar 21A3/28G5
Lees 21F1
Legacy .20E4
Legbourne Road 17A3
Leicester Belgrave Road 16F3
Leicester Humberstone Road 16F3
Leicester Humberstone 16F3
Leicester London Road 16F3
Leicester West Bridge 16F3
Leigh (Staffs) 15D4
Leigh Court 9B3
Leigh 20B2/24F2/45C3
Leigh-on-Sea 6A5
Leighton Buzzard 10D1
Leire Halt 16G4
Leiston 12C2
Leith Central 30F2
Leith Citadel 30F2
Leith North 30F2
Leith Walk West 30F2
Lelant .1E4
Lemington 27B5/28A3
Lenham 6C4
Lennoxtown 29B5
Lentran 36D5
Lenwade 18E4
Lenzie Junction for
   Garngaber Junction 29B5/44D5
Leominster 9B1
Leslie 30A2/34G5
Lesmahagow 30D5
Letchworth 11E2
Letham Grange 34D3
Lethenty 37E3
Letterston 13F1
Leuchars Junction 34F4
Leuchars Old 34E4

Leven 30A1/34G4
Levenshulme North 45A3
Levenshulme South . . .20C1/24G1/45A3
Leverton .16A2
Levisham 22A5/28G2
Lewes 5F4
Lewiefield Halt 27A2
Lewisham 40E3
Lewknow Bridge Halt 10F3
Leyburn 21A2/27G5
Leycett 15C3/24F1
Leyland 20A3/24E3/45D1
Leysmill .34D3
Leyton Midland Road 40B3
Leyton 40B3
Leytonstone High Road 40B2
Leytonstone 5A4/40A2
Lezayre 23A3/25G4
Lhanbryde 36C1
Lichfield City 15E5
Lichfield Trent Valley High Level . .15E5
Lichfield Trent Valley Low Level . . .15E5
Lidlingtopn 10C1
Liff 34E5
Lifford 9A4
Lifton 1A5
Lightcliffe 21E2/42B1
Lightmoor Platform 15F2
Lilbourne 10A4
Limpley Stoke 3B3
Linan Bay 34D3
Linby 16C4/41E4
Lincoln Central 16A1
Lincoln East 16A1
Lincoln Holmes 16A1
Lincoln St Marks 16A1
Lincoln West 16A1
Lindal 24B4
Lindean .30E1
Lindores 34F5
Lingfield .5D4
Lingwood 18F2
Linley Halt 15F2
Linlithgow 30B4
Linthwaite 21E2/42D1
Linton .11D4
Lintz Green 27C5
Linwood 44G3
Liphook .4D1
Liscard & Poulton 45F3
Liskeard .1D4
Liss 4D1
Litchfield (Hants) 4B3
Little Bytham 16E1/17E1
Little Eaton 16C5/41F2
Little Kimble 10E2
Little Mill Junction 8B3/43A2
Little Mill 31F5
Little Salkeld 27D1
Little Somerford 9G4
Little Steeping 17B3
Little Stretton Halt 14C1
Little Sutton 20D4/45F5
Little Weighton 22D4
Littleborough 21E1
Littlehampton 5G1
Littlehaven Halt 5E2
Littlemore 10E4
Littleport 10A4/17G4
Littlestone Holiday Camp
   (Maddieson's) 6E3
Littleton & Badsey 9C4
Littleworth 17E2
Liverpool Alexandra &
   Langton Dock 45F3/45G3

Liverpool Bankfield 45G4
Liverpool
   Brunswick 20C4/24G4/45F4/45G5
Liverpool Canada Dock 45F3/45G4
Liverpool Central 29C4/24G4/45F4
Liverpool Crown Street 45F4
Liverpool Exchange & Tithebarn
   Street 20C4/24G4/45F4/45G5
Liverpool Great Howard Street 45G4
Liverpool Huskisson 45F3/45G4
Liverpool
   James Street (HL/LL) 45F4/45G5
Liverpool Lime Street . .20C4/24G4/45F4
Liverpool North Docks 45G4
Liverpool North Mersey 45G3
Liverpool Park Lane 45F4/45G5
Liverpool Riverside 45G5
Liverpool Sandon Dock 45G4
Liverpool Wapping 45G5
Liverpool Waterloo Dock 45F3/45G5
Liversedge Central 21E2/42C2
Liversedge Spen 21E2/42B2
Livingston 30C4
Llafar Halt 19F3
Llamberis 19E2
Llanaber Halt 13A5
Llanarthney Halt 13G5
Llanbadarn 13C5
Llanbedr & Pensarn 19G2
Llanbister Road 14D2
Llanbradach 8B4/43B3
Llanbrynmair 14B4
Llandaff for Whitchurch 8C4/43B4
Llandanwg Halt 19G2
Llandebie 7A3/43G1
Llandecwyn Halt 19F2
Llandenny 8A3
Llanderfel 19F5
Llandilo .13G5
Llandilo Bridge 13G5
Llandinam 14C3
Llandogo Halt 8A2/9E1
Llandovery 14F5
Llandow Halt 43D5
Llandow Wick Road Halt 43D5
Llandre .13C5
Llandrillo 19F5
Llandrindod Wells 14D3
Llandudno Juntion 19D4
Llandudno 19C3
Llandyssul 13F4
Llanelly .7B3
Llanerchymedd 19C1/23G1
Llanfair Caereinion 14B3
Llanfair .19D2
Llanfairfechan 19D3
Llanfalteg 13G2
Llanfaredd Halt 14E3
Llanfechain Halt 14A2
Llanfyllin 14A3
Llanfyrnach 13F3
Llangadock 14F5
Llangammarch Wells 14E4
Llangefni 19D1
Llangeinor 7B5/43D3
Llangelynin Halt 13B5
Llangennech 7B3
Llanglydwen 13G2
Llangollen 20F5
Llangorse Lake Halt 14F3
Llangower Halt 19F4
Llangunllo 14D2
Llangwyllog 19C1
Llangybi 13E5
Llangybi 19F1

Llangyfellach 7B4
Llangynwyd 7B5/43E3
Llanharan 8C5/43D4
Llanharry 8C5/43C4
Llanhilleth 8B4/43B2
Llanidloes 14C4
Llanilar .13D5
Llanishen 8C4/43B4
Llanmorlais 7B3
Llanpumpsaint 13F4
Llanrhaiadr Mochnant 14A3/20G5
Llanrhystyd Road 13C5
Llanrwst & Trefriw 19E4
Llansamlet North 43F3
Llansamlet South 43F3
Llansantffraid 14A2
Llansilin Road 14A2/20G5
Llanstephan Halt 14F3
Llantarnam 8B3/43A3
Llantrisant 8C5/43C4
Llantwit Fadre 8C5/43C4
Llantwit Major 8D5/43D5
Llanuwchllyn 19G4
Llanvihangel (Mon) 14G1
Llanvihangel 8A3/43A1
Llanwern 8C3
Llanwnda 19E2
Llanwrda 14F5
Llanwrtyd Wells 14E4
Llanybyther 13F5
Llanymynech Junction 14A2/20G5
Llanymynech 14A2
Lletty Brongu 7B5/43D3
Llong 20E5
Llwngwril 13A5
Llwydcoed 8A5/43D2
Llwynpia 8B5/43D3
Llynclys 14A2/20G4
Llys Halt 19G4
Llysfaen Siding 19D4
Loanhead 30C2
Loch Awe 32F2
Loch Leven 30A3/33G5
Loch Skerrow Halt 25B5
Lochailort 32B5
Locharbriggs 26B3
Lochburn 44E4
Lochee West 34E4
Lochee 34E4
Locheilside 32B3
Lochgelly 30A3
Lochluichart 35C4
Lochmaben 26A3
Lochmill 30B4
Lochside 29C3
Lochty 34F3
Lochwinnoch 29C3
Lockerbie 26A3
Lockington 22C4
Lockwood 21E2/42D1
Loddington 10A2
Loddiswell 2E4
Lodge Hill 3B2/8E2
Lofthouse & Outwood Goods .21E3/42B4
Lofthouse & Outwood 21E3/42B4
Loftus 28E3
Logierieve 37e4
Login 13G2
Londesborough 22D5
(London) Blackfriars 40C5
London Bridge 5B3/40D4
(London) Broad Street 5A3/40C4
(London) Cannon Street 5B3/40C4
(London) Charing Cross 5B3/40C5
(London) Euston 5A3/40C5

(London) Fenchurch Street ...5A3/40C4
London Fields 40B4
(London) Holborn Viaduct 5B3/40C5
(London) King's Cross 5A3/40C5
(London) Liverpool Street ...5A3/40C4
(London) Marylebone 5A3/39C5
(London) Paddington 5B3/39C5
London Road (Glasgow) 44D3
London Road (Guildford) 5C1
(London) St Pancras 5A3/40C5
(London) Victoria 5B3/39D5
(London) Waterloo 5B3/40D5
Long Buckby 10B3
Long Eaton 16D4/41G3
Long Marston 9C5
Long Marton 27E2
Long Melford 12D5
Long Parish 4C4
Long Preston 24C1
Long Stanton 11C3
Long Sutton & Pitney 3D1/8F2
Long Sutton 17E3
Long Witton 27A4
Longbenton Halt 27B5
Longbridge 9A4
Longcliffe 15C5
Longcross 5B1
Longdon Halt 15E2
Longdown 2B3
Longforgan 34E5
Longhirst 27A5
Longhope 8A1/9D1
Longhoughton 31F5
Longmorn 36D2
Longniddry 30B1
Longport 15C3/24E1
Longridge 24D2
Longside 37D5
Longsight for Belle Vue 45A3
Longswood & Milnbridge ...21E2/42D1
Longton Bridge 20A3/24E3
Longton 15C3/24F1
Longtown 26B1
Longville 15F1
Lonmay 37C4
Looe 1D4
Lords bridge 11C3
Lossiemouth 36C2
Lostock Gralam 15A2/20D2/45C5
Lostock Hall 20A3/24E3
Lostock Junction 20B2/24F2/45C2
Lostwithiel 1D3
Loth 38G4
Loudwater 5A1/10F2
Loughborough Central 16E4
Loughborough Derby Road 16E4
Loughborough Junction 40E5
Loughborough Midland 16E4
Loughor 7B3
Loughton 5A4/11G3
Lount Colliery 16E4
Louth 17A3/22G2
Low Bentham Timber Siding 24B2
Low Gill 27G1
Low Moor 21D2/42B2
Low Row 27C1
Low Street 5B5
Lowdham 16C3
Lower Darwen 20A2/24E2
Lower Edmonton
  (High Level) 5A4/11G3
Lower Edmonton
  (Low Level) 5A4/11G3
Lower Ince 45D2
Lower Pontnewydd 8B3/43A3

Lower Sydenham 40F3
Lowestoft Central 12A1/18G1
Lowestoft Kirkley 12A1/18G1
Lowestoft North 12A1/18F1
Lowthorpe 22C3
Lowton St Mary's 45C3
Lubenham 16G3
Lucker 31E4
Luckett 1C5
Ludborough 22F2
Luddendenfoot 21E1
Luddington 22E5
Ludgershall 4B5
Ludlow 9A1
Luffenham 16F1
Lugar 29F5
Lugton 29D4
Luib Houses 35D2
Lumphanan 37G2
Luncarty 33E5
Lundin Links 34G4
Lustleigh 2C4
Luthrie 34F5
Luton Bute Street 11E1
Luton Hoo for New Mill End 11F1
Luton Midland Road 11E1
Lutterworth 10A4
Luxulyan 1D3
Lydbrook Junction 8A2/9E1
Lydd Town 6E3
Lydd-on-Sea Halt for Dungeness ..6E3
Lydford 1C5
Lydney Junction 8B1/9E2
Lydney Town 8A1/9E2
Lydstep Halt 7D2
Lye 9A3/15G3
Lyghe Halt 5D5
Lyme Regis 3F1
Lymeside 26C1
Lymington Pier 4F4
Lymington Town 4F4
Lymm 15A2/20C2/24G2/45C4
Lympstone 2B3
Lyndhurst Road 4E4
Lynedoch Street 29B3
Lyng Halt 3D1/8F3
Lytham 20A4/24E4
Mablethorpe 17A4
Macbiehill 30D3
Macclesfield Central ...15A3/20D1/45A5
Macclesfield
  Hibel Road 15A3/20D1/45A5
Macduff 37C2
Machen 8B4/43B3
Machynlleth 14B5
Macmerry (Gladsmuir) 30B1
Maddaford Moor Halt 1B5
Madderty 33F4
Madeley (Shrops) 15F2
Madeley (Staffs) 15C3/24F1
Madeley Market 15F2
Maentwrog Road 19F3
Maerdy 8B5/43D2
Maesbrook 14A2/20G4
Maesteg Castle Street 7B5/43E3
Maes-y-Crugiau 13F4
Maesycwmmer 43B3
Magdalen Green 34E4
Magdalen Road 17E4
Maghull 20B4/24F4/45F2
Magor 8C3
Maiden Lane 40B5
Maiden Newton 3F2
Maidenhead 4A1/5/B110G2
Maidens 29G3

Maidstone Barracks 6C5
Maidstone East 6C5
Maidstone Tovil 6C5
Maidstone West 6C5
Maindy North Road Halt 43B4
Malden for Coombe 5B3/39F3
Malden Manor 39G3
Maldon East & Heybridge 12F5
Maldon West 12F5
Mallaig 32A5
Malmesbury 9F3
Malpas 15C1/24E3
Malswick Halt 9D2
Maltby 21G5
Malton 22B5
Malvern Link 9C3
Malvern Well 9C3
Manchester Ancoats 45A3
Manchester Central ..20B1/24F1/45A3
Manchester Cornbrook 45B3
Manchester Dean Lane .20B1/24F1/45A2
Manchester Docks Station 45B3
Manchester Docks 45B3
Manchester Ducie Street 45A3
Manchester Exchange ..20B1/24F1/45A3
Manchester
  London Road 20B1/24F1/45A3
Manchester Oldham Road 45A3
Manchester Oxford Road 45A3
Manchester Victoria ..20B1/24F1/45A3
Manea 10A3/17G3
Mangotsfield 3A3/8C1/9G2
Manley 45E5
Manningford Halt 4B5
Manningham 21D2/42A2
Manningtree 12E4
Manod 19F3
Manor Park 40B2
Manorbier 7D2
Manors 28A1
Mansfield Central 16B4/41D4
Mansfield Town 16B4/41D4
Mansfield Woodhouse 16B4/41D4
Mansion House 40C5
Manton 16F2
Marazion 1F4
March 10A3/17F3
Marchington 15D5
Marchwiel 20E4
Marchwood 4E4
Marden 6D5
Mardock 11F3
Marfleet 22D3
Margam Goods & Coal Depot 43E3
Margate 6B21
Marine Colliery Platform 43B1
Marishes Road 22A5
Market Bosworth 16F5
Market Drayton 15D2/24F2
Market Harborough 16G2
Market Rasen 17A1/22G3
Market Weighton 22D5
Markham Village Halt 43B2
Markinch 35G5
Marks Tey 12E5
Marlborough High Level 4A5
Marlborough Low Level 4A5
Marlesford 12C2
Marlow 10G2f
Marple 21G1
Marsden 21F1
Marsh Brook 14C1
Marsh Gibbon & Poundon 10D3
Marsh Lane & Strand Road 45F3
Marsh Mills 2D5

Marshfield 8C4/43A4
Marske .28E3
Marston Gate 10E2
Marston Lane Siding 14E1
Marston Magna 3D2/8G2
Marston Moor 21C4
Marteg Halt 14D4
Martham for Rollesby 18E1
Martin Mill 6D1
Martock 3D2/8G2
Marton 10A5
Mary Tavy & Blackdown 1C5
Maryfield 34E4
Maryhill Park 29C5/44E4
Marykirk 34C3
Maryland Point 40B2
Maryport Elizabeth Dock 26D3
Maryport 26D3
Masbury Halt 3B2/8E1
Masham 21A3
Massingham 18E5
Mathry Road 13F1
Matlock Bath 16B5/41D1
Matlock 16B5/41D1
Mauchline 29E4
Maud .37D4
Mauds Bridge Siding 22F5
Mauldeth Road for Withington 45A3
Mawcarse Junction 33G5
Maxton 31E1
Maxwell Park 44E3
Maxwelltown 26B4
Maybole 29F3
Mayfield 5E5
Maze Hill for
   National Maritime Museum 40D3
Meadow Hall 42F4
Measham 16E5
Medge Hall 22F5
Medstead & Four Marks 4C2
Meigle 34D5
Melangoose Mill 1D2
Melbourne 16D5
Melcombe Regis 3G3
Meldon 27A5
Meldreth & Melbourn 11D3
Meledor Mill 1D2
Meliden 19C5
Melksham 3A4
Melling 24B2
Mellis .12B4
Mells Road 3B3/8E1
Melmerby 21A3
Melrose 31E1
Meltham 21F2/42D1
Melton Constable 18D4
Melton Crossing Halt 22E4
Melton Mowbray North 16E2
Melton Mowbray Town 16E2
Melton 12D3
Melyncourt Halt 43E2
Menai Bridge 19D2
Menheniot 1D4
Menston 21D2
Menstrie & Glenochil 30A5
Menthorpe Gate 21D5
Meole Brace 15E1
Meols Cop 20A4/24E4/45F1
Meols 20C5/24G5
Meopham 5B5
Merchiston 30G2
Mersey Road & Aigburth 45F3
Merstham 5C3
Merstone 4F3
Merthyr High Street 43C2

Merthyr Vale 8B5/43C2
Merthyr 8A5/43C2
Merton Abbey 39F5
Merton Park 39F4
Methil 30A2/34G4
Methley North 21E4/42B5
Methley South 21E4/42B5
Methven Junction 33E4
Methven 33E4
Mexborough 21F4
Micheldever 4C3
Mickle Trafford East 15B1/24D3
Micklefield 21D4/42A5
Micklehurst 21F1
Mickleover for Radbourne . . .16D5/41G1
Mickleton 27E4
Midcalder 30C3
Middle Drove 17F4
Middle Stoke Halt 6B5
Middlesbrough 28E4
Middleton Junction 20B1/24F1/45A2
Middleton Road 24C3
Middleton Towers 17E5
Middleton 20B1/24F1/45A2
Middleton-in-Teesdale 27E3
Middleton-on-the-Wolds 22C4
Middlewich 15B2/24D2
Middlewood Higher 15A4
Middlewood Lower 15A4
Midford 3B3/8D1
Midge Hall 20A3/24E3
Midgham 4A3
Midhurst 4D1
Midsomer Norton & Welton 3B3/8E1
Midsomer Norton South 3B3/8E1
Midville 17C3
Milborne Port 3D3/8F1
Milcote for Weston-on-Avon &
   Welford-on-Avon 9B5
Mildenhall 11B5
Mile End 40C3
Mileage Yard 39C1
Miles Platting 20B124F1/45A3
Milford & Brocton 15E4
Milford Haven 7D1
Milford .5D1
Milkwall 8A2/9E1
Mill Hill Broadway 5A3
Mill Hill East for Mill Hill Barracks . .5A3
Mill Hill 4F3
Mill Lane Platform 3A4
Millbay 1Dy
Millbrook 10C1/11D1
Millbrook 4E4
Miller's Dale 15A5
Millerhill 30C2
Millfield 28C5
Millhouses & Ecclesall 16A5/41A2
Milliken Park 29C4
Millisle 25D4
Millom 24A5
Millwall Docks 40D3
Milnathort 33G5
Milngavie 29B4/44E5
Milnrow 20B1/45A1
Milnthorpe 24A3
Milton of Campsie 29B5
Milton Range Halt 6B5
Milton 15C3/24E1
Milverton 8F4
Mindrum 31E3
Minehead 8E5
Minera 20E5
Minety & Ashton Keynes 9F4
Minffordd 19F2

Minikie 34D4
Minster 6C2
Minsterley 14B1
Mintlaw 37D4
Mirfield 21E2/42C2
Mislingford 4E3
Misson Siding 21G5
Misterton 22G5
Mistley 12E4
Mitcham Junction 5B3/39G5
Mitcham 5B3/39G5
Mitcheldean 9D2
Mitchell & Newlyn Halt 1D1
Mithian Halt 1D1
Mitre Bridge 39C4
Moat Lane Junction 14C3
Mobberley 15A3/20C1/45B4
Moffat .30F3
Moira .16E5
Mold .20D5
Mollington 15B1/24D4
Mollington 20D4
Monckton Main Colliery 42D4
Monifieth 34E4
Monk Bretton 21F3/42E4
Monk Fryston 21D4
Monks Risborough &
   Whiteleaf Halt 10E2
Monkseaton 28D5
Monkton & Came Halt 3F3
Monkton 29E3
Monkwearmouth 28C5
Monmore Green 15F3
Monmouth May Hill 8A2/9E1
Monmouth Troy 8A2/9E1
Monsal Dale 15A5
Montacute 3D2/8G2
Montgomery 14B2
Montgreenan 29D3
Monton Green 45B3
Montpelier 3F1
Montrave 34G4
Montrose East 34C2
Montrose 34C2
Monument Lane 13C3
Monument 40C4
Monymusk 37F2
Moor Row 26F3
Moorgate 40C4
Moorhampton 14E1
Moorhouse & South Kirkby . .421F4/2D5
Moorside & Wardley 45B2
Moorswater 1D4
Moorthorpe & South Kirkby .21F4/42D5
Moortown for Caistor 22F3
Morar .32B5
Morchard Road 2A4
Morcott 16F1
Morden Road Halt 39F5
Morden South 39G4
Morebath Junction Halt 7F5
Morebath 8F5
Morecambe Euston Road 24B3
Morecambe Promenade 24B3
Moresby Parks 26E3
Moreton 20C5/24G4
Moreton 3F3
Moretonhampstead 2B4
Moreton-in-Marsh 9D5
Moreton-on-Lugg 9C1
Morley Low 21E3/42B3
Morley Top 21E3/42B3
Mormond 37C4
Morningside 30C5
Morpeth 27A5

Morris Cowley 10E4
Morriston Halt 7B4/43G2
Mortehoe & Woolacombe 7E3
Mortimer 4A2
Mortlake for East Sheen 5B2/39E3
Morton Road 17E1
Moseley 9A4
Moses Gate 45B2
Moss Bank 20B3/24F3/45D3
Moss Side 24D4
Moss .20E4
Mossend 30C5/44B3
Mossley Hill for
    Aigburth 20C4/24G4/45F4
Mossley 21F1
Mosspark West 44F3
Mosstowie 36C2
Moston 20B1/24F1/45A2
Mostyn 20C5
Motherwell Central 30C5/44B2
Motspur Park 39G4
Mottingham 40E2
Mottisfont 4D4
Mouldsworth 15B1/24D3/45D5
Moulton 17E3
Moulton 27F5
Mount Florida 44E3
Mount Hawkee Halt 1E1
Mount Melville 34F4
Mount Vernon North 44C3
Mount Vernon South 44C3
Mount Vernon 29C5
Mountain Ash Cardiff Road 43C2
Mountain Ash Oxford Street 43C2
Mountain Ash 8B5/43C2
Mountfield Halt 6E5
Mow Cop & Scholar Green . .15B3/24E1
Moy .36E4
Much Wenlock 15F2
Muchalls 34A1
Muir of Ord 35D5
Muirend 29C5/44E2
Muirkirk 29E5
Mulben 36D1
Mumbles Pier 7B3/43G3
Mumbles Road 7B3/43G3
Mumby Road 17A4
Muncaster Mill 26G3
Mundesley-on-Sea 18D2
Munlochy 36D5
Murrayfield 30G2
Murrow East 17F3
Murthly 33E5
Murton Lane 21C5
Murton 28C5
Musselburgh 30B2
Muswell Hill 5A3/40A5
Muthill 33F4
Mytholmroyd 21E1
Naburn 21C5
Nafferton 22C3
Nailsea & Backwell 3A2/8D2
Nailsworth 9F3
Nairn 36D4
Nancegollan 1F5
Nannerch 20D5
Nanstallon Halt 1D3
Nantclwyd 19E5
Nantgaredig 13G4
Nantgarw Colliery 43C4
Nantlle 19E2
Nantmawr 20G5
Nantwich 15C2/24E2
Nantybwch 8A4/43C1
Nantyderry 8A3/43A2

Nantyffyllon 7B5/43E3
Nantyglo 8A4/43B1
Nantymoel 7B5/43D3
Nantyronen 14C5
Napsbury 11G1
Napton & Stockton 10B4
Narberth 7C3
Narborough & Pentney 17E5
Narborough 16F4
Nassington 10A1/16F1/17F1
Navenby 16B1/17C1
Navigation Road 45B4
Nawton 21A5
Neasden 5A2/39B4
Neath Abbey 7B4/43F2
Neath General 7B4/43F2
Neath Riverside 43F2
Needham 12C4
Neen Sollars 9A2
Neepsend 21G3/42G4
Neilston High 29C4/44G2
Neilston Low 29C4/44G2
Nelson & Llancaiach 8B5/43C2
Nelson 24D1/21B1
Neptune Street 22A2
Nertherton 13B1/15G4
Nerwhaven 30F2
Nesscliff & Pentre 14A1
Neston North 20D4/45F5
Neston South 20D4/45F5
Netherburn 30D5
Nethercleugh 26A3
Netheredge Halt 8B2/9F1
Netherfield & Colwick 16C3/41F4
Netherton 21E2/42D1
Netherton 29C4/44F2
Netherton 30A3
Nethertown 26F3
Nethy Bridge 36F3
Netley .4E3
New Barnet 5A3/11G2
New Basford 41F4
New Beckenham 40F3
New Biggin 27E1
New Bolingbroke 17C3
New Brighton 20C4/24G4/45F3
New Clee 22F2
New Cross Gate 40D3
New Cross 40D3
New Cumnock 29F5
New Dale Halt 15E2
New Eltham 5B4/40E1
New Galloway 26B5
New Hey 21F1
New Holland Pier 22E3
New Holland 22E3
New Hythe 6C5
New Lane 20A4/24E3/45E1
New Longton & Hutton 20A3/24E3
New Luce 25C3
New Machar 37F4
New Mills Central 15A4
New Milton for Milford-on-Sea 4F5
New Passage Halt 8C2/9G1
New Romney & Littlestone-on-Sea . . .6E3
New Romney (RHDR) 6E3
New Southgate & Friern Barnet 40A5
New Tredegar 8A4/43B2
New Wandsworth 39E5
Newark Castle 16C2
Newark Northgate 16C2
Newbiggin-by-the Sea 28A5
Newbridge 43B2
Newbridge-on-Wye 14E3
Newburgh 34F5

Newburn 27B5/28A3
Newbury 4A3
Newbury Park 40A1
Newbury Racecourse 4A3
Newbury Westfields Halt 4A3
Newby Wiske 21A3/28G5
Newcastle Central 27B5/28A1
Newcastle Emlyn 13F3
Newcastle under Lyme 15C3/24F1
Newcastleton 27A1
Newchapel & Golden Hill . . .15C3/24E1
Newchurch 4F3
Newchurch Halt 45C3
Newent 9D2
Newhaven Harbour 5G4
Newhaven Town 5F4
Newhouse 30C5/44A3
Newick & Chailey 5E4
Newington 30G2
Newington 6B4
Newland Halt 9B3
Newlay & Horsforth 21D3/42A3
Newmains 30C5
Newmarket 11C4
Newmilns 29E4
Newnham Bridge 9A2
Newnham 8A1/9E2
Newpark 30C3
Newport (Essex) 11E4
Newport (Shrops) 15E2
Newport (Yorks) 28E4
Newport Alexandra Dock 8C3/43A4
Newport Dock Street 43A3
Newport High StreeT 8B3/43A3
Newport on Tay East 34E4
Newport on Tay West 34E4
Newport Pagnell 10C2
Newport 4F3
Newquay 1D1
Newseat Halt 37D5
Newsham 28A5
Newsholme 24C1
Newstead East 16C4/41E4
Newstead 16C4/41E4
Newthorpe, Greasthorpe &
    Shipley Gate 41F3
Newton Abbot 2C3
Newton for Hydge 21G1
Newton Heath 20B1/24F1/45A2
Newton Kyme 21C4
Newton Poppleford 2B2
Newton St Cyres 2B3
Newton Stewart 25B4
Newton Tony 4C5
Newton 29C5/44C3
Newtongrange 30C2
Newtonhill 34A1
Newton-le-Willows . . .20C2/24G2/45D3
Newtonmore 33A2
Newton-on-Ayr 29F3
Newtown Halt 18E1
Newtown 14C3
Newtyle 34D5
Neyland 7D2
Nidd Bridge 21C3
Niddrie 30B2
Nigg .36C4
Nine Elms 40D5
Nine Mile Point 8B4/43B3
Nisbet 31E2
Nitshill 44F3
Nocton & Dunston 16B1/17B1
Noel Park & Wood Green 40A5
Norbiton for Kingston Hill . . .5B2/39F3
Norbury for Ellastone 15C5

Norbury 40F5
Norham 31D3
Normacot 15C4
Normanby Park 22E4
Normans Bay Halt 5F5
Normanton 21E3/42C4
North Acton 39C3
North Berwick 31B1
North Blyth 28A5
North Camp 4B1/5C1
North Cave 22D4
North Connel Halt 32E4
North Dock (Sunderland) 28C5
North Drive 17E2
North Dulwich 40E4
North Ealing 39C3
North Eastrington Halt 22D5
North Elmham 18E4
North Filton Platform . . .8C2/9G1
North Grimston 22B5
North Harrow 5A2/39A1
North Hayling 4E2
North Howden 22D5
North Kelsey 22F3
North Middleton 27A4
North Queensferry 30B3
North Rode 15B3/24D1
North Seaton 27A5
North Sheen 39E3
North Shields 28D5
North Skelton 28E3
North Tawton 2B5
North Thoresby 22F2
North Walsham Main 18D2
North Walsham Town 18D2
North Weald 11G3
North Wembley 39B2
North Woolwich 5B4/40D1
North Wootton 17E5
North Wylam 27B5
Northallerton Town 28G5
Northallerton 21A3/28G5
Northam 4E4
Northampton Bridge Street 10B2
Northampton Castle 10B2
Northenden 45A4
Northfield 9A4
Northfields 39D2
Northfleet 5B5
Northiam for Beckley & Sandhurst . .6E5
Northolt Park for Northolt Village . .39B2
Northolt 39B1
Northorpe 22G4
Northorpe North Road 42C2
Northumberland Park 40A4
Northwich 15A2/20D2/45C5
Northwick Park 39A2
Northwood Halt 9A3
Northwood Hills 5A2
Norton Bridge 15D3/24G1
Norton Bridge for Eccleshall .15D3/24G1
Norton Fitzwarren 8F4
Norton Junction 9C3
Norton on Tees 28E5
Norton 21E5
Norton-in-Hales 15C2/24C2
Norwich City 18F3
Norwich Thorpe 18F3
Norwich Victoria 18F3
Norwood Junction &
    South Norwood 40G4
Nostell 21E4/42C5
Notgrove 9D4
Nottage Halt 7C5/43E4
Notting Hill Gate 39C4

Nottingham Arkwright Street 16D4/41G4
Nottingham London Road 41G5
Nottingham Manvers Street 41F5
Nottingham Midland 16D3/41G4
Nottingham Racecourse 41F5
Nottingham Victoria 16C4/41F4
Notton & Royston 21E3/42D4
Nuneaton Abbey Street 16F5
Nuneaton Trent Valley 16F5
Nunhead Coal Depot 40E4
Nunhead 40D4
Nunnington 21A5
Nunthorpe 28F4
Nursling 4D4
Nutbourne Halt 4E1
Nutfield 5D3
Oakamoor 15C4
Oakengates 15E2
Oakengates Market Street 15E2
Oakenshaw 21E3/42C4
Oakham 16E2
Oakington 11C3
Oakleigh Park for East Barnet .5A3/11G2
Oakley Street 8A1/9E2
Oakley 10B1/11C1
Oakley 30A4
Oakley 4B3
Oaksey Halt 9F4
Oakworth 21D1
Oban 32F4
Ochiltree 29F4
Ockendon 5A5
Ockley & Capel 5D2
Offord & Buckden 11C2
Ogbourne 5A5
Ogilvie Village Halt 43C2
Ogmore Vale 7B5/43D3
Okehampton 2B5
Old Colwyn 19D4
Old Ford 40C3
Old Hill 13C1/15G4
Old Kilpatrick 44G5
Old Leake 17C3
Old North Road 11C2
Old Roan 20B4/24F4/45F3
Old Trafford 45B3
Old Woods Halt 14A1/15E1/20G3
Oldbury & Bromford Lane 13B2
Oldbury & Langley Green 13C2
Oldbury 13B2/15G4
Oldfield Park 3A3/8D1
Oldham Central 21D1/45A2
Oldham Clegg Street 21D1
Oldham Glodwick Road 21D1
Oldham Mumps 21D1
Oldham Werneth 21F1/45A2
Oldham 21F1
Oldland Common 3A3
Oldmarch Halt 13E5
Oldmeldrum 37E3
Ollerton 16B3
Olney 10B2
Olton 9A5/15G5
Ongar 11G4
Onibury 9A1/14C1
Onllwyn 7A5/43E1
Ordens Halt 37C2
Ordsall Lane for Salford 45B3
Oreston 1D5
Ormesby 28E4
Ormiston 30C1
Ormskirk 20B4/24F3/45E2
Orpington 5B4/40G1
Orrell Park 45F3
Orrell 20B3/24F3/45D2

Orton Waterville 10A1/17F1
Orton 36D1
Orwell 12D3
Osbaldwick 21C5
Osmondthorpe Halt 42A2
Ossett 21E3/42C3
Osterley 5B2/39D2
Oswestry 20G5
Otford 5C5
Otley 21D2
Otterby Halt 22F2
Otterham 1B3
Otterington 21A3/28G5
Otterspool 45F3
Ottery St Mary 2B2
Ottringham 22E2
Oughty Bridge 21G3/42F3
Oulton Broad North 12A1/18G1
Oulton Broad South 12A1/18G1
Oundle 10A1/16G1/17G1
Outwell Basin 17F4
Outwell Village 17F4
Ovenden 21E2/42B1
Over & Wharton 15B2/24D2
Overton 29B3
Overton 4B3
Overton-on-Dee 20F4
Overtown Siding 30D5
Oxenholme 24A3/27G1
Oxenhope 21D1
Oxford General 10E4
Oxford Rewley Road 10E4
Oxhey 24D3
Oxshott for Fairmile 5C2
Oxted & Limpsfield 5C4
Oxton 30C1
Oyne 37E2
Oystermouth 43G3
Padbury 10D3
Paddock Wood 5D5
Padeswood & Buckley 20E4
Padgate 20C2/24G2/45C4
Padiham 24D1
Padstow 1C2
Paignton 2D3
Paisley Canal 44G3
Paisley East 44F3
Paisley Gilmour Street 44G3
Paisley King Street Depot 44G3
Paisley St James 44G3
Paisley West 44G3
Paisley 29C4
Palace Gates (Wood Green) . . .5A3/40A5
Pallion 28C5
Palmers Green & Southgate 5A3
Palnure 25C4
Pampisford 11D4
Pandy 14G1
Pangbourne 4A2/10G3
Pannal 21C3
Pans Lane Halt 3B5
Pant Glas 19E1
Pant 14A2/20G4
Pant 8A5/43C1
Panteg & Griffiths Town . . .8B3/43A2
Pantydwr 14D4
Pantyffordd 43E1
Pantyffynnon 7A3/43G1
Pantysgallog Halt 43C1
Pantywaun Halt 43C1
Par 1D3
Parbold for Newburgh . .20B3/24F3/45E2
Parham 12C2
Park Bridge 21F1
Park Drain 22F5

Park Hall Halt 20F4
Park Parade 21A2
Park Street & Frogmore 11G1
Park (Aberdeenshire) 34A2/37G3
Park (Furness) 24B5
Park (Manchester) 45A3
Parkend 8A1/9E2
Parkeston Quay 12E3
Parkgate & Rawmarsh 21G4/32F5
Parkgate 20D4/45F5
Parkhead Stadium 44D4
Parkhill 37F4
Parkhouse Halt 26C1
Parkstone .3F5
Parsley Hay 15B5
Parson Street 3G1
Parsons Green 39D4
Partick Central 29C4/44E4
Partick Hill 29C4/44E4
Partick West 29C4/44E4
Partington 20C2/24G1/45C3
Parton (Kirkud) 26B5
Parton 26E3
Partridge Green 5E2
Paston & Knapton 18D2
Patchway 8C1/9G1
Pateley Bridge 21B2
Patna 29F4
Patney & Chirton 3B5
Patricroft 20B2/24F1/45B3
Patrington 22E2
Patterton 29C4/44F2
Paulsgrove Halt 4E2
Peacock Cross 44B2
Peak Forest for Peak Dale 15A5
Peakirk 17F2
Peartree & Normanton 16D5/41G2
Peasley Cross 45D3
Pebworth Halt 9C5
Peckham Rye 40D4
Peebles East 30D2
Peebles West 30D2
Peel Road Halt 23B2
Peel 23B2
Pegswood 27A5
Pelaw Junction 28C5
Pellon 21E2/42B1
Pelton 27C5
Pemberton 20B3/24F3/45D2
Pembrey & Burry Port 7B2
Pembridge 14E1
Pembroke Dock 7D2
Pembroke Town 7D2
Penallt Halt 8A2/9E1
Penally 7D3
Penarth Dock 8D4/43B5
Penarth Town 8D4/43B5
Pencader .13F4
Pencaitland 30C1
Pencarreg Halt 13E5
Penclawdd 7B3
Pencoed 8C5/43D4
Penda's Way 42A2
Pendlebury 45B2
Pendleton (Broad Street) 45B3
Pendre 13B5
Pengam 8B4/43B2
Penge East 40F4
Penge West 40F4
Penhelig Halt 13B5
Penicuik .30C2
Penistone 21F3/42E3
Penmaenmawr 19D3
Penmaenpool 14A5
Penmere Platform 1F1

Penns for Warmley 15F5
Penpergwm 8A3/43A1
Penpont Halt 14F4
Penrheol 8B4/43B3
Penrhiwceiber 8B5/43C2
Penrhiwfelin 43B3
Penrhyndeudraeth 19F2
Penrith for Ullswater Lake 27E1
Penruddock 26E1
Penryn 1F1
Pensford 3A2/8D1
Penshaw .28C5
Penshurst .5D4
Pensycynor Halt 43F2
Pentebach 8B5/43C2
Pentir Rhiw 8A5/14G3/43C1
Penton 26B1
Pentre Halt 43D2
Pentwynmawr Halt 43B2
Penwortham (Cop Lane) 20A3/24E3
Penybont .14D3
Penychain for
    Pwllheli Holiday Camp 19F1
Penyffordd for Leeswood 20E4
Penygraig 8B5/43D3
Penygroes 19E1
Penzance .1F4
Peplow 24G2
Percy Main 28D5
Perivale .39C2
Perranporth Beach Platform 1D1
Perranporth 1D1
Perranwell 1E1
Perry Barr 13B3/15G4
Pershore .9C4
Perth 33F5
Pesall 15F4
Peswet 4B5
Peterborough East 10A2/17F2
Peterborough North 10A2/17F2
Peterhead 37D5
Petersfield 4D2
Peterston 8C5/43D4
Petrockstow 1A5
Petts Wood 40G1
Petworth .5E1
Pevensey & Westham 5F5
Pevensey Bay Halt 5F5
Philorth Bridge Halt 37C4
Philorth Halt 37C4
Philpstoun 30B3
Pickburn & Brodsworth 21F4
Pickering .22A5
Pickhill Halt 20F4
Pickhill 21A3
Picton 28F5
Piddington 10B2
Piercebridge 27E5
Piershill 30F1
Pill 3A2/8C2/9G1
Pilling 24C3
Pilmoor 21B4
Pilning 8C2/9G1
Pilot Halt .6E3
Pilsley 16B4/41D3
Pinchbeck 17E2
Pinewood Halt 4A3
Pinhoe 2B3
Pinkhill 30G3
Pinmore .25A3
Pinner 5A2/39A1
Pinwherry 25A3
Pinxton North 16C4/41E3
Pinxton South 16C4/41E3
Pipe Gate 15C2/24F2

Pitcaple 37E3
Pitlochry .33C3
Pitmedden 37F4
Pitsea 6A5
Pitsford & Brampton 10B3
Pittenweem 34G3
Pittington 28D5
Pittshill 15C3/24E1
Plains 30C5/44A4
Plaistow & West Ham 40C2
Plaistow .40C2
Plank Lane 45C3
Plashetts .27A2
Plas-y-Court Halt 14A1
Platt Bridge 45D2
Plawsworth 27C5
Plealey Road 14B1
Plean for Cowie 30A5
Pleasington 20A2/24E2
Pleasley East 16B4/41D4
Pleasley West 16B4/41D4
Plessey 27B5
Plocton 35E1
Plodder Lane for
    Farnworth 20B2/24F2/45B2
Pluckley 6D4
Plumley 15A2/20D2/45B5
Plumpton 27D1
Plumpton .5F3
Plumstead 40D1
Plumtree .16D3
Plym Bridge Platform 2D5
Plymouth Friary 1D5
Plymouth North Road 1D5
Plympton .2D5
Plymstock 1D5
Pochin Pits 43B2
Pocklington 22C5
Point Pleasant 28B5
Pokesdown for
    Eastern Bournemouth 4F5
Polegate 5F5
Polesworth 16F5
Pollington 21E5
Pollokshaws East 44E3
Pollokshaws West 44E3
Polsloe Bridge Halt 2B3
Polton 30C2
Pomathorn 30C2
Ponders End 5A3/11G3
Ponfeigh .30E4
Pont Llanio 13E5
Pont Lliw 7B3/43G2
Pont Yates 7A3
Pontardawe 7A4/43F2
Pontardulais 7A3
Pontdolgoch 14D3
Pontefract Baghill 21E4/42C5
Pontefract Monkhill 21E4/42C5
Pontefract Tanshelf 21E4/42C5
Ponteland 27B5
Pontesbury 124B1
Ponthenry 7A3
Ponthir 8B3/43A3
Pontllanfraith High Level 8B4/43B3
Pontlottyn 43C2
Pontnewydd 43A2
Pontrhydyrun Halt 43A3
Pontrhythallt 19D2
Pontrilas .14G1
Pontsarn for Vaynor 8A5/43C1
Pontsticill 8A5/43C1
Pontwalby Halt 43D2
Pontyberem 7A3
Pontycymmer 7B5/43D3

Pont-y-Pant 19E3
Pontypool Clarence Street 43A2
Pontypool Crane Street 8B4/43A2
Pontypool Road 8B3/43A2
Pontypool 8B3/43A2
Pontypridd 8B5/43C3
Pontyrhyll 7B5/43D3
Pool Quay 14A2
Poole 3F5
Pool-in-Wharfedale 21C3
Poppleton 21C4
Port Clarence 28E4
Port Dinorwic 19D2
Port Dundas 44E4
Port Eglinton Depot 44F1
Port Elphinstone 37F3
Port Erin 23C1
Port Glasgow 29B3
Port Gordon 37C1
Port Isaac Road 1C3
Port of Menteith 29A5
Port Soderick 23C2
Port St Mary 23C1
Port Sunlight 45F4
Port Talbot Central 43F3
Port Talbot Dock 7B4/43F3
Port Talbot General 7B4/43F3
Portbury 3A2/8C2/9G1
Portchester 4E3
Porth 8B5/43C3
Porthcawl 7C5/43E4
Porthlethen 34A1/37G4
Porthywaen 14A2/20G5
Portishead 3A2/8C2/9G1
Portknockie 37C1
Portland 3G3
Portmadoc 19F2
Portobello 30G1
Porton .4C5
Portskewett 8B2/9F1
Portslade & West Hove 5F3
Portsmouth & Southsea 4E2
Portsmouth Arms 7G3
Portsmouth Harbour 4E2
Portsmouth 20A1/24E1
Portsoy 37C2
Possil Park 44E4
Possil .44E4
Postland for Crowland 17E2
Potter Heigham Bridge Halt 18E2
Potter Heigham 18E2
Potterhanworth 16B1/17B1
Potterhill 29C4/44G3
Potters Bar & South Mimms 11G2
Potto .28F4
Potton 11D2
Powerstock 3F2
Poyle Estate Halt 5B1
Poyle Halt for Stanwell Moor 5B1
Poynton 15A3/20C1/45A4
Praed Street 39C5
Praze 1E5
Prees 15D1/24F3
Prescot 20C3/24G3/45E3
Prestatyn 19C5
Prestbury 15A3/20D1/45A5
Presteign 14E2
Presthope 15F1
Preston Brook 15A1/20C3/45D5
Preston Junction 20A3/24E3
Preston Park 5F3
Preston Road 20C4/24G4/45F3
Preston Road 39A3
Preston 24D3
Prestonpans 30B1

Prestwich 20B1/24F1/45B2
Preswick 29E3
Priestfield 13A1
Princes Dock 44E4
Princes End & Coseley 13B1/15F4
Princes Risborough 10F2
Princes Street (Perth) 33F5
Princetown 2C5
Priory Halt 12E3
Prittlewell 6A4
Privett .4D2
Probus & Ladock Platform 1E2
Prudhoe 27C4
Pudsey Greenside 21D2/42A2
Pudsey Lowtown 21D2/42A2
Pulborough 5E1
Pulford Siding 20E4
Pulham Market 12A3/18G3
Pulham St Mary 12A3/18G3
Puncheston 13F1
Purfleet 5B5
Purley .5C3
Purley Oaks 5C3
Purton .9F4
Putney Bridge 39E4
Putney 5B3/39E4
Puxton & Worle 3A1/8D3
Pwllheli 19F1
Pye Bridge 16C4/41E3
Pye Hill & Somercoates for
  Pye Bridge 16C4/41E3
Pyle 7C5/43E4
Pylle 3C3/8E1
Quainton Road 10E2
Quakers Drove 10A3/17G3
Quakers Yard High Level 8B5/43C2
Quakers Yard Low Level 8B5/43C2
Queenborough 6B4
Queen's Park 39B5
Queens Park 44E3
Queens Road Peckham 40D4
Queens Road, Battersea 39D5
Queensbury 21D2/42B1
Queensferry 20D4
Quintrel Downs Platform 1D1
Quorn & Woodhouse 16E4
Quy 11C4
Racks .26B3
Radcliffe Black Lane . . .20B1/24F1/45B2
Radcliffe Bridge 20B1/24F1/45B2
Radcliffe Central 45B2
Radcliffe-on-Trent 16D3
Radipole Halt 3G3
Radley 10F4
Radstock North 3B3/8E1
Radstock West 3B3/8E1
Radway Green & Bartholmey .15C3/24E1
Radyr 8C4/43C4
Raglan Road Crossing Halt 8A3
Raglan .8A3
Rainford Junction 20A3/24F3/45E2
Rainford Village 20B3/24F3/45E2
Rainham 6B5
Rainhill 20C324G4/45E4
Ramsbottom 20A1/24E1/45B1
Ramsden Dock 24B5
Ramsey East 11B2
Ramsey North 10A2/17G2
Ramsey 23A3/25G4
Ramsgate 6B2
Rankinston 29F4
Rannoch 32D1/33C1
Ranskill 16A3
Raskelf 21B4
Ratby .16F4

Rathen 37C4
Ratho .30B3
Rauceby 16C1/17C1
Raunds 10A1/11B1
Ravelrig 30C3
Raven Square 14B2
Ravenglass 26G3
Ravensbourne 40F3
Ravenscar 28F1
Ravenscourt Park 39D4
Ravensthorpe & Thornhill 42C3
Ravenstonedale 27F2
Rawcliffe 21E5
Rawtenstall 20A1/24E1
Rawyards 44A4
Raydon Wood 12D4
Rayleigh 6A5
Rayne .11E5
Rayners Lane 39B1
Raynes Park 5B3/39F4
Raynham Park 18D5
Reading Central 4A2
Reading General 4A2
Reading South 4A2
Reading West 4A2
Rectory Road 40B4
Red Rock 20B3/24F2/45D2
Redbourn 11F1
Redbrook 8A2/9E1
Redcar Central 28E3
Redcar East 28E3
Redcastle 36D5
Redding 30B4
Reddish North 45A3
Reddish South 45A3
Redditch 9B4
Redheugh 28A1
Redhill .5C3
Redland 3F1
Redmarshall 28E5
Redmile 16D2
Redmire 21A1/27G4
Rednal & West Felton 20G4
Redruth 1E5
Reedham (Surrey) 5C3
Reedham (Norfolk) 18F2
Reedley Hollow Halt 24D1
Reednesss Junction 22E5
Reedsmouth 27A3
Reepham (Lincs) 16A1/17B1
Reepham (Norfolk) 18E4
Reigate .5C3
Renfrew Ferry 44F4
Renfrew Fulbar Street 44F4
Renfrew Potterfield 44F4
Renfrew South 29C4/44F4
Renishaw Central 41B3
Renton 29B3
Repton & Willington 16D5
Resalrig Siding 30F1
Resolven 7B5/43E2
Reston for Coldingham & St Abbs . .31C3
Retford 16A3
Rhayader 14D4
Rhewl .19E5
Rhigos Halt 43D1
Rhiwderyn 8C4/43A3
Rhiwfron 14C5
Rhoose 8D5/43C5
Rhos 20F4
Rhosgoch 19C1/23G1
Rhosneigr 19B2/19D1
Rhostyllen 20E4
Rhosymedre Halt 20F4
Rhu 29B3

Rhuddlan 19D5
Rhydowen 13F3
Rhydryonen 13B5
Rhydymwyn 20D5
Rhyl 19C5
Rhymney Bridge 8A5/43C1
Rhymney 8A5/43C1
Ribblehead 24A1
Riccarton & Craigie 29E4
Riccarton Junction 31G1
Richmond 27F5
Richmond 5B2/39E3
Rickmansworth
   Church Street 5A1/10F1/11G1
Rickmansworth
   High Street 5A1/10F1/11G1
Riddings Junction 26B1
Riddlesdown 5C3
Ridgmont 10C1
Rifing Mill 27C4
Rifle Range Halt 45F5
Rigg 26B2
Rillington 22B5
Rimington 24C1
Ringley Road 24F1/45B2
Ringstead & Addington 10A1
Ringwood .4E5
Ripley Valley 21C3
Ripley 16C5/41E2
Ripon 21B3
Rippingale 17D1
Ripple 9C3
Ripponden & Barkisland 21E1
Risca 8B4/43A3
Rishton 24D2
Roade 10B2
Roath Coal & Mileage Depot 43B4
Roath 8C4/43B4
Robertsbridge 6E5
Robin Hood 21E3/42B4
Robin Hoods Bay 28F1
Roby 20C4/24G3/45E4
Rocester .15D5
Rochdale 20B1/45A1
Roche 1D2
Rochester .6B5
Rochford 6A4
Rock Ferry 20C4/24G4/45F4
Rockingham Colliery 21F3
Rockingham 16F2
Roding Valley 5A4
Rodmarton Platform 9F3
Rodwell 3G3
Rogart 36A5
Rogate 4D1
Rogerstone 8B4/43B3
Rolleston Junction 16C2
Rolvenden 6E4
Romaldkirk 27E4
Roman Bridge Halt 19E3
Romford (Essex) 5A4
Romiley .21G1
Romney Sands (RHDR) 6E3
Romset 4D4
Rookery Bridge 15B2/24E2
Roose 24B5
Ropley 4C2
Rose Grove 24D1
Rose Hill Marple 21G1
Rose Lane 30F2
Rosemill .34E5
Rosemount 33D5
Rosewell & Hawthornden 30C2
Roskear Siding 1E5
Roslin 30C2

Rossett 20E4
Rossington 21F5
Rosslyn Castle 30C2
Rosslynlee 30C2
Ross-on-Wye 9D1
Rosyth Halt 30B3
Rothbury .31G4
Rotherfield & Mark Cross 5E5
Rotherham Central 21G4/42F5
Rotherham Holmes 21G4/42F5
Rotherham Masborough 21G4/42F5
Rotherhithe 40D4
Rothes 36D1
Rothienorman 37E3
Rothiemay 37D1
Rothley 16E4
Rothwell 21D3/42B4
Round Oak 15G3
Rowfant 5D3
Rowlands Castle 4E2
Rowlands Gill 27C5
Rowley Regis & Blackheath . .13C2/15G4
Rowrah 26E3
Rowsley 16B5/41C1
Roxburgh 31E2
Roy Bridge 32B2
Royal Oak 39C1/39C5
Roydon 11F3
Royds Green Lower 42B4
Royston & Notton 21F3/42D4
Royston 11D3
Royton Junction 21F1
Royton 21F1
Ruabon 20F4
Rubery 9A4
Ruddington 16D4/41G4
Rudgwick .5E2
Rudyard Lake 15B4
Rufford 20A3/24E3/45E1
Rugby Central 10A4
Rugby Midland 10A4
Rugeley Town 15E4
Rugeley Trent Valley 15E4
Ruislip 5A2
Rumbling Bridge 30A4/33G4
Rumworth & Daubhill 45C2
Runcorn Docks 15A1/20C3/45E4
Runcorn 15A1/24C3/45E4
Rushcliffe Platform 16D4
Rushden .10B1
Rushey Platt 9G5
Rushton .15B4
Rushwick Halt 9B3
Ruskington 17C1
Ruspidge 8A1/9E2
Ruswarp .28F2
Rutherford 31E1
Rutherglen 29C5/44D3
Ruthin 19E5/20E5
Ruthwell .26B3
Ryde Esplanade 4F3
Ryde Pier Head 4F3
Ryde St John's Road 4F3
Rye Harbour 6E4
Rye Hill & Burstwick 22E2
Rye House 11F3
Rye 6E4
Ryeford 9E3
Ryhall & Belmisthorpe 16E1/17F1
Ryhope East 28C5
Ryhope 28C5
Rylstone .21C1
Ryston 10A4/17F4
Ryton 27B5
Saddleworth 21F1

Saffron Walden 11D4
St Agnes 1E1
St Albans Abbey 11F1
St Albans City 11F1
St Andrews Docks (Hull) 22A2
St Andrews Road 8C2/9G1
St Andrews 34F4
St Anne's Park 3A3/8C1
St Annes-on-the-Sea 24D4
St Asaph .19D5
St Athan 8D5/43D5
St Bees 26F4
St Blazey 1D3
St Boswells 31E1
St Botolphs 12E4
St Briavels 8A2/9E1
St Budeaux Ferry Road 1D5
St Budeaux Victoria Road 1D5
St Clears 7A1/13G3
St Columb Road 1D2
St Combs 37C5
St Cyrus .34C2
St Denys 4D4
St Devereux 14F1
St Erth 1F4
St Fagans 8C4/43B4
St Fort 34E4
St Germains Halt 23B2
St Germans 1D5
St Harmons Halt 14D4
St Helens Central 20C3/24G3/45D3
St Helens Junction 20C3/24G3/45D3
St Helens Shaw Street .20C3/24G3/45D3
St Helier .39G4
St Ives (Cambs) 11B2
St Ives (Cornwall) 1E4
St James Deeping 17F2
St James Park Halt 22B3
St James Street (Walthamstow) . . .40A3
St James' Park 40D5
St John's .23B2
St Johns Chapel 27D3
St Johns Wood 39C5
St Kew Highway 1C2
St Keynes Halt 1D4
St Leonards Warrior Square 6F5
St Leonards West Marina 6F5
St Margarets for Stansted Abbotts . .11F3
St Margarets 39B2
St Marmocks 29E4
St Mary Cray 5B4/40G1
St Mary's Bay 6C3
St Mary's Crossing Halt 9F3
St Mary's 10A2/17G2
St Michaels 20C4/24G4/45F4
St Monance 34G3
St Neots .11C2
St Olaves .18F1
St Pancras (Goods) 40B5
St Peters .28A1
St Rollox 29C5/44D4
Sale 20C1/24G145B3
Salford Priors 9B4
Salford 20B1/24F1/45A3
Salhouse .18E2
Salisbury Fisherton 4C5
Salisbury Milford 4D5
Salisbury .4C5
Saltaire 21D2/42A1
Saltash 1D5
Saltburn .28E3
Saltcoats Central 29D3
Saltcoats North 29D3
Saltfleetby 17A3/22G1
Saltford 3A3/8D1

Saltley 13B4/15G5
Saltmarshe 22E5
Saltney Ferry 20D4
Saltney 20D4
Saltoun 30C1
Salwick 24D3
Salzcraggie Halt 38F4
Sampford Courtenay 2B5
Sampford Peverell 2A2/8G5
Sandal 21E3/42C4
Sandbach Ettiley Heath 15B2/24E2
Sandbach 15B2/24E2
Sanderstead 5C3
Sanderton 10F2
Sandford & Banwell 3B1/8D3
Sandhills 45G4
Sandholme 22D5
Sandilands 30E4
Sandling for Hythe 6D3
Sandon 15D4
Sandown 4F3
Sandplace Halt 1D4
Sandsend 28F2
Sandside 24A3
Sandtoft 22F5
Sandwich 6C2
Sandy 11D2
Sandyford Halt 44G4
Sanquhar 30F5
Santon 23C2
Sarnau 7A2/13G3
Sarsden Halt 10D5
Saughton 30B3
Saughtree 27A1/31G1
Saundersfoot 7D3
Savernake High Level 4A5
Savernake Low Level 4A5
Sawbridgeworth 11F3
Sawley Junction for Long Eaton . .16D4
Sawley 16D4
Saxham & Risby 11C5
Saxilby 16A1
Saxmundham 12C2
Scafell Halt 14C3
Scalby 22A4/28G1
Scalford 16E2
Scarborough Central 22A4/28G1
Scawby & Hibaldstow 22F4
Scholes 21D3/42A4
Scopwick & Timberland 17C1
Scorrier 1E1
Scorton 27F5
Scotby 26C1
Scotscalder 38D3
Scotsgap 27A4
Scotstoun East 29C4/44F4
Scotstoun West 29C4/44F4
Scotstounhill 29C4/44F4
Scotswood 27B5/28A2
Scratby Halt 18E1
Scruton 21A3/28G5
Sculcoates 22A1
Scunthorpe & Frodingham 22F4
Sea Mills 3A2/8C2/9G1
Seaburn 28C5
Seacombe (Goods) 45F3
Seacombe 45F3
Seacroft 17B4
Seaford 5F4
Seaforth 20B4/24F4/45F3
Seaham 28C5
Sealand 20D4
Seamer 22A4
Seascale 26F3
Seaton (Cumb) 26E3

Seaton (D&S) 28C5
Seaton (Rutland) 16F1
Seaton Carew 28E4
Seaton Delaval 28D5
Seaton Junction 2B1
Seaton 2B1
Seaton-on-Tees 28E4
Sebastopol 43A2
Sedbergh 24A2/27G2
Sedgebrook 16D2
Sedgefield 28E5
Sedgeford 17D5
Seend .3B4
Seer Green for Penn 5A1/10F1
Sefton & Maghull 20B4/24F4/45F2
Sefton Park 20C4/24G4/45F4
Seghill 28D5
Selby 21D5
Selham 5E1
Selhurst 5B3/40G5
Selkirk 30E1
Sellafield 26F3
Selling 6C3
Selly Oak 15G4
Selsdon 5C3
Semington Halt 3B4
Semley 3D4
Senghenydd 8B4/43C3
Sessay 21B4
Sesswick Halt 20F4
Settle 24B1
Settrington 22B5
Seven KIngs 5A4
Seven Sisters 7A5/43E1
Sevenoaks 5C4
Severn Beach 8C2/9G1
Severn Bridge 8A1/9E2
Severn Tunnel Junction 8B2/9F1
Sexhow 28F4
Shackerstone 16F5
Shadwell 40C4
Shalford 5D1
Shandon 29A3
Shankend 31F1
Shanklin 4G3
Shap .27F1
Shapwick 3C1/8E3
Sharlston Colliery 42C4
Sharlston 21E4/42C5
Sharnal Street 6B5
Sharnbrook 10B1/11C1
Sharpness Lower Dock & Basin .8B1/9F2
Sharpness 8B1/9F2
Shaugh Bridge PLatform 2D5
Shaw & Compton 21F1
Shawclough & Healey . .20A1/24E1/45A1
Shawford for Twyford 4D3
Shawlands 44E3
Sheepbridge Iron Works 41B2
Sheepridge 16A5/41B2
Sheerness-on-Sea Dockyard 6B4
Sheerness-on-Sea 6B4
Sheffield Midland/
    Pond Street . . .16A5/21G3/41A2/42G4
Sheffield Nunnery 41A2/42G4
Sheffield Park 41A2/42G4
Sheffield Park 5E4
Sheffield Queens Road .16A5/41A2/42G4
Sheffield
    Victoria 16A5/21G3/41A2/42G4
Sheffield
    Wharf Street . .16A5/21G3/41A2/42G4
Shefford 11D1
Shelford 11D3
Shenfield & Hutton Junction . .5A5/11G4

Shenstone 15F5
Shenton 16F5
Shepherd's Well 6C2
Shepherds Bush 39C4
Shepherds 1D1
Shepley & Shelley 21F2/42D2
Shepperton 5B2
Shepreth 11D3
Shepshed 16E4
Shepton Mallet Charlton Road . .3C3/8E1
Shepton Mallet High Street . . .3C3/8E1
Sherborne 3xx/8G1
Sherburn Colliery 28D5
Sherburn-in-Elmet 21D4
Sheringham 18C3
Shettleston 29C5/44C3
Shide .4F3
Shieldhill 26A3
Shields Road 44F1
Shifnal 15F2
Shildon 27E5
Shillingstone 3E4
Shilton 10A5
Shincliffe 28D5
Shiplake 10G2
Shipley & Windhill 21D2/42A1
Shipley 21/D242A1
Shippea Hill 11B4
Shipston-on-Stour 9C5
Shipton for Burford 10D5
Shirebrook North 16B4/41C4
Shirebrook South 16B4/41C4
Shirehampton 3A2/8C2/9G1
Shireoaks 16A4/41A4
Shirley 9A5
Shoeburyness 6A4
Sholing 4E4
Shoreham (Kent) 5C5
Shoreham-by-Sea 5F3
Shorncliffe 6D2
Shortlands 5B4/40F3
Shoscombe & Single Hill Halt . .3B3/8D1
Shottle 16C5/41F1
Shotton Colliery 28D5
Shotton 20D4
Shotts East 30C4
Shotts 30C5
Shrawardine 14A1
Shrewsbury Abbey Foregate 15E1
Shrewsbury Abbey 15E1
Shrewsbury Coton Hill 15E1
Shrewsbury General 15E1
Shrewsbury New Yard 15E1
Shrewsbury West 15E1
Shrivenham 9F5
Shustoke 16G5
Sible & Castle Hedingham 11E5
Sibsey 17C3
Sidcup 5B4
Sidmouth Junction 2B2
Sidmouth 2B2
Sigglesthorne 22D3
Sileby 16E3
Silecroft 24A5
Silkstone 21F3/42E3
Silloth 26C3
Silver Street for Upper Edmonton . .40A4
Silverdale 15C3/24F1
Silverdale 24B3
Silverton 2A3
Silvertown 40C2
Simonstone 24D1
Sinclairtown 30A2
Sinderby 21A3
Singer 29C4/44F4

Sirhowy 8A4/43C1
Sittingbourne & Milton Regis 6C4
Six Mile Bottom 11C4
Skares .29F4
Skegness 17B4
Skelbo Halt 36A4
Skellingthorpe 16B1
Skelmanthorpe 21F3/42D3
Skelmersdale 20A3/24F3/45E2
Skewen 7B4/43F2
Skinningrove 28E3
Skipton 21B1
Skipwith 21D5
Skirlaugh 22D3
Slade Green 5B4
Slaggyford 27C2
Slaithwaite 21E2/42D1
Slateford 30G3
Sleaford 16C1/17C1
Sledmere & Fimber 22B4
Sleights 28F2
Slinfold .5E2
Sling 8A2/9E1
Slingsby 21B5
Sloane Square 39D5
Slough 5B1/10G1
Smallford 11F2
Smeaton 30B2
Smeeth Road 17F4
Smeeth .6D3
Smethwick Junction 13B2
Smethwick 13C2
Smitham 5C3
Smithy Bridge 20A1/21E1/45A1
Snaefell 23B3
Snailham Halt 6E4
Snaith .21E5
Snape .12C2
Snaresbrook 5A4/40A2
Snarestone 16E5
Snatchwood Siding 43A2
Snelland 17A1
Snettisham 17D5
Snodland 6C5
Snowdon 19E2
Snowdown & Nonington Halt 6C2
Soham .11B4
Soho & Winson Green 13C3
Soho Pool 13B3
Soho 13C3/15G4
Sole Street 5B5
Solihull .9A5
Somerleyton 12A1/18F1
Somersham 11B3
Somerton 3D2/8F2
Sorbie .25D4
South Acton 39D3
South Aylesbury Halt 10E2
South Bank 28E4
South Bermondsey 40D4
South Cave 22D4
South Cerney 9F4
South Croydon 5C3
South Dock (Sunderland) 28C5
South Ealing 39D2
South Eastrington 22E5
South Elmsall 21F4/42D5
South Gosforth 27B5
South Greenford 39C2
South Hampstead 39B5
South Harrow 5A2/39B1
South Hetton 28D5
South Howden 22E5
South Kensington 39D5
South Kenton 39A2

South Lambeth 40D5
South Leigh 10E5
South Leith Docks 30F1
South Leith 30F1
South Lynn 17E4
South Merton 39F4
South Milford 21D4
South Molton 7F4
South Queensferry 30B3
South Rhondda 8C5/43D4
South Ruislip 5A2/39B1
South Shields 28D5
South Tottenham & Stamford Hill . .40A4
South Willingham & Hainton 17A2
South Witham 16E1
South Woodford 5A4/40A2
Southall 5B2/39C1
Southam & Long Itchington 10B4
Southam Road & Harbury 10B5
Southampton Central 4E4
Southampton Terminus 4E4
Southbourne Halt 4E1
Southburn 22C4
Southcoats 22A1
Southease & Rodmell Halt 5F4
Southend 43G3
Southend-on-Sea Central 6A4
Southend-on-Sea East 6A4
Southend-on-Sea Victoria 6A4
Southerndown Road 7C5/43D4
Southfields 39E4
Southfleet for Springhead 5B5
Southill 11D1
Southminster 12G5
Southport
   Chapel Street 20A4/24E4/45F1
Southport
   Kensington Road 20A4/24E4/45F1
Southport St Lukes 20A4/24E4/45F1
Southrey 17B1
Southwater 5E2
Southwell 16C3
Southwick 28C5
Southwick 5F2
Sowerby Bridge 21E2/42C1
Spalding Town 17E2
Sparkford 3D2/8F1
Spean Bridge 32B2
Speech House Road 8A19E2
Speen for Donnington 4A3
Speeton 22B3
Spennymoor 27D5
Spetchley 9B3
Spetisbury 3E4
Spey Bay 36C1
Spiersbridge 44F3
Spilsby 17B3
Spinkhill 16A441B3
Spital 20C4/45F4
Spitalfields (Coal) 40C4
Spitalfields (Goods) 40C4
Spofforth 21C3
Spon Lane for
   West Bromwich 13B2/15G4
Spondon 16D5/41G2
Spooner Row 12A4/18F4
Spring Road 15G5
Spring Vale 20A2/24E2
Springburn Park 29C5/44D4
Springburn 44D4
Springfield 34F5
Springside 29E3
Sprotborough 21F4
Sprouston 31E2
Sproxton 16D1

Squires Gate 24D4
Stacksteads 20A1/24E1
Staddlethorpe 22E5
Stafford Common 15D3/24G1
Stafford Doxey Road 15E3/24G1
Stafford 15E3/24G1
Stainby 16D1
Staincross 21F3/42D4
Staines Central 5B2
Staines West 5B1
Stainforth & Hatfield 21F5
Stainland &
   Holywell Green 21E2/42C1
Staintondale 28G1
Stairfoot for Ardsley 42E4
Staithes 28E2
Stalbridge 3D3/8F1
Staley & Millbrook 21F1
Stalham 18D2
Stallingborough 22F2
Stalybridge South 21A2
Stalybridge 21F1
Stamford Bridge 22C5
Stamford Brook 39D4
Stamford East 16F1/17F1
Stamford Hill 40A4
Stamford Town 16F1/17F1
Stanbridgeford 10D1
Standon Bridge 15D3/24F1
Standon 11E3
Stanford-le-Hope 5A5
Stanhope 27D4
Stanley (Perthshire) 33E5
Stanley Bridge Halt 3A5
Stanley 42B4
Stanley 45F3
Stanlow & Thornton 45E5
Stanner 14E2
Stannergate 34E4
Stanningley 21D2/42A2
Stannington 27A5
Stansted 11E4
Stanton Gate 16D4/41G3
Stanwardine Halt 20G4
Staple Edge Halt 8A1/9E2
Staple Hill 3A3/8C1/9G2
Stapleford & Sandiacre 16D4/41G3
Staplehurst 6D5
Stapleton Road 3F1
Star Crossing Halt 20D5
Starbeck 21C3
Starcross 2C3
Staveley Central 41B3
Staveley Works 16A4/41B3
Staveley 27G1
Staverton Halt 3B4
Staverton 2D4
Steele Road 27A1
Steeplehouse 16C5/41E1
Steer Point 2E5
Steeton & Silsden 21C1
Stepney (Hull) 22A1
Stepney East 40C4
Stepney Green 40C3
Stepps 29C5/44C4
Stevenage 11E2
Stevenston 29D3
Steventon 10F4
Stewartby Halt 10C1/11D1
Stewarton 29D4
Steyning 5F2
Stickney 17C3
Stillington 28E5
Stirling 30A5
Stirling East 30A5

Stixwould 17B2
Stobcross 44E4
Stobs .31F1
Stockbridge 4C4
Stockcross & Bagnor Halt 4A4
Stockport Edgeley 20C1/24G145A4
Stockport Tiviot Dale 45A4
Stockport 21G1
Stocksfield 27C4
Stocksmoor 21F2/42D2
Stockton Brook 15C3/24E1
Stockton North Shore 28E5
Stockton South 28E5
Stockton 28E5
Stogumber 8F5
Stoke Canon 2B3
Stoke Edith 9C2
Stoke Ferry 10A5/17F5
Stoke Golding 16F5
Stoke Junction Halt 6B5
Stoke Mandeville 10E2
Stoke Newington 40B4
Stoke on Trent 15C3/24F1
Stoke Works 9B4
Stoke .11D5
Stokesley 28F4
Stone 15D3/24G1
Stonea 10A3/17G3
Stonebridge Park 39B3
Stoneferry 22D3
Stonegate 5E5
Stonehaven 34A1
Stonehouse Burdett Road 9E3
Stonehouse Pool 1D5
Stonehouse 30D5
Stonehouse 9E3
Stoneleigh 5C3
Storeton for Barnston . .20C4/24G4/45F4
Stottesdon 15G2
Stoulton 9C3
Stourbridge Junction 9A3/15G3
Stourbridge Town 9A3/15G3
Stourpain & Durweston Halt 3E4
Stourport-on-Severn 9A3
Stow Bardolph 17F4
Stow Bedon 12A5/18F5
Stow Park 16A2
Stow 30D1
Stowmarket 12C4
Stow-on-the-Wold 9D5
Stranraer Harbour 25C2
Stranraer Town 25C2
Strata Florida 14D5
Stratford Market 40B2
Stratford 40B2
Stratford-on-Avon 9B5
Stratford-on-Avon General 9B5
Stratford-on-Avon Old Town 9B5
Strathaven Central 29D5
Strathblane 29B5
Strathbungo 44E3
Strathcarron 35E2
Strathcathro 34C3
Stratheyre 33F2
Strathmiglo 34F5
Strathord 33E5
Stratton Park Halt 9F5
Stratton 9F5
Stravithie 34F3
Strawberry Hill 5B2/39F2
Streatham Common 40F5
Streatham Hill 40E5
Streatham 40F5
Streetly 15F4
Strenshall 21B5

Stretford 45B3
Stretton & Cley Mills 15C5
Stretton 16B5/41D2
Strichen 37D4
Strines .15A4
Strome Ferry 35E1
Stroud Wallbridge 9E3
Stroud .9E3
Struan .33C3
Stubbins 20A1/24E1/45B1
Studley & Astwood Bank 9B4
Sturmer 11D5
Sturminster Newton 3E3
Sturton 16A2
Styal 15A3/20C1/45A4
Suckley .9B2
Sudbury & Harrow Road 39B2
Sudbury Hill Harrow 39B2
Sudbury Hill 39B2
Sudbury Town 39B2
Sudbury (Staffs) 15D5
Sudbury 12D5
Sulby Bridge 23A3/25G4
Sulby Glen 23A2/25G4
Sully 8D4/43B5
Summer Lane 21F3/42E3
Summerseat 20A1/24E1/45B1
Summerston 29B5/44C5
Sunbury 5B2
Sunderland Central 28C5
Sundridge Park 40F2
Sunilaws 31D2
Sunningdale for Windlesham 5B1
Sunniside Depot 27D5
Sunnymeads 5B1
Surbiton 5B2/39G2
Surfleet 17D2
Surrey Docks 40D4
Sutton Bingham 3E2
Sutton Bridge 17E4
Sutton Coldfield 15F5
Sutton Common 5C3
Sutton Harbour 1D5
Sutton Junction 16B4/41D4
Sutton Park 15F5
Sutton Scotney 4C3
Sutton Siding 21D4
Sutton .11B3
Sutton .5C3
Sutton-in-Ashfield Central . . .16B4/41D4
Sutton-in-Ashfield Town 16B4/41D4
Sutton-on-Hull 22D3
Sutton-on-Sea 17A4
Swadlincote 16E5
Swaffham 18E5
Swaffham Prior 11C4
Swainsthorpe 18F3
Swale Halt 6B4
Swalwell 27C5/28B3
Swan Village 13B2/15F4
Swanage 3G5
Swanbourne 10D2
Swanbridge Halt 43B5
Swanley .5B4
Swanscombe Halt 5B5
Swansea Victoria 43G3
Swansea Bay 7B4/43G3
Swansea Docks 43G3
Swansea High Street 7B4/43G3
Swansea Rutland Street 7B4/43G3
Swansea St Thomas 43G3
Swanwick 4E3
Swavesey 11B3
Sway 4E5
Swaythling 4D4

Swimbridge 7F4
Swinderby 16B2
Swindon 9G5
Swindon Town 9G5
Swine 22D3
Swineshead 17D2
Swinton (Lancs) 20B1/24F1/45B2
Swinton Central 21F4/42F5
Swinton Town 21F4/42F5
Swiss Cottage 39B5
Sydenham Hill 40F4
Sydenham 40F4
Sykehouse 21E5
Sylfaen .14B2
Symington 30E4
Symond's Yat 8A2/9E1
Syon Lane 39D2
Syston .16E3
Tackley Halt 10D4
Tadcaster 21D4
Tadworth & Walton on the Hill 5C3
Taff's Well 8C4/43C4
Tain 36B4
Takeley .11E4
Talacre .20C5
Talerddig 14B4
Talgarth 14F3
Talley Road 13G5
Tallington 17F1
Talsarnau 19F2
Talwrn Bach Halt 19G2
Tal-y-Cafn & Eglwysbach 19D4
Talyllyn .14G3
Tamerton Foliot 1D5
Tamworth High Level 15F5
Tamworth Low Level 15F5
Tanfield Lea Colliery 27C5
Tanfield 21A3
Tannadice 34C4
Taplow 5A1/10G2
Tarbolton 29E4
Tarset .27A2
Tattenhall Road 15B1/24E3
Tattenhall 15B1/24E3
Tattenham Corner 5C3
Tattershall 17C2
Tauchers Halt 36D1
Taunton .8F4
Tavistock 1C5
Taynuilt 32E3
Tayport 34E4
Tebay .27F1
Teddington for Bushy Park 5B2/39F2
Teigl Halt 19F3
Teigngrace Halt 2C3
Teignmouth 2C3
Temple Hirst 21E5
Temple Sowerby 27E1
Templecombe 3D3/8F1
Templeton 7C3
Tempsford 11C2
Tenbury Wells 9A1
Tenby .7D3
Tenterden Town 6D4
Tern Hill 15D2/24G2
Terrington 17E4
Teston Crossing Halt 6C5
Tetbury .9F3
Teversall East 16B4/41D3
Teversall Manor 16B4/41D3
Tewkesbury Quay 9D3
Tewkesbury 9D3
Teynham 6C4
Thame .10E3

Thames Ditton	.5B2/39G2
Thameshaven	.6A5
Thankerton	.30E4
Thatcham	.4A3
Thatto Heath	.20C3/24G3/45E3
The Hawthorns (West Bromwich) Platform	.13B3
The Lakes Halt	.9A5
The Mound	.36A4
Theale	.4A2
Theddingworth	.16G3
Theddlethorpe	.17A3/22G1
Thelwall	.15A2/20C2/24G2/45C4
Theobalds Grove	.11G3
Thetford Bridge	.12B5
Thetford	.12B5
Theydon Bois	.11G3
Thirsk Junction	.21A4
Thirsk Town	.21A4
Thongs Bridge	.21F2/42D1
Thorganby	.21D5
Thorington	.12E4
Thorn Falcon	.8F4
Thornaby	.28E4
Thornbury	.8B1/9F2
Thorncliffe Iron Works	.21F3/42F2
Thorne North	.21E5
Thorne South	.21F5
Thorner	.21D3
Thorney & Kingsbury Halt	.3D1/8F3
Thorney	.17F2
Thorneyburn	.27A2
Thornford Bridge Halt	.3E2
Thornhill for Dewsbury	.42C3
Thornhill	.30G4
Thornley Colliery	.28D5
Thornliebank	.29C4/44E2
Thornton Abbey	.22E3
Thornton Dale	.22A5
Thornton Heath	.5B3/40G5
Thornton-in-Craven	.21C1
Thornton Junction	.34G5
Thornton	.21D2/42A1
Thornton-Cleveleys	.24D4
Thorntonhall	.29D5/44E2
Thorp Arch	.21C4
Thorp Gates Siding	.21D5
Thorpe Bay	.6A4
Thorpe Cloud	.15C5
Thorpe Culvert	.17B4
Thorpe	.10A1/11B1
Thorpe-in-Balne	.21F5
Thorpe-le-Soken	.12E3
Thorpe-on-the-Hill	.16B1
Thorverton	.2A3
Thrapston Bridge Street	.10A1/11B1
Thrapston Midland Road	.10A1/11B1
Three Bridges	.5D3
Three Cocks	.14F2
Three Counties	.11E2
Three Oaks & Guestling Halt	.6E5
Threlkeld	.26E1
Throsk	.30A5
Thurcroft	.16A4/21G4/41A4
Thurgarton	.16C3
Thursford	.18D4
Thurso	.38C3
Thurstaston	.20C5
Thurston	.12C5
Thuxton	.18F4
Tibbermuir	.33E4
Tibshelf & Newton	.16B4/41D3
Tibshelf Town	.16B4/41D3
Tickhill & Wadworth	.21G5
Tiddington	.10E3

Tidenham	.8B2/9F1
Tidworth	.4B5
Tilbury Riverside	.5B5
Tilbury Town for Tilbury Docks	.5B5
Tile Hill	.10A5
Tilehurst	.4A2/10G3
Tillicoultry	.30A4
Tillietudelem	.30D5
Tillynaught	.37C2
Tilton	.16F2
Timperley	.20C1/24G145B3
Tingley	.21E3/42B3
Tinkers Green Halt	.20G4
Tinsley	.21G4/42G4
Tintern	.8B2/9F1
Tipton Five Ways	.13B1
Tipton Owen Street	.13B1
Tipton St Johns	.2B2
Tiptree	.12F5
Tirphil	.8B4/43C2
Tirydail	.7A3/43G1
Tisbury	.3D4
Tisted	.4C2
Titley	.14E1
Tiverton Junction	.2A2/8G5
Tiverton	.2A3/7G5
Tivetshall	.12A3/18G3
Tochieneal	.37C1
Toddington	.9D4
Todmorden	.20A1/21E1
Tollcross	.44D3
Toller	.3F2
Tollerton	.21B4
Tolworth	.5C2
Tomatin	.36E4
Tonbridge	.5D5
Tondu	.7xx/43D4
Tonfanau	.13B5
Tonge & Breedon	.16D4
Tongham	.4B1/5C1
Tonteg Platform	.43C3
Tonypandy & Trealaw	.43D3
Tonyrefail	.8B5/43D3
Tooting	.39F5
Topcliffe	.21A4
Topsham	.2B3
Torksey	.16A2
Torpantau	.8A5/14G3/43C1
Torphins	.34A3/37G2
Torquay	.2D3
Torrance	.29B5/44D5
Torre	.2D3
Torrington	.7G3
Torryburn	.30A4
Torver	.24F4/26G2
Totnes	.2D4
Tottenham	.40A4
Totteridge & Whetstone	.5A311G2
Tottington	.20A1/24E1/45B1
Totton for Eling	.4E4
Towcester	.10C3
Tower Hill	.1A5
Tower Hill	.40C4
Towesey Halt	.10E3
Towiemore	.37D1
Town Green & Aughton	.20B4/24F4/45F2
Towneley	.24D1
Towyn Wharf	.13B5
Towyn	.13B5
Trabboch	.29F4
Trafford Park & Stretford	.20C1/24G1/45B3
Tram Inn	.14F1
Tranent	.30B1

Trawscoed	.13D5
Trawsfynydd Lake Halt	.19F3
Trawsfynydd	.19F3
Treamble	.1D1
Treborth	.19D2
Trecynon Halt	.43D2
Tredegar	.8A4/43B1
Trefant	.19D5
Treforest Estate	.43C3
Treforest Halt	.43C3
Treforest	.8B5/43C3
Tregaron	.14D5
Tregarth	.19D2
Trehafod	.8B5/43C3
Treherbert	.7B5/8B5/43D2/43D3
Trelewis Platform	.43C2
Tremains Platform	.43D4
Trench Crossing	.15E2
Trench Halt	.20F4
Trenholme Bar	.28F5
Trent	.16D4
Trentham Gardens	.24F1
Trentham	.15C3/24F1
Treorchy	.43D2
Treowen Halt	.43B2
Tresmeer	.1B4
Trevil Halt	.8A4/43B1
Trevor	.20F5
Trewerry & Trerice Halt	.1D1
Trimdon	.28D5
Trimley	.12E3
Trimsaran	.7A3
Tring	.10E1
Troedyrhiew Garth	.7B5/43E3
Troedyrhiw	.43C2
Troon	.29E3
Troutbeck	.26E1
Trowbridge	.3B4
Trowell	.16C4/41F3
Trowse	.18F3
Truro Newham	.1E1
Truro	.1E1
Trusham	.2C3
Truthall Halt	.1F5
Tue Brook	.20C4/24G4/45F3
Tufnell Park	.40B5
Tullibardine	.33F4
Tulloch	.32B1
Tulse Hill	.5B3/40E5
Tumble	.7A3
Tumby Woodside	.17C2
Tunbridge Wells Central	.5D5
Tunbridge Wells West	.5D5
Tunstall	.15C3/24E1
Turnberry	.29G2
Turnchapel	.1D5
Turnham Green	.39D3
Turnhouse	.30B3
Turriff	.37D3
Turton & Edgeworth	.20A2/24E2/45B1
Turvey	.10B1
Tutbury	.15D5
Tuts Hill Halt for Beachley	.8B2/9F1
Tuxford Central	.16B2
Tuxford North	.16B2
Twechar	.29B5
Tweedmouth	.31D3
Twenty	.17E2
Twickenham	.5B2/39E2
Twizell	.31D3
Twyford	.4A1/10G2
Ty Croes	.19D1
Tydd	.17E3
Tyddyn Bridge Halt	.19F4
Ty-Glas	.43B4

Tygwyn 19F2
Tyldesley 20B2/24F2/45C2
Tyllwyn Halt 43B1
Tylorstown 8B5/43D2
Tylwch 14C4
Tyndrum Lower 32E1
Tyndrum 32E1
Tyne Dock 28D5
Tynehead 30C1
Tynemouth 28D5
Tynycwm 43A3
Tytherington 8B1/9F2
Uckfield 5E4
Uddingston Central 44C3
Uddingston East 44C3
Uddingston West 44C3
Udny 37E4
Uffculme 2A2/8G5
Uffington & Barnack 17F1
Uffington 10F5
Ulceby 22E3
Ulleskelf 21D4
Ullesthorpe 16G4
Ulverston Glaxo Works 24B4
Ulverston 24B4
Umberleigh 7F3
Underwood Mineral Depot 44G3
Undy Halt 8B2
Union Mills Halt 23B2
Unstone 16A5/41B2
Up Exe Halt 2A3
Uphall 30C3
Uplawmoor 29D4/44G2
Upminster Bridge 5B5
Upminster 5B5
Upney 5A4
Upper Bank 7B4/43G3
Upper Boat Halt 43C3
Upper Halliford Halt 5B2
Upper Holloway 40B5
Upper Lydbrook 8A2/9E1
Upper Pontnewydd 8B3/43A3
Upper Port Glasgow 29B3
Upper Warlingham 5C3
Uppermill 21F1
Uppingham 16F2
Upton & Blewbury 10F4
Upton & North Elmsall 21E4/42D5
Upton-by-Chester Halt 45F5
Upton Magna 15E1
Upton Park 40B2
Upton 20C5/24G4/45F4
Upton-on-Severn 9C3
Upwell 17F4
Upwey & Broadwey 3G3
Upwey Goods 3F3
Upwey Wishing Well Halt 3F3
Urmston 20C1/24G1/45B3
Urquhart 36C1
Ushaw Moor 27D5
Usk .8B3
Usworth 28C5
Uttoxeter 15D5
Uxbridge High Street 10G1
Uxbridge Vine Street 10G1
Valley 19B2
Varteg 8A4/43A2
Vauxhall & Duddeston 13C4
Vauxhall 40D5
Velvet Hall 31D3
Venn Cross 8F5
Ventnor 4G3
Verney Junction 10D3
Verwood 3E5
Victoria 8A4/43B2

Virginia Water for Wentworth 5B1
Vobster 3B3/8E1
Vulcan Halt 45D3
Wadborough 9C3
Waddington 16B1/17B1
Waddon for Beddington and
Bandon Hill 5C3
Wadebridge 1C2
Wadhurst 5E5
Wadsley Bridge 21G3/42G4
Wainfleet 17C4
Wainhill Halt 10F2
Wakefield Kirkgate 21E3/42C4
Wakefield Westgate 21E3/42C4
Wakerley & Barrowden 16F1
Walcut 15E1
Waleswood 16A4/41A3
Walford Halt 9D1
Walkden 20B1/24F1/45B2
Walker 28D5
Walkerburn 30E1
Walkergate 28B5
Walkeringham 22G5
Wall Grange & Longsdon 15C4
Wall .27B3
Wallasey Grove Road . .20C4/24G4/45G3
Wallasey Village 20C4/24G4/45G3
Wallingfen 22D5
Wallingford 10F3
Wallington 5C3
Wallsend 28D5
Walmer 6C2
Walpole 17E4
Walsall 13A2
Walsall Long Street 13A2
Walsall Midland Road 13A3
Walsall Wood 15F4
Walsden 21E1
Walsingham 18D5
Waltham (Lincs) 22F2
Waltham Cross & Abbey 11G3
Waltham-on-the-Wold 16D2
Walthamstow (Hoe Street) 40A3
Walthamstow 40A3
Walton & Anfield 45F3
Walton Junction 45F3
Walton 42C4
Walton-on-Naze 12E3
Walton-on-Thames 5C2
Walton-on-the-Hill 20C4/24G4/45F3
Walworth Road 40D5
Wamphray 26A3/30G3
Wanborough for Normandy 5C1
Wandsworth Common 39E5
Wandsworth Road 40E5
Wandsworth Town 39E5
Wansford 10A1/17F1
Wanstead Park 40B2
Wanstrow 3C3/8E1
Wantage Road 10F5
Wapping 40C4
Warblington Halt 4E2
Warboys 11B2
Warcop 27E2
Wardhouse 347E2
Wardleworth 20A1/21E1/45A1
Ware 11F3
Wareham 3F4
Wargrave 4A1/10G2
Wark 27B3
Warkworth 31F5
Warminster 3C4
Warmley 3A3/8C1
Warmsworth 21F5
Warnham 5D2

Warrenby Halt 28E4
Warrington
Arpley 15A2/20C2/24G2/45C4
Warrington
Bank Quay 20C2/24G2/45D4
Warsop 16B4/41C4
Warthill 21C5
Wartle 37E3
Warwick Road 39D4
Warwick Road (Lancs) 45B3
Warwick (Milverton) 10B5
Warwick 10B5
Washford 8E5
Washington 28C5
Waskerley 27D4
Wassand 22D3
Watchet 8E5
Water Orton 15F5
Waterbeach 11C3
Waterfall 23B2
Waterfoot for Newchurch . . .20A1/24E1
Waterhouses 27D5
Wateringbury 6C5
Waterloo Halt 43B3
Waterloo 20B4/24F4/45F4
Waterside 29F4
Watford High Street 5A2/11G1
Watford Junction 5A2/11G1
Watford North 11G1
Watford West 11G1
Wath Central 21F4/42E5
Wath North 42E5
Watlington 10F3
Watten 38D2
Watton 18F5
Watton-at-Stone 11F2
Wattstown 43D3
Waverton 15B1/24E3
Wavertree & Edge Hill 45F3
Wavertree 45F3
Wearhead 27D3
Weaste 45B3
Weatherhill Quarry 27D4
Weaverthorpe 22A4
Wednesbury Central 13A2/15F4
Wednesbury Town 13A2/15F4
Wednesfield 15F4
Wednesfield Heath 15F4
Weedon 10B3
Weeley 12E3
Weeton 21C3
Welbury 28F5
Welford & Kilworth 10A3/16G3
Welford Park for
Wickham & Weston 4A4
Wellfield 28D5
Welling 5B4/40E1
Wellingborough London Road 10B2
Wellingborough Midland Road 10B2
Wellington (Somerset) 8G4
Wellington 15E2
Wellow 3B3/8D1
Wells Priory Road 3C2/8E2
Wells Tucker Street 3C2/8E2
Wells .3C2
Wells-next-the-Sea 18C5
Welnetham 12C5
Welsh Hook Halt 13G1
Welshampton 20F4
Welshpool 14B2
Welton 10A3
Welwyn Garden City 11F2
Welwyn North 11F2
Wem 15D1/24G3
Wembley Central 5A2/39B2

Wembley Hill 39B3	Westenhanger 6D3	Whitehurst 20F4
Wembley Park 5A2/39B3	Westerfield 12D3	Whiteinch Park 44F4
Wembley Stadium 39B3	Westerham 5C4	Whiteinch Riverside 44F4
Wemyss Bay 29C2	Westerton 44E5	Whitemoor 10A3/17F3
Wemyss Castle 30A2/34G5	Westfield 30B4	Whiterigg 30C5/44A4
Wendling 18E5	Westgate-in-Weardale 27D3	Whithorn 25D4
Wendover 10E2	Westgate-on-Sea 6B3	Whitland 7A1/13G3
Wenford Bridge 1C3	Westhoughton 45C2	Whitley Bay 28D5
Wennington 24B2	Westhouses & Blackwell 16B4/41D3	Whitley Bridge 21E5
Wensley 21A2/27G4	Westmill 11E3	Whitlingham 18F3
Wenvoe 8C4/43C5	Westminster 40D5	Whitlock's End Halt 9A5
Wern Las Siding 14A1/20G4	Westmoor 14E1	Whitmore 15C3/24F1
Wern Siding 19F2	Weston & Ingestre 15D4	Whitney-on-Wye 14E2
West Acton 39C3	Weston (Lincs) 17E2	Whitrope Siding 31G1
West Allerton 45E4	Weston Milton Halt 3B1/8D3	Whitstable & Tankerton 6B3
West Auckland 27E5	Weston 3A3/8D1	Whitstone & Bridgerule 1A4
West Bay 3F1	Weston-on-Trent 16D5	Whittington High Level 20F4
West Brinstead 5E2	Weston-Rhyn 20F4	Whittington Low Level 20F4
West Brompton 39D5	Weston-sub-Edge 9C5	Whittlesea 10A2/17G2
West Bromwich &	Weston-super-Mare General 3B1/8D3	Whittlesford 11D3
Spon Lane 13B2/15G4	Weston-under-Penyard Halt 9D2	Whitton 39E1
West Calder 30C4	Wetheral 27C1	Whitwell & Reepham 18E4
West Cornforth 28D5	Wetherby 21C4	Whitwell 16A4/41B4
West Cross 43G3	Wetwang 22C4	Whitwick 16E4
West Croydon 5C3/40G5	Weybourne 18C4	Whitworth 20A1/24E1/45A1
West Derby 45F3	Weybridge 5C2	Whyteleaf 5C3
West Drayton & Yiewsley 5B2/10G1	Weyhill .4B4	Whyteleaf South 5C3
West Dulwich 40E4	Weymouth Quay 3G3	Wick 38D2
West Ealing 39C2	Weymouth Town 3G3	Wickenby 17A1
West Exe Halt 2A3	Whaley Bridge 15A4	Wickford Junction 6A5
West Fen Drove 10A3/17G3	Whalley 24D2	Wickham Bishops 12F5
West Ferry 34E4	Whaplode 17E3	Wickham Market 12C2
West Gosforth 27B5	Wharram 22B5	Wickham 4E3
West Green 40A4	Whatstandwell 16C5/41E2	Wickwar 8B1/9F2
West Hallam for Dale Abbey 41F3	Whauphill 25C4	Widdrington 27A5/31G5
West Halton 22E4	Wheathampstead 11F2	Widford 11F3
West Ham 40C2	Wheatley Park 21G2	Widmerpool 16D3
West Hampstead Midland 39B5	Wheatley 10E3	Widnes Central 15A1
West Hampstead 39B5	Wheatley 21E2/42B1	Widnes 20C3/24G3
West Harrow Halt 39A1	Wheldrake 21C5	Widney Manor 9A5
West Hartlepool 28D4	Whelley 45D2	Wigan Central 45D2
West Hoathley 5E3	Wherwell 4C4	Wigan North Western 45D2
West Horndon 5A5	Whetstone 16F4	Wigan Wallgate 45D2
West India Docks 40C3	Whifflet East 44B3	Wighton Halt 18D5
West Jesmond 27B5/28A1	Whifflet High Level 44B3	Wigston Magna 16F3
West Kensington 39D4	Whifflet Low Level 44B3	Wigston South 16F3
West Kilbride 29D2	Whifflet 30C5	Wigton 26C4
West Kirby 20C5/24G5	Whimple 2B2	Wigtown 25C4
West Leigh & Bedford 45C3	Whistlefield 29A3	Wilbraham Road 45B3
West Leigh Siding 45C3	Whitburn 30C4	Wilburton 11B3
West Malling 6C5	Whitby Town 28F2	Willaston 15C2/24E2
West Meon 4D2	Whitby West Cliff 28F2	Willenhall Bilston Street 15F4
West Moors for Frendown 1C5	Whitchurch Down Platform 1C5	Willersey Halt 9C5
West Pennard 3C2/8E2	Whitchurch Halt 3A2/8D1	Willesden Green 39B4
West Rounton Gates 28F5	Whitchurch North 4B3	Willesden Junction HL 39C4
West Runton 18C3	Whitchurch Town 4B3	Willesden Junction Main 39C4
West St Leonards 6F5	Whitchurch 15C1/24F3	Willesden Junction New 39C4
West Stanley Goods 27C5	White Bear 20A3/24F2/45D1	Williamwood 44E2
West Stanley 27C5	White City 39C4	Willington Quay 28B5
West Street 44F1	White Colne 12E5	Willington 11D1
West Sutton 5C3	White Fen 10A3/17G3	Willington 27D5
West Timperley 45B4	White Hart Lane 40A4	Williton 8E5
West Vale 21E2/42C1	White Notley 11F5	Willoughby 17B3
West Weybridge 5C1	Whitebrook Halt 8A2/9E1	Wilmcote 9B5
West Wickham 5B4/40G3	Whitechapel 40C4	Wilmington 22A1
West Worthing 5F2	Whitecraigs 29C5/44E2	Wilmslow 15A3/20C1/45A5
West Wycombe 10F2	Whitecroft 8A1/9E1	Wilnecote 15F5
Westbourne Park 39C5	Whitedale 22D3	Wilpshire 24D2
Westbury (Salop) 14A1	Whitefield 20B1/24F1/45B2	Wilsden 21D2/42A1
Westbury on Severn Halt 8A1	Whitegate 15B2/24D2	Wilsontown 30C4
Westbury 3B4	Whitehall Halt 2A2/8G4	Wilstrop Siding 21C4
Westcliffe-on-Sea 6A4	Whitehaven Bransty 26E3	Wilton North 3C5
Westcombe Park 40D2	Whitehaven Corkickle 26E3	Wilton South 3C5
Westcraigs for	Whitehaven Preston Street 26E3	Wimbledon Chase 39F4
Harthill & Blackridge 30C4	Whitehouse 37F2	Wimbledon Park 39E4

Wimbledon 5B3/39F4
Wimblington 10A3/17G3
Wimborne 3E5
Wincanton 3D3/F1
Winchburgh 30B3
Winchcombe 9D4
Winchelsea 6E4
Winchester Chesil 4D3
Winchester City 4D3
Winchfield 4B1
Winchmore Hill 5A3
Wincobank 42F4
Windermere Lakeside 24A4/26G1
Windermere 26G1
Windmill End 13C1/15G4
Windsor & Eton Central 5B1/10G1
Windsor & Eton Riverside . . .5B1/10G1
Windsor Street Wharf 13B4
Winestead 22E2
Wingate 28D5
Wingfield 16C5/41E2
Winkhill 15C4
Winnersh Halt for
  Sindlesham & Hurst 4A1
Winnington 15A2/45C5
Winscombe 3B1/8D3
Winsford & Over 15B2/24D2
Winsford 15B2/24D2
Winslow 10D2
Winson Green 13C3/15G4
Winston for Staindrop 27E5
Winterbourne 8C1/9G2
Wintersett 42D4
Winterton & Thealby 22E4
Winton 30B1
Wirksworth 16C5/41E1
Wisbech East 17F3
Wisbech North 17F3
Wisbech St Mary 17F3
Wishaw Central 30C5/44A2
Wishaw South 30D5/44A2
Wishford 3C5
Wistanstow Halt 14C1
Wistow 21D5
Witham 12F5
Witham 3C3/8E1
Withcall 17A2
Withernsea 22E2
Withington &
  West Didsbury 20C1/24G1/45A3
Withington 9C1
Withington 9E4
Withnell 20A2/24E2
Withymoor Basin 13C1
Witley .5D1
Witney 10E5
Wittersham Road 6E4
Witton for Villa Park 13B4
Witton-le-Wear 27E5
Witton Gilbert 27D5
Wiveliscombe 8F5
Wivelsfield 5E3
Wivenhoe 12E4
Wixford 9B4
Wnion Halt 14A5/19G4
Woburn Sands 10C1
Woking 5C1
Wokingham 4A1
Woldingham 5C3
Wolf's Castle Halt 13G1
Wolferton 17D5
Wollerton Halt 15D2/20G2

Wolsingham 27D4
Wolverhampton High Level 15E3
Wolverhampton Low Level 15E3
Wolverhampton Victoria Basin 15E3
Wolverhampton Walsall Street 15E3
Wolverton 10C2
Wombourn 15F3
Wombridge 15E2
Wombwell Central 21F4/42E5
Wombwell West 21F3/42E4
Womersley 21E4
Wooburn Green 5A1/10F2
Wood End 9A5
Wood Green 5A3/40A5
Wood Street (Walthamstow) 40A3
Woodborough 3B5
Woodbridge 12D3
Woodburn 27A3
Woodbury Road 2B3
Woodchester 9F3
Woodend 26F3
Woodford Halse 10B4
Woodford 5A4
Woodgrange Park 40B2
Woodhall Halt 29B3
Woodhall Junction 17B2
Woodhall Spa 17B2
Woodham Ferrers 11G5
Woodhay 4A3
Woodhead 21F2/45F5
Woodhouse 16A4/21G4/41A3/42G5
Woodhouse Mill .16A4/21G4/41A3/42G5
Woodkirk 21E3/42B3
Woodland 24A5/26G2
Woodlands Road Halt 45A2
Woodley 21G1
Woodmansterne 5C3
Woodside Park 5A3
Woodside Siding (Halebank)
  Coal Depot 15A1/45E4
Woodside 5B3
Woodside 20C3/40G4
Woodville Road Halt 43B4
Woodville 16E5
Woofferton 9A1
Wookey 3B2/8E2
Wool 3F4
Wooler 31E3
Woolfold 20B1/24F1/45B1
Woolston 4E4
Woolwich Arsenal 40D1
Woolwich Dockyard 5B4/40D2
Wootton Bassett 9G4
Wootton Rivers Halt 4B5
Wootton Wawen Platform 9B5
Worcester Foregate Street 9B3
Worcester Park 5B3/39G4
Worcester Shrub Hill 9B3
Workington Central 26E3
Workington Main 26E3
Worksop 16A3/41B5
Worleston Coal Depot 15B2/24E2
Worlington Golf Links Halt 11B5
Wormald Green 21B3
Wormit 34E4
Worplesdon 5C1
Worsborough 42E4
Worsley 45B3
Worstead 18E2
Worthing Central 5F2
Worthington 16E5
Wortley 21F3/42F3

Wrabness 12E3
Wrafton 7F3
Wragby 17A1
Wrangaton 2D5
Wraysbury 5B1
Wrea Green 24D4
Wrenbury 15C2/24E3
Wressle 21D5
Wretham & Hockham 12A5/18G5
Wrexham Central 20E4
Wrexham Exchange 20E4
Wrexham General 20E4
Wrington 3B2/8D2
Wrotham & Boro' Green 5C5
Wroxall 4G3
Wroxham 18E2
Wryde .17F3
Wye 6D3
Wyke & Norwood Green 21E2/42B1
Wylam 27B5
Wylde Green 15F5
Wyllie Halt 43B3
Wylye .3C5
Wymondham 18F4
Wyndham Halt 43D3
Wynn Hall Siding 20F4
Wyre Dock 24C4
Wyre Forest 9A2
Wyre Halt 9C4
Wyrley & Cheslyn Hay 15E4
Yalding .5C5
Yardley Wood 9A5
Yarm .28F5
Yarmouth Beach 18F1
Yarmouth Fishmarket 18F1
Yarmouth South Town 18F1
Yarmouth Vauxhall 18F1
Yarnton 10E4
Yate 8C1/9G2
Yatton 3A1/8D3
Yaxham 18E4
Yaxley & Farcet 10A2/17G2
Yeadon 21D2
Yealmpton 2E5
Yeathouse 26E3
Yeldham 11D5
Yelvertoft & Stanford Park 10A3
Yelverton 2D5
Yeo Mill Halt 7F5
Yeoford 2B4
Yeovil Junction 3D2/8G2
Yeovil Pen Mill 3D2/8G2
Yeovil Town 3D2/8G2
Yetminster 3E2
Ynys 19F1
Ynysddu 8B4/43B3
Ynyshir 8B5/43C3
Ynyslas 13B5
Ynysybwl 8B5/43C3
Yockleton 14A1
Yoker Ferry 29C4/44F4
Yoker High 29C4/44F4
York Foss Island 21A4
York Road 40C5
York 21C5
Yorkhill Sidings 44E4
Yorton 15E1/24G3
Ystalyfera 7A4/43F1
Ystrad (Rhondda) 8B5/43D2
Ystrad Mynach 8B4/43B3
Ystradgynlais 7A5/43E1
Ystradowen 8C5/43D4